"What a treasure Kelley and Brennan's *Talking Is a Gift* is to anyone seeking to improve their speaking and communication abilities. This user-friendly text is packed with practical application, moving the reader into a speaker with useful steps and tools. Many thanks to them for writing this fine book!"

Karen Allen
President's wife, Midwestern Baptist Theological Seminary

"I greatly appreciate the message of this book: that speaking is a privilege and a gift. As one who has struggled to get out of the gate in speech preparation, I am very excited to have this practical and academic reference book. *Talking Is a Gift* is a must read for the women I coach and mentor."

Becky Badry
Founder, Women in Leadership Coaching, Women's Ministry Consultant

"Whether you are speaking to hundreds of women from a platform or leading a small group in your living room, *Talking Is a Gift* will equip you to clearly communicate and connect with your audience. The authors give you proven skills to develop your talk, communicate your vision, and inspire others toward action. This book is a must read and practical resource for every woman desiring to engage the hearts and minds of others."

Lisa Bryant
Director of Women's Ministry, Thomas Road Baptist Church, Lynchburg, VA

"In the book, *Talking Is a Gift*, Rhonda Kelley and Monica Rose Brennan spotlight the art of using their words to help women develop skills for effective communication. Not only will this book be beneficial on the academic level, it will be a valuable tool for women's ministry leaders to communicate God's Word and message in Bible studies and special events."

Mary Cox
Women's Ministry Director, North Metro First Baptist Church, Lawrenceville, GA

"Help! I can't put this book down! Written by two of our nation's top experts in Christian communication, *Talking Is a Gift* is a treasured resource. This intellectual yet fun-to-read tome provides detailed instruction, spiritual inspiration, and great encouragement for both novice and experienced speakers."

Diana Davis
Syndicated columnist/author/Christian speaker, www.dianadavis.org

"In *Talking Is a Gift*, Dr. Kelley and Dr. Brennan share straightforward advice which will benefit even the most timid and inexperienced speaker. *Talking Is a Gift* will challenge the reader to think before she opens her mouth, prepare thoroughly, and then speak out with the bold confidence of knowing she is doing her very best."

Deb Douglas
Minister to Women, First Baptist Bossier City, LA, LifeWay Ministry Multiplier

"*Talking Is a Gift* is a much-needed resource for women's ministry leaders currently serving in local churches as well as a great academic text for training the next generation of women's leaders. The benefits of this text stem from the insights of two Christian leaders with varied experiences ranging from speaking at women's events to teaching in college and seminary classrooms."

Stephanie Edge
Associate Professor, Union University
Director of Women's Ministry, Poplar Heights Baptist Church, Jackson, TN

"Wow! Rhonda Harrington Kelley and Monica Rose Brennan have provided speakers with an amazing resource to take their speaking careers to the next level. These ladies know what they are talking about and address all of the important areas of speaking. Can't wait to get my copy!"

Linda Gilden
CLASSEMINARS, Inc. Speaker Trainer and Director of Writing Programs

"What an extraordinary resource Rhonda and Monica have given us! There is no aspect of effective communication that is not covered here—from the mechanics of preparation to fear of speaking, to nonverbal communication. Women leaders will find this book invaluable in helping them move their speaking skills to the next level!"

Susie Hawkins
Author/speaker/president's wife, GuideStone Financial Resources, Dallas, TX

"Drs. Kelley and Brennan have written a superb guide to public speaking and communication specifically for women. Their incredible insights and practical advice will challenge the minds and bless the hearts of all their readers—women and men alike. Don't miss *Talking Is a Gift*—and indeed so is this book."

Ed Hindson
Distinguished Professor, School of Religion, Liberty University

"In *Talking Is a Gift*, Rhonda Kelley and Monica Rose Brennan have stepped up with a practical guide to understanding communication, in hopes of broadening our ability to say what we mean, mean what we say, and do it in a way that invites others to listen and respond with clarity and purpose. So, whether you talk a lot or a little, to large crowds or just anyone who'll listen, you'll find this timely resource supportive, compelling, and effective in your growth as a communicator."

Judi A. Jackson
Associate Dean of Students; Coordinator of Women's Programs
Adjunct Professor, New Orleans Baptist Theological Seminary

"*Talking Is a Gift* affords a rich resource for women whose roles in Christian ministries call upon them to do public speaking for devotionals and Bible studies, as well as drama and oral interpretation. Women's ministry leaders, Bible study leaders, and mission group leaders will profit from this helpful guide to help female speakers perform these roles more effectively in the Lord's work."

Steve Lemke
Provost/Professor of Philosophy and Ethics,
New Orleans Baptist Theological Seminary

"I wholeheartedly recommend *Talking Is a Gift*. Gleaned insights from timeless truths of public speaking woven with fresh practices of the most engaging voices of our day will arm women to confidently present well. This volume will equip women in any context from Bible study to the board room. A much needed tool for women to lead and teach more powerfully."

Kathy Ferguson Litton
Consultant for Ministry to Pastors' Wives, North American Mission Board

"*Talking Is a Gift* is an incredible collection of essential tips for any speaker. The authors are not only gifted in speaking but also in the art of communicating through the written word. I am thrilled to endorse this valuable resource and would recommend this book to anyone who longs to effectively communicate their message to an audience."

Jaye Martin
President, Jaye Martin Ministries, Houston, TX

"I wish I could have been in Rhonda or Monica's classes when I went to seminary. I also would have loved to have had *Talking Is a Gift* as a textbook. Now, this valuable resource will be a great tool for training the woman who senses a call to the ministry of proclamation and wants to fulfill that call within the giftedness she has as a woman."

Leighann McCoy
Women's Ministry Leader; pastor's wife, Thompson Station Church, Franklin, TN

"*Talking Is a Gift* is a valuable resource for any woman who wants to glorify God through a speaking and teaching ministry. Kelley and Brennan have masterfully created this very practical book with an eye toward all aspects of oral communication for women by women. I look forward to using it as a textbook in my classes."

Denise O'Donoghue
Women's Life Director, Southeastern Baptist Theological Seminary

"Finally, a book about communication and public speaking designed specifically for women. *Talking Is a Gift* is a very concise, thorough book that addresses the full gamut of public speaking from organizing a speech to verbal presentation and the appearance of the speaker. As a professor of women's ministry for two colleges, this book will be a 'must have' textbook in my public speaking class."

Judy Patrick
Women's Ministry Professor, University of Mobile/Baptist College of Florida

"The need for Spirit-empowered communication that is clear, accurate, and inspirational is paramount in a media culture of ambiguous signals and shallow theology. No one is more qualified to speak into the fog than Rhonda Kelley and Monica Brennan. These two ladies bring a wealth of experience and expertise together in *Talking Is a Gift: Communication Skills for Women*. This book is a timely resource that is incredibly practical and impressively substantive, while at the same time being insightfully sensitive to the unique role of those who communicate woman to woman."

Jim Shaddix
Professor of Preaching, Southeastern Baptist Theological Seminary
Pastor of Teaching and Training, The Church at Brook Hills, Birmingham, AL

"Whether I am on a platform or a playground, *Talking Is a Gift: Communication Skills for Women* teaches and equips me to fulfill my mission effectively. This is the instruction book I will read again and again as I strive to deliver meaningful messages with impact and application. If you are a woman, you probably have the 'gift of talking,' so use *Talking Is a Gift* to sharpen and polish that gift."

Debbie Stuart
Church and Leadership Development Director, Women of Faith

"Communication is absolutely essential for any woman in ministry! Whether communication is one-on-one or in small groups or to large groups, communication is the absolute foundation for any ministry. Both Rhonda Kelley and Monica Brennan are my friends, and this book starts with their ability to communicate in every way. So, this book is more than research; it is the lives of two women who communicate, and they both do it well in this book."

Elmer L. Towns, Ph.D.
Cofounder, Liberty University, Lynchburg, VA

"Needed. That is the word that came to mind as I read the description of this book. It was needed when I started out a number of years ago; it is needed now. In a variety of ways, the authors present a variety of methods, speaking and preparation techniques, and skills for use by speakers in a variety of places. This book is totally useful."

Janie Wise
Women's Missions and Ministry Strategist, Louisiana Baptist Convention

Rhonda Harrington Kelley
and Monica Rose Brennan

TALKING
Is a GIFT

Communication Skills *for* Women

PUBLISHING GROUP
NASHVILLE, TENNESSEE

Talking Is a Gift: Communication Skills for Women
Copyright © 2014 by Rhonda Harrington Kelley and Monica Rose Brennan

B&H Publishing Group
Nashville, Tennessee

ISBN: 978-1-4336-9085-3

Dewey Decimal Classification: 302.2
Subject Heading: COMMUNICATION \ WOMEN \ PUBLIC SPEAKING

Printed in the United States of America

1 2 3 4 5 6 7 8 9 10 • 19 18 17 16 15 14

BP

From Rhonda:
To Chuck,
a godly, loving husband,
who is my greatest source of encouragement.
To my family,
who taught me to speak
and never fails to listen when I share my passions.

From Monica:
To my husband, Michael,
who always encourages me to write for God's glory.
To my daughter Elizabeth Rose,
who is a constant inspiration to influence the next generation.
To my family,
whose love for communicating God's truth continues to shape my life.

TABLE OF CONTENTS

ACKNOWLEDGMENTS

Any project involves many people. The writing of this comprehensive book has required support from everyone we know—families, friends, and colleagues. Please accept our deepest gratitude for your love, prayers, and diligent work. Our dream would not have become reality without your invaluable help!

Heartfelt thanks to our husbands for their keen insights, volunteer editing, and personal assistance during our months of writing. We appreciate our parents, siblings, and other family members who have encouraged us and provided many relevant illustrations for our speaking and writing ministries. It is a joy to share life with our precious families.

Many thanks to the schools where we teach—New Orleans Baptist Theological Seminary and Liberty University—who have provided our educational training as well as professional experience. It is a blessing to serve the Lord alongside the wonderful people at these schools.

Thank you to Dorothy Patterson for mentoring us in ministry and writing such a gracious foreword for this book. Thanks also to these friends who reviewed chapters in their areas of expertise: Vanee Daure (Microphones and Media), Yvette Peevy (Articulation and Voice), and Brent Ramsey (Appearance and Clothing). It is a privilege to have such gifted friends.

A huge thank you to Judi Jackson whose diligent work as content editor made this final work stronger. Thanks also to Natalee Morris, Taran Holland, and Laura Landry for their invaluable help as research assistants, as well as Boyd Guy for his excellent work on designing select illustrations. It is a pleasure to work with such committed Christians.

And, special thanks to B&H Academic (Jim Baird and Chris Cowan) for publishing this book that has been in our hearts for years. We pray that every word will empower the readers to fulfill their callings to Christian ministry as effective teachers and speakers. May God speak through you faithfully!

Blessings to all,
Rhonda Harrington Kelley
Monica Rose Brennan

FOREWORD

Nothing is more basic to relationships or to learning on every level than communication, especially when you have the opportunity and giftedness to provide information and encouragement from the public platform. In building and nurturing personal relationships and in my role as a professor presenting to women the truths of Scripture and preparing those who are my students for the public platform, *Talking Is a Gift: Communication Skills for Women* is the volume for which I have been waiting.

This unique book is especially welcome to the world of women's studies. It is written by Christian women who, as experienced communicators, challenge other Christian women to achieve excellence in communicating on every level. They equip readers to present their messages more effectively whether from the public platform, in small study groups, in the professional arena of the marketplace, or in personal conversations with family and friends.

Kelley and Brennan have wisely started with laying the foundation for communication skills, including nonverbal as well as verbal components. They have not been afraid to weigh in on thorny issues in the modern cultural scene, such as the gender debate, and they have not overlooked the fact that genuine communication includes *hearing and listening!*

In the classroom, as well as in private study, a woman who is serious about wanting to communicate more effectively looks for instruction ranging from preparation to delivery to evaluation in order to improve her skills. These authors show clearly that to do your best on the platform demands excellence—a task that does not just come naturally if you want to be among the best. They draw attention to uncovering and polishing any natural giftedness while looking beyond what is natural to pursue with determination the strengthening of any weaknesses and the stretching to consider other factors such as appearance, gestures, posture, and clothing, which can add to a speaker's effectiveness.

If you are a novice and a bit reticent to jump into speeches or any connection to the public platform, this volume will take you from the foundations of verbal and nonverbal communication to the pinnacle of successful ministry in a series of focused chapters that build one upon the other. If you are already in demand as a speaker and seem to have natural gifts for this arena, you will be challenged to polish and take your ministry a bit further. You may be intrigued by the chapters on drama and oral interpretation, which will awaken your creativity to "something new—at least for you—under the sun!"

This volume is one that keeps on giving—pulling you back on course in your personal communication with those you love and others with whom you interact in the course of life. But there is more—you will also be inspired to make your communication worthy of being a part of the marketplace of ideas and ultimately to share your life message effectively. Yes, I will have my personal desk copy of *Talking Is a Gift*, but I must also recommend it as a textbook in our women's programs on the seminary campus, and I want my teenage granddaughters to have copies to read and absorb as part of their preparation for communicating effectively on all levels. This volume is for every woman's personal library of resources!

Dorothy Kelley Patterson
Professor of Theology in Women's Studies
Southwestern Baptist Theological Seminary
Fort Worth, TX

INTRODUCTION BY RHONDA KELLEY

I do believe that talking is a spiritual gift! My precious husband has always teased me about my spiritual gifts which are not in the Bible—sleeping, shopping, and *talking*. I respond to him in jest about his spiritual gift of discernment which encourages me to develop my spiritual gifts. So, I sleep late whenever possible, take his credit card to the mall, and talk from morning until night. I love my gifts!

Seriously, I do believe that talking is an essential spiritual gift for ministry to others. The Bible teaches that the Holy Spirit empowers every believer with spiritual gifts to accomplish his work (Rom 12:3–8; 1 Cor 12:4–11, 27–31; Eph 4:11–13; 1 Pet 4:9–10). Ken Hemphill defines a spiritual gift in his book, *You Are Gifted!* A spiritual gift is "an individual expression of grace enabling every believer to participate fully in the edification of the church and the advance of the kingdom."[1] Talking is simply a talent when used for personal pleasure, but it is a spiritual gift when used to benefit others. Spiritual gifts have been given to believers for the good of others, the work of the kingdom, and the glory of God. Talking is an essential God-given ability that enables the believer to use her gifts of teaching, encouraging, prophesying, and leading in service to others.

God used the Scripture 1 Peter 4:9–10 to help me understand that my husband is right; talking is one of my spiritual gifts! It is very interesting that Peter is the disciple who wrote about talking as a spiritual gift. Peter often spoke when he had nothing to say. He spoke before he thought about his words. In fact, in the Gospel accounts of the transfiguration of Jesus, Peter spoke words though "he did not know what he should say" (Mark 9:6). Do you identify with Peter? I do. I often speak when I have nothing to say, but I speak anyway.

Later in his first epistle, Peter discussed spiritual gifts as he challenged believers to minister with urgency to others in the end times. He specifically identifies the gifts of hospitality, serving, and speaking as gifts used "to serve others, as

---

[1] Kenneth Hemphill, *You Are Gifted: Your Spiritual Gifts and the Kingdom of God* (Nashville: Broadman and Holman, 2009), xvi.

good managers of the varied grace of God" (1 Pet 4:10). Peter says that a person's speech "Should be as one who speaks God's words . . . so that God may be glorified through Jesus Christ in everything" (1 Pet 4:11). Talking should bring glory to God!

The purpose of this book is to provide a comprehensive communication textbook for women to whom the Lord has given the gift of talking. It is written to provide information and insight about the process of communication, especially public speaking, for women in undergraduate and graduate academic programs as well as lay leaders in the church. Written from a Christian woman's perspective, it will include general discussions of interpersonal, verbal, and nonverbal communication. Specific topics of discussion will include gender communication, devotional preparation, the appearance and wardrobe of a speaker, as well as speech skills and voice care. Unique features will be chapter discussion questions, informational charts, glossary of terms, and a companion blog available at talkingisagift.wordpress.com. In select chapters, you will also find QR codes. By scanning these codes with your mobile device, you can view video clips of us speaking on the topic addressed in that chapter. To view our full-length teaching on communication, visit www.mininstrygrid.com.

As a speaker, teacher, and writer, my heart's desire is to continue improving my God-given gift of talking in my life and ministry in order to serve and glorify God to the best of my ability. I am grateful to know that you have a similar desire. With personal discipline and systematic study plus the work of the Holy Spirit, our spiritual gift of talking can join with the spiritual giftedness of others to accomplish God's work here on earth. Then, our talking will bring glory to God and good to his people!

Introduction by Monica Brennan

I specifically remember my parents spending a lot of time speaking to others after church when I was a little girl. With my father being the pastor and my mother the pastor's wife, there always seemed to be a line of people waiting to speak to them. At the time, their conversations seemed to last an eternity, and I remember thinking, *Why do they always have so much to say to others?* However, I also remember looking into the faces of my parents as they communicated and seeing so much joy as they took time to talk with each unique person. It is from their example that I believe the Lord instilled in my heart a love for people and a love for sharing God's truth with others. I was only four years old when I approached a woman standing in the line of McDonald's and asked her if she had Jesus in her heart and was going to heaven. I terrified this stranger as she replied, "Well, I hope so!" I had a message that the Lord placed in my heart, and I had urgency to present the truth! It is my prayer that as you read *Talking Is a Gift*, you will experience a great urgency as I did to share the Word of God effectively with others.

Talking Is a Gift is a much-needed resource for today's female Christian leader. Learning how to communicate effectively should be an ongoing, lifetime pursuit. It is essential for an effective women's ministry. This book is designed to train women's ministry leaders as well as future Christian women's leaders to share God's unchanging Word effectively and to present truth passionately. The ultimate goal behind speaking effectively is to help listeners come to know Christ and grow in spiritual maturity.

I have met many women who love the Lord and desire to be used of him but have difficulty when it comes to getting in front of an audience. I have also met women who have excellent speaking skills but do not know how to prepare a message or outline for a speaking engagement. Regardless of how much training or lack of training that you have, this book will be an excellent help to you in ministry.

I have had the wonderful honor and privilege of working with a communication expert, Rhonda Kelley, on this writing project. I have learned so much from her expertise that is contained on each page of this book. At the beginning of this writing project, I meditated on Psalm 45:1, which says, "My heart is moved by a noble theme as I recite my verses to the king; my tongue is the pen of a skillful writer." I believe this book is filled with good themes and pray it will be a great blessing in the lives of women for many years to come as they endeavor to be more effective communicators. As women read this book, I pray they will become further equipped by the Lord to proclaim his Word to women and to impact many lives for eternity!

Part I

INTERPERSONAL COMMUNICATION

What Is Involved in Talking with Others?

Part one of this book will examine foundational principles of communication as an introduction to a focus on public speaking. Interpersonal communication will be the specific focus of the first part of the book with attention given to the discussion of communication and gender, process and product, hearing and listening. The first three chapters will introduce concepts, define terms, and suggest principles. This textbook, which is written specifically for women, begins with the discussion of the influence of gender on communication. It also establishes an understanding about the nature and function of the communication process. The first part concludes with the assertion of the importance of attention and a differentiation between hearing and listening.

The premise of this book is that talking is a spiritual gift given by God to some believers for the purpose of ministry to others. When speech is used to teach, proclaim, or encourage, it is truly ministry. Quentin Schultze supports this premise in his book, *An Essential Guide to Public Speaking*. He challenges readers to become servant speakers who faithfully serve audiences as they develop their own character and practice technical methods. According to Schultze, "Faith, virtue, and skill are the keys to servant speaking."[1] Ministering the gift of talking and becoming a servant speaker begin with understanding the foundations of communication.

---

[1] Quentin Schultze, *An Essential Guide to Public Speaking: Serving Your Audience with Faith, Skill, and Virtue* (Grand Rapids: Baker Academics, 2006), 10.

Chapter 1

COMMUNICATION AND GENDER

"Even if they grow up in the same neighborhood,
on the same block, or in the same house,
girls and boys grow up in different worlds of words."[1]

I n the beginning God created" (Gen 1:1). He created the heavens and earth, land and sea, day and night, sun and moon, birds and fish. Then he created male and female. Since man and woman were created by God in the beginning, it seems right to begin this book with a discussion of gender and communication.

"So God created man in His own image; He created him in the image of God; He created them male and female" (Gen 1:27). From the beginning, God created mankind, both male and female, in his own image. Equal in worth and value, men and women are different in role and function. Men and women are different biologically and emotionally; different in nature and personality; different in assignments and responsibilities. Scientists continue to determine that the brains of men and women function differently, that women think and problem solve in different ways and for different reasons than men.

---

[1] Deborah Tannen, *You Just Don't Understand: Women and Men in Conversation* (New York: HarperCollins, 2001), 43.

Since communication is a unique human behavior, it can be assumed that gender differences impact an individual's communication style. Differences do not imply superiority or inferiority; instead, differences reflect God's unique design for the genders to complement or complete each other. Men and women differ in the way they think, feel, act, and talk. Some of the most striking differences between the sexes are the unique ways that men and women interact verbally. In this chapter, we will explore some of these gender communication differences.

Gender

In recent years, the communication styles of men and women have been studied scientifically, and linguists have documented perceived differences. The primary purpose of these intensive investigations is not to determine which communicative style is best or to motivate others to change completely, but to identify differences for the purpose of understanding and adaptation. As men and women better recognize differences in communicative styles, they can work to improve their own communication with members of the opposite sex.

Deborah Tannen, professor of linguistics, was one of the first to document in professional and popular writing a discussion of gender communication. In her book, *You Just Don't Understand*, Tannen reported striking differences in the way that boys and girls, as well as men and women, communicate. After studying male and female communication patterns, she concluded that men and women have different conversational styles and that both styles are equally valid. Since there are gender differences in ways of speaking, we need to identify and understand them.[2]

Differences in gender communication begin in early childhood. Tannen found this to be apparent in conversation as early as three years of age. As language is being developed, little girls talk to be liked; little boys often talk to boast. Little girls make requests; little boys make demands. Little girls talk more indirectly; little boys talk directly. It seems that little boys communicate more with actions, while little girls use words. Little boys prolong verbal conflict, while little girls tend to diffuse conflict.[3]

According to Tannen, "Even if they grow up in the same neighborhood, on the same block, or in the same house, girls and boys actually grow up in different worlds of words."[4] Children learn to communicate from parents and peers, often

---

[2] Ibid., 17.
[3] Ibid., 43–47.
[4] Ibid., 43.

imitating their same-sex models. Language and communication are considered learned behaviors that develop through a combination of nature and nurture, genetic predisposition, and environmental stimulation. As a result, communication differences between boys and girls are expected and emerge early in childhood. Boys and girls both want to get their messages across and use language differently in order to do so.[5]

It is very important in life and ministry to understand the different ways that males and females communicate. Speech is often the basis for a person's first impression. Judgments about a person may be made dependent upon communication style and pattern alone. Men often judge women based on male conversational style and vice versa. Miscommunication between men and women is common and can be very challenging because men and women expect different responses from each other. These communication differences are noted during same-gender and opposite-gender conversations as well as during one-on-one and small-group interactions. Parents, spouses, coworkers, neighbors, ministers, and church members need to be aware of differences in gender communication.

One example of major miscommunication took place in the garden of Eden between Adam and Eve (see Genesis 3). Disaster occurred as Eve entered into a conversation with a serpent while Adam said nothing. What resonated in Adam's mind? Did Eve expect a response? Perhaps during this interaction, there was miscommunication and uncertainty of each other's responses producing a terribly wrong perception.

Communication affects all relationships involving male-female verbal interaction. Relationships can suffer if the differences are not understood. Gender communication impacts relationships between father and daughter, mother and son, husband and wife, employer and employee, and pastor and member. In vocational or business settings, men and women may be at the same level of employment, but they communicate differently. On church committees, men and women communicate differently. A balance is needed between men and women who are serving together if they are to communicate effectively. Gender differences will never change; therefore, we must understand unique communication styles.

Genderlect

Tannen, in her study of gender communication, coined the term *genderlect* to acknowledge that the conversation styles of men and women are not right or wrong, superior or inferior; they are just different. Genderlect is "a variety of

---

[5] Ibid., 46.

speech or conversational style used by a particular gender."[6] The term is based on two root words: gender and dialect. *Gender* refers to the male and female sexes. *Dialect* refers to the unique language of people in a specific area. Thus, genderlect refers to the language of the sexes. Communication between men and women can literally be considered cross-cultural communication.

Suzette Haden Elgin described genderlect as "a variety of a language that is not tied to geography or to family background or to a role, but to the speaker's sexual gender."[7] She suggested communication techniques to combat gender style differences in her book entitled *Genderspeak*. John Gray, a relationship psychologist, wrote a book entitled *Men Are from Mars, Women Are from Venus*, implying that men and women are so different that one might conclude they are from different planets. Men and women speak entirely different languages.[8]

Before exploring the characteristics of gender communication, several assumptions must be accepted. First, men and women have different conversational styles. Evidence supports this assumption and this book will accept it. Second, both male and female communication styles are valid. Strengths and weaknesses are inherent in the patterns of both genders. Third, the goal in gender communication is not to change the style of communication but to adapt to the differences. The discussion is not about right or wrong but about differences. Understanding and adaptation are important to effective communication between the genders.

Studies by Tannen and others have revealed a number of distinctives in the ways that men and women communicate. While these are generalizations, they apply to most men and most women. Men and women do seem to express themselves in different ways and for different reasons. Here is a summary of the most apparent gender communication distinctions.

1. *Men use communication to maintain* **status***; women to maintain* **intimacy***.* Men typically talk for the purpose of establishing their own credibility. They talk about their positions, accomplishments, work activities, and sporting events in order to demonstrate they are "king of the mountain." On the other hand, women talk to connect with other people and build relationships. They talk most about family and friends in order to develop closeness in conversation. Men are most often introduced by their title or occupation, while women are usually introduced based on their marital status, personal relationships, or family background.

---

[6] *American Heritage Dictionary of the English Language*, 4th ed. (Houghton Mifflin, 2009), s.v. "genderlect."

[7] Suzette Haden Elgin, *Genderspeak: Men, Women, and the Gentle Art of Verbal Self-Defense* (New York: John Wiley and Sons, 1993), 22.

[8] John Gray, *Men Are from Mars, Women Are from Venus* (New York: Harper Collins, 1992), 10.

As a little girl, I (Monica) remember sitting beside my grandfather, whom I affectionately called "Paw Paw Bill," in church every Sunday on the second pew. He was known as a man of few words. Although he did not say a lot, I knew it thrilled him for me to sit beside him in church. I will never forget the warm, big smile that would appear on his face as I walked toward him. His expression alone made me feel so loved and special. When he did speak, he would ask me how school was going or how I liked voice lessons. I would always reply back with long responses that often led away from the subject entirely and centered around more personal things going on in my life. At times, I would wait for a response back from him, but he would simply nod his head and grin. I began to think he just really enjoyed hearing his granddaughter talk. Although my grandfather would ask me about things I considered impersonal (school or work), I always remember feeling closer to him after our conversations. Why? Because women form connections through conversations!

2. *Men offer **solutions** to problems; women **complain** about problems.* While women often want to talk about their problems to receive empathy and understanding, men are naturally problem solvers. Men rise to the challenge of resolving a problem while women find relief in discussing it.

I (Rhonda) experience this communication difference in my marriage relationship. I love being busy, involved in a variety of activities. Of course, life often gets intense and I get tired. When I comment to my husband that I am weary, he immediately begins to point out the things I have been doing that I could quit doing. He wants to fix my problem of fatigue by solving my problem of over-activity. I just want to talk about it and get a little sympathy because I do not plan to stop any of my activities. I have learned to call my mother who always has a listening ear!

This tendency in men and women can cause a lot of conflict if we fail to see it as a gender difference in how we communicate. So often, when I (Monica) am going through a difficult time or have an important decision to make, I need to think it through before I am ready to form a conclusion. I lived off campus with my younger brother, Jeremy, for one year while I was in college. It is a wonder we did not end up killing one another! I would come home to the place we were renting just needing to talk. Now, you probably can imagine how much joy this would give my brother. He really had no choice in listening to me, but he always wanted to offer a solution to the problem and still does to this day. Often his advice was really good, but I was not ready to take action, as my brother would strongly suggest, to make a certain problem go away. I just wanted to verbalize my thoughts.

3. *Men give **information**; women give **affirmation**.* Men tend to talk only when they have something to say. Women love to talk even when they have nothing to say because it helps them stay connected. The content of male conversation is typically facts and figures, while women fill their conversations with praise and encouragement. Men fill their word count with nouns, while women fill theirs with adjectives and adverbs.

Conversations with my parents demonstrate this gender communication difference. When I (Rhonda) talk with my mother by telephone, she tells me every single detail of her day, often repeating them for emphasis. She may tell me goodbye six or seven times as she thinks of more things to say. When I talk with my dad, he often ends the conversation abruptly in the middle of a sentence because he has finished talking. These differences always give me a laugh.

I (Monica) love giving lots of detail about any given subject. My husband has joked with me concerning how many adjectives and adverbs I use to describe my day. I have even made up words to describe what I want to say! When we go home at the end of our teaching day, I am ready to discuss all the events of the day while my husband would prefer to listen to the evening news. Our compromise is to share news about our day *during* dinner while recording the news to watch *after* dinner.

4. *Men **report-talk**; women **rapport-talk**.* Because men talk to give information, it sounds like they are giving a verbal report. They list facts and figures as they move to the bottom line. Women talk to build relationships and give affirmation, so they "rapport-talk." They talk to establish connections and negotiate relationships.

Communication in church business meetings often demonstrates this difference. While men provide the quantitative information, women often offer stories about the ministries. When presenting our women's ministry budget to our church committee, I (Rhonda) found myself enthusiastically talking about the life changes in our Bible study and the evangelistic impact of our mission project when it dawned on me that the men just wanted to know how much money we needed for the budget next year.

I (Monica) have seen this difference many times in my relationship with my husband. When we were first married, my husband and I would talk about many aspects of each Sunday's church service: the worship, the message, and the people with whom we had conversations. I would ask my husband who he talked to after church and I wanted a report on how they were doing. On one occasion, he looked at me and said, "Well, we were having a conversation about motorcycles, so I really do not know how he is doing." I wondered how my husband could enter into a conversation with someone and remain unaware of how they felt. Now I understand better that this reflects a gender difference in how we communicate. When I enter into conversations with others (even complete strangers), I work to build a connection with a person in the hope that I might possibly help or encourage them.

5. *Men* **lecture**; *women* **listen**. Since men give information and report-talk, their speech sometimes sounds like a lecture. Men typically speak with confidence and passion, so their conversation may sound dogmatic. Women, who give affirmation and rapport-talk, usually listen in order to maintain that relationship. They listen not only to the words being spoken but to the way they are spoken.

My dad was a well-known evangelist as I (Rhonda) was growing up. When he returned home, Dad talked with us as if he were preaching a sermon. My sister and I would often joke about his same song, second verse approach. We would pretend to push the play button on the tape recorder as Dad preached to us in conversation that often sounded like a lecture.

My husband and I (Monica) are both professors. Many times when my husband is talking to me about something he read in an article or watched on the news, it sounds as if he is teaching in a classroom and not talking to me as his wife. On occasion, just to be funny, I will raise my hand as he is talking and say, "Professor, may I ask you something?" While we both laugh, we are reminded how challenging it is for him not to be in "lecture mode."

6. *Men* **use conflict** *to negotiate status; women* **avoid conflict** *to establish connection.* Men are much more comfortable dealing with conflict than are women. For men, conflict allows an opportunity to win and assume a higher status. For women, conflict might interfere with connection and harm a relationship. Men can engage in a heated discussion which is quickly forgotten, while women often experience hurt feelings when there is difference or discord.

I (Monica) hate conflict of any kind. On many occasions, I have seen that my husband, father, grandfather, or brothers do not mind it. I remember my mother becoming so uptight with the way my father was driving when I was a little girl. However, my father had a valid explanation. On one occasion, he was in the passing lane and got behind an extremely slow-moving vehicle. Instead of keeping a reasonable distance, he followed the vehicle closely until the driver moved over into the other lane. I thought my mother was going to have a heart attack. I will never forget her words, "Honey, what if that is a church member?" My mother was definitely more concerned with maintaining relationships with the people in the congregation where my father served as pastor than with teaching a person a lesson on the road. My father would say that he felt it necessary to show them they needed to pull over into the slower lane.

7. *Men **interrupt**; women **overlap**.* The notion that women talk too much and interrupt men has been contradicted in research about gender communication. During conversation, men frequently interrupt to insert a comment or reestablish status. Women, on the other hand, often overlap. Two or more women can talk at once without a perception of interruption or a violation of rights. Women are comfortable talking at the same time, while men interrupt to become the speaker.

Several years ago, I (Rhonda) was invited to speak for a women's conference at a church where my friend's husband was pastor. Susan and Bill picked me up at the airport and immediately we girls began talking. I moved to the middle of the backseat so I could look at Susan while talking with her. As we spoke enthusiastically, I could see Bill's face in the rearview mirror. He was driving and kept trying to open his mouth to get a word into our conversation. I finally said, "Just jump right in if you want to talk!" Susan and I were overlapping, but Bill could not bring himself to interrupt us.

Recently, I (Monica) hosted a baby shower for one of my dear friends. We had a houseful of joyful and excited women. My husband decided to stay home in our finished basement. During the shower, he came upstairs for a brief moment. I remember looking at the expression on his face which seemed to scream, "This is not the place for me." The many conversations going on at once seemed like chaos to him. Meanwhile, we women were enjoying our conversations immensely.

8. *Men talk more in **public**; women talk more in **private**.* There is an assumption that women talk more than men. Men are typically the source of this statement of fact! Study after study has demonstrated that men and women use approximately the same number of words per day. However, men use most of their words in public and women use most of their words in private. While husbands use their words at work, wives save their words for their husbands when they get home.

My husband and I (Monica) naturally share about our days when we are having dinner or after our little girl falls asleep. On one occasion, I could tell my husband's day had been very long and exhausting. I suggested we find an interesting movie on television so we could relax. With relief, he shared with me that his throat was sore because he had been on the phone all day talking to people: he did not have the energy to have another long conversation. I started laughing inside at the thought of how women can talk for hours and not think twice about it. In fact, a lot of women become energized from their conversations and rarely reach a point where they feel too tired to communicate!

9. *Men talk more about their **accomplishments**; women are hesitant to **boast**.* In general, men do not have a problem bragging about their achievements. It is a natural part of maintaining status. However, women do not boast because they do not want to harm relationships by asserting themselves as better.

In several different group settings, my (Rhonda) husband has enthusiastically described his amazing interception during the last play of the last football game of his senior year of high school and his game-winning touchdown like they occurred yesterday. He is so very proud of his defensive play! While I was head cheerleader and won first place in our cheerleading competition during my own senior year, I rarely share that with others. As a woman, I have that innate desire to build relationships and not elevate my own accomplishments.

I (Monica) am reminded of a friend in college who was an excellent athlete. He wanted to share his accomplishments with others. At first, he came across to me as being very proud, but then I realized that he felt comfortable sharing about sports and deep inside he was longing for affirmation. There were things he vocalized that I would never have said simply because I would not want anyone to feel inferior or jealous. As a woman, I consider the feelings and emotions of others with the words I choose.

10. *Men **use** silence; women **avoid** silence.* Men seem very comfortable remaining silent in the company of others. Women assume that silence implies anger, boredom, or hurt feelings. In their research, Tannen and her colleagues found little boys could be in the same room with each other and never speak a word. However, little girls immediately began talking.[9] Silence may be golden to men, but silence is often uncomfortable for women.

I (Rhonda) have learned in my marriage that my husband loves silence. When we get in the car for a road trip, I immediately think that I have him to myself and we can talk without interruptions. Chuck looks forward to road trips for a different reason. He is eager for silence, for time to himself that excludes conversation. Early in our marriage, this difference hurt my feelings, but I have learned to adapt. Now, I enjoy my naps in the car while he enjoys his thinking.

My (Monica) father is a very passionate preacher of the gospel. He does not hold back from proclaiming the truth when he delivers the Word of God. I grew up with my father as my pastor, and I had the privilege of being under solid teaching since my birth. The majority of people in the congregation would always assume that my father's personality was extroverted and bold; however, he is a true introvert at heart. On many occasions, when my parents would host a

---

[9] Tannen, *You Just Don't Understand*, 43–47.

get-together for the church family at our home, my father would seem very low-key. My mother is more of a social butterfly and an extrovert. At times, people would ask if anything was wrong with my father because he had such a different temperament than when behind the pulpit. My father would politely explain that nothing was wrong, that he was simply relaxing and enjoying their company. While exercising his spiritual gift of preaching, confidence would emerge, but his true personality is more relaxed.

11. *Men speak with **confidence**; women often **apologize**.* Rarely do men hesitate when they speak. They typically speak with confidence because they only speak when they have something to say. However, women can be very hesitant as they speak, often apologizing even when they know they are right. They frequently say "I'm sorry" to express sympathy and concern though it is perceived as lack of confidence. Carol Kent titled her public speaking book, *Speak Up with Confidence.*[10] She encourages other women to communicate more effectively and to speak confidently without apology.

This particular gender communication difference was illustrated to me (Rhonda) when I was in a seminary administrative meeting about the design of a new building on campus. Our interior designer suggested a particular shade of green for the carpet, when one administrator confidently informed us that "there are thirty-two different shades of green in Ireland." Interested, I asked him how he knew that fact. A little bit stunned by the challenge, he responded, "Well, I do not know that there are exactly thirty-two, but there are a lot of different greens in Ireland." He spoke with such confidence though he did not have facts.

On many occasions, I (Monica) have found myself apologizing simply because I am more concerned about a relationship or hurt feelings than with the actual topic of discussion. Men often can become so engrossed in the subject matter that they tend to lose sight of the feelings of others. Early in our marriage, my husband and I were having a discussion about politics. He spoke so firmly that I thought for sure he was very upset. Although the conversation was just between the two of us and I agreed with what he was saying, I began to apologize for bringing up the topic that frustrated him so severely. He immediately responded by saying he was not upset at all but was simply stating the facts.

12. *Men use body language **indirectly**; women use body language **very directly**.* While talking, girls and women often sit close to each other, look at each other directly, and may even touch. Boys and men typically sit at angles to each other, are less likely to look at each other while talking, and rarely touch or stand closely during conversation.

---

[10] Carol Kent, *Speak Up with Confidence: A Step-by-Step Guide for Speakers and Leaders* (Colorado Springs, CO: NavPress, 2007).

During college, I (Rhonda) recognized the difference in the way men and women use body language when the leader of one of our student organizations stepped back when I began to talk with him. I noticed this same reaction when others spoke to him, too. One day I mentioned it to him, and John said he was uncomfortable when people violated his body space. Stepping back was his way of saying that he was uncomfortable with direct body language or close proximity. I have not had the same experience with women through the years.

When I (Monica) have conversations with women, one-on-one or in a group, I like to be close enough to see their expressions. Body language is another way women feel connected. I remember my mother as well as other older ladies in our church coming up and putting their arms around me when I was a teen, asking how they could pray for me specifically. As my mother would put her arm around me and begin to pray, I felt a warmth come over me. I felt like I could share with her all of the struggles I was experiencing.

The different ways that men and women view the world impact their communication styles. Communication, and especially genderlect, is a continual balancing act between independence and intimacy. These language differences are challenging but also bring balance between men and women according to God's divine design.

Gender Communication Differences	
Men use communication to . . .	**Women use communication to . . .**
maintain status	maintain intimacy
offer solutions to problems	complain about problems
give information	give affirmation
report-talk	rapport-talk
lecture	listen
use conflict to negotiate status	avoid conflict to establish connection
interrupt	overlap
talk more in public	talk more in private
talk more about their accomplishments	talk, remaining hesitant to boast
use silence	avoid silence
speak with confidence	speak, often apologizing
use body language indirectly	use body language very directly

Judith Tingley found that men and women express gender communication differences in *content*, *style*, and *structure*. *Content* refers to *what* men and women talk about. Men often talk about sports, money, and business; women most often discuss people, feelings, and relationships. *Style* refers to *why* men and women talk. Men often express themselves to give specific information, converse for competition, and talk to resolve problems. Women most often express themselves to promote understanding, converse to support, and talk to connect. *Structure* refers to *how* men and women talk. Men typically use precise words that are to the point without descriptive details. Women use more detailed descriptions, apologetic tones, and vague generalizations. While these characteristics may be generalizations, they have been found to be true consistently when communication patterns of men and women are studied.[11]

Genderflex

Communication between those speaking different languages requires translation and adaptation. When men and women communicate, their primary languages require some understanding and consideration. Tingley has described this necessary process of adaptation as "genderflex." In the book by the same name, *genderflex* is defined as an active process: "to temporarily use communication behavior typical of the other gender in order to increase potential for influence."[12] Because of the natural way men and women communicate, temporary adaption to a different style of communication is necessary when talking with someone of the opposite gender. The primary goal of this adjustment is effective communication with members of the opposite sex.

Genderflex is necessary in life and ministry. Researchers have concluded that in mixed groups women make more adjustments in communication than men. Women tend to talk about topics of more interest to men when both genders are present. They also adjust their style and structure more easily in order to be understood and appreciated. These studies demonstrate that male-female conversations are more like men's conversations than they are like women's.[13]

In the context of the Christian community, several strategies for improving gender communication can be employed:[14]

---

[11] Judith C. Tingley, *Genderflex: Men and Women Speaking Each Other's Language at Work* (New York: AMACOM, 1994), 22–38.

[12] Ibid., 16.

[13] Tannen, *You Just Don't Understand*, 237.

[14] Rhonda H. Kelley, "Communication between Men and Women in the Context of the Christian Community," *Faith and Mission* 15, no. 1 (Fall 1996): 49–56.

Content, Style, and Structure in Gender Communication		
	Men	**Women**
Content (*What* do they talk about?)	• sports • money • business	• people • feelings • relationships
Style (*Why* do they talk?)	• give specific information • converse for competition • talk to resolve problems	• promote understanding • converse to support • talk to connect
Structure (*How* do they talk?)	• precise words • to the point • without descriptive details	• detailed descriptions • apologetic tones • vague generalizations

1. *Become aware of your own communication style.* Each person has a unique style of communication. Listen to your own speech. Evaluate your words, your tone of voice, and your body language. Compare your own communication style with that of individuals whom you judge to be effective communicators. Self-evaluation is an important first step in improving communication between genders.

My (Monica) husband has helped me realize that at times when I am speaking to him, I tend to talk really fast. Also, I might begin a conversation with him while I am doing other things such as cleaning or cooking, leading him to say, "Honey, remember I am not in the same room as you are. I cannot hear you." Other times, he has asked me to repeat something because I was talking so fast. I must admit when I get excited, I can talk at a rapid pace! I began to realize that this often would frustrate him, so I have learned to speak less rapidly and with more focus—even though I may be excited and eager to share something with him. I simply cannot have a long conversation with my husband while I am in the kitchen and he is in our living room!

2. *Understand the communication style of the opposite sex.* Become familiar with the unique communication style of the other gender. Listen carefully to your father, your husband, your son, your brothers, and your male friends. Make observations about their conversation. What do they say? How do they say it?

When do they speak? Why do they speak? Discuss these conversational differences with them at an appropriate time, not when conflict arises. Try to determine if your perceptions are accurate. Then you are ready to make some changes in order to communicate more effectively with the opposite sex.

My (Monica) husband and I recently experienced the joy of welcoming our first baby. I was thankful that we were able to share the first week together as we entered into this new phase of life. We had opportunities to share with one another freely because he was right there with me. When my husband left for work, I would observe a wide array of new experiences with our precious baby girl. I just could not wait for him to arrive home so I could share with him. Some days my husband would come home late due to the demands at work. I would be so ready and eager to begin our conversations, but I could tell he was ready to just sit down and relax. At first, it made my heart sad because I had so looked forward to communicating with him and really felt I needed to talk. I even wondered if my husband cared about sharing with me. I wanted him to have time to relax, but at the same time I could not wait to enter into conversation. He asked me if something was wrong when I reluctantly suggested he just sit down and relax. When I asked him if something was wrong, he began to laugh. Nothing was wrong at all. He simply was gathering his thoughts before we communicated. I realized yet again how different men and women are. I also understood that it was not that my husband did not care, but he definitely needed some time to regroup. He also became more aware of the need I had to share about the day and how I felt more connected to him when we communicated with one another. Although communication is vital in any relationship, it is important to be able to discern when it is most effective and best received.

3. *Adjust to different conversational styles.* While it may seem difficult to change the way you communicate since you have been talking that way for so long, remember that communication is a learned behavior. Behaviors can be changed. Communication styles can be modified. Both men and women should work on improving their communication and should continue to do so throughout their lifetimes.

Discernment is very important when it comes to speaking with those who have different conversational styles. I (Monica) remember one occasion when my brother, Brady, and I were having lunch together with a lot of other people after church one Sunday. There were so many conversations going on at once! My brother was speaking to me about a particular subject, and then two women began to enter into dialogue with me by asking me different questions at the same time. I felt compelled to juggle all three conversations. I remember looking at my brother, saying, "I'm sorry. I will come back to you in just a second."

I spoke very quickly with no thought to his feelings. I later apologized because I felt I came across in a way that was very rude, although I had simply tried to have a conversation with everyone at once. I will never forget my brother's response: "That's okay, sis. It was not as much what you said but how you said it." I felt so horrible and apologized again. My conversational style had not taken his into account. I had come across as rude. I needed improvement.

4. *Alter your conversational style to fit the context.* Effective communication is adapted appropriately to fit the setting. Some comments are best made in private while others can be shared in public. Some conversations are more appropriate in a casual setting than in a formal one. Some statements are fit for a group of people while others should be made only when talking one-on-one. The context dictates the conversational style.

This is especially true when you are speaking with women. As women, we often tend to share about extremely personal things. Some of the topics we discuss are definitely more appropriate one-on-one and in private than they are in a public setting. Women can become hurt if things are said in public that they had wished would have stayed in private. I (Monica) have seen many instances at women's conferences when someone will get up in front of a group to discuss prayer requests. Personal issues often become gossip, and many women can get their feelings hurt. We need to be very careful to fit our conversations with the contexts.

5. *Do not assume that the opposite sex understands your message.* Even when you believe your message has been clearly communicated, it is dangerous to assume that the listener understands—especially if the listener is a male. Just because it is clear to you does not mean that it is clear to others. In fact, one of the biggest mistakes in communication is assumption. It is always better to explain the message thoroughly than run the risk of being misunderstood. Special effort should be taken to clarify the meaning across genders.

Women are often misunderstood simply because we have a tendency to assume that the opposite gender understands what we mean even if we do not fully vocalize it. I (Monica) have seen this numerous times as I have talked with various young women who are interested in dating certain young men whom they believe are likewise interested in them. I respond that a man will usually pursue when he is ready, and she should not assume anything otherwise. Assumption can be the cause for many hurt feelings and misunderstandings. Communication always clears up wrong assumptions.

6. *Do not criticize others who communicate in a different way.* It is a human tendency to think "my way is the best way." In the area of communication, remember that different conversational styles are not bad. Different is simply

different. Accept the differences and adjust when needed. Learn from the ways other people communicate.

If we simply understand that we are different, then a lot of conflict and misunderstandings can be avoided. I (Monica) communicate differently than my husband, but that does not mean that my way is better. We are simply different. When those of both genders come to understand this fact, we can learn to laugh at ourselves instead of becoming frustrated when we have differences.

Talking Point

Men and women have different—though equally valid—
communication styles.

Let's Talk about It

1. What are some of the unique ways men and women communicate?
2. Give an example of a time in your life when you saw firsthand the miscommunication that can take place between a man and a woman.
3. Define and describe *genderlect* and *genderflex*.
4. List the most apparent gender communication differences. Give a personal example of at least one.
5. Identify one way you need to improve your gender communication. Set a goal or two to help accomplish the objective.

Chapter 2

PROCESS AND PRODUCT

"Speaking is innate, writing is an invention."[1]

Human communication is a creation of God, an innate ability to convey thoughts to others. The process of human communication is very complex as people attempt to create meaning by using symbolic behavior and words in a specific situation to achieve understanding. Humans use words to express thoughts to another person. Though many animals communicate within their species, humans alone have the unique ability to express complex thoughts and concepts verbally and nonverbally.

Communication is essential to life and relationships. It has been said that most of us spend up to seventy percent of our waking hours engaged in some form of communication.[2] Most of a person's day is filled with words. Communication skills are vital to personal and professional relationships as thoughts and feelings are verbalized in an effort to connect and convince others. Meaning is created through communication among human beings.

Communication is one of the most rapidly expanding disciplines in modern education. Speech communication often includes courses on organizational, cultural, intrapersonal, interpersonal, and public communication. It integrates

---

[1] Steven Pinker and Paul Bloom, "Natural Language and Natural Selection," *Behavioral and Brain Sciences* 13, no. 4 (1990): 707–84.

[2] C. David Mortensen, ed., *Communication Theory* (New York: Harper and Row, 2007), xxiii.

aspects of both social sciences and the humanities. The discipline may overlap with sociology, psychology, anthropology, biology, political science, economics, and public policy. It may apply to outside disciplines including ministry, business, engineering, architecture, mathematics, and information science. Many different career paths are possible with college degrees in communication. In addition, oral communication is utilized in most professions and lifestyles.

Communication skills have the power to help people achieve their goals and accomplish their dreams. In his book, *Secrets of Great Communicators*, Jeff Myers suggests there are six ways communication skills can help dreams come true.[3] He believes people with excellent communication skills will have a tremendous advantage over those without them. It has been said that seven out of ten jobs require effective speech skills. Consider these factors that support the impact of good communication on life and work:

1. It gives a stronger sense of purpose.
2. It helps people become more aware of the world at large.
3. It creates better learners.
4. It creates better thinkers.
5. It helps people develop greater poise in social situations.
6. It helps people better relate to one another.

These and other reasons should encourage the pursuit of communicative excellence.

Queen Esther provides an excellent biblical example of an effective communicator. She had many serious concerns to express, which necessitated an audience with the king. She discreetly planned the appropriate time to pour out her deep burden and revealed the plot to kill her beloved people (Esther 7). Her conversation with the king literally saved the Jews in Persia.

Effective communication is especially important for those in ministry. General public speaking techniques are needed in sermon delivery, teaching, and speaking. Speech is no longer taught in many high schools and colleges. A small minority of students have involvement on drama teams or debate teams, but many adults enter careers and ministry with no training in public speaking and little experience in formal communication. In an effort to develop the spiritual gift of talking, this chapter will explore types of communication, steps in communication, and misunderstandings about communication.

---

[3] Jeff Myers, *Secrets of Great Communicators: Simple, Powerful Strategies for Reaching Your Audience* (Nashville: B&H, 2006), 15–17.

Types of Communication

In the beginning, God spoke the world into being. His divine communication accomplished his creation. To his human creations, made in his image, God gave the gift of communication. The word *communication* comes from the Latin *communis,* which means "to share, to make common, or to have a common faith."[4] For Christians, communication is more than the exchange of ideas. It is sharing faith with others through God-given speaking abilities. God also empowers his children to communicate with him through prayer and with each other in many different ways.

In his book, *Basic Oral Communication,* Glenn Capp discussed the three basic types of oral communication: *intrapersonal, interpersonal,* and *nonverbal.* While each aspect of communication is separate, they are related in the total process.[5] A description of each type of communication follows.

Intrapersonal communication occurs throughout the day when an individual engages in mental dialogue. It is typical for thoughts to be formulated and communicated internally during daily tasks. Language is developed and communication is improved during this type of communication. People often rehearse what is to be said before saying it. Intrapersonal communication helps a speaker anticipate feedback and construct meaning before speaking. It promotes confidence and clarity when a message is shared.[6]

As a speech pathologist, I (Rhonda) often employed play therapy with children who were delayed in language development. They were encouraged to verbalize words and phrases as they played with toys. Playtime became an opportunity for them to rehearse speech before communicating with others. What began as simple statements of action typically became expression of thoughts and feelings. Children communicate with themselves in play much like adults dialogue internally during intrapersonal communication.

Interpersonal communication occurs when a person talks with other people. (It includes one-on-one conversations, talking within a group and public speaking situations.) Interpersonal communication takes place during life and ministry. Speakers work together toward a consensus in thought, state beliefs or convictions, and work to solve problems.[7] Throughout the day, people talk

---

[4] Merriam-Webster Online Dictionary (Merriam-Webster, Incorporated, 2013), s.v. "communicate." Accessed 18 March 2013, http://www.merriam-webster.com/dictionary/communicate.

[5] Glenn R. Capp, Carol C. Capp, and G. Richard Capp Jr., *Basic Oral Communication,* 5th ed. (Englewood Cliffs, NJ: Prentice Hall, 1990), 5–6.

[6] Ibid.

[7] Ibid.

to each other privately or in groups. In ministry, communication takes place in counseling sessions, support groups, Bible studies, or larger gatherings. The public speaking aspect of interpersonal communication will be the focus of this book once foundational principles have been presented.

Teaching a Bible study employs the use of interpersonal communication. The teacher may begin speaking to a larger group of women and then engage in dialogue with one individual in the class who asks a specific question. Sometimes small group discussion takes place within the larger group of students. Bible teachers may also be given the opportunity to speak to even larger gatherings as God gives a message of truth. Navigating between person-to-person and person-to-persons communication requires skill and practice.

Nonverbal communication involves actions, not words. Body movements, posture, positioning, gestures, facial expression, eye contact, and vocal tone accompany words to explain or emphasize the meaning of the message. Verbal expression can be strengthened by the addition of a hand gesture, the change in tone of voice, a look of surprise, or increase in volume. Nonverbal cues can carry as much meaning—if not more—than words.[8]

A pantomime demonstrates the power of communicating thoughts without words. The mime creatively acts out a story or message. With skill in gesture, expression, and movement, a mime communicates nonverbally. Similarly, speakers often use gesture, expression, and movement to enhance the message. Effective communicators deliberately work on improving nonverbal communication for conversation and public speaking.

I (Monica) will never forget the different facial expressions my mother would use on my siblings and me from the choir loft of our church on Sunday mornings. Although we were told to be on our best behavior and to sit quietly on the second pew, at times we would begin to misbehave. All my mother had to do was raise her right eyebrow and look sternly into our eyes. Although she was unable to communicate with us by words, we knew exactly what she meant!

In summary, the three overarching types of communication are:

- *Intrapersonal*—communication that happens within a person throughout her daily tasks.
- *Interpersonal*—communication with other persons.
- *Nonverbal*—communication conveyed through actions and expressions.

---

[8] Ibid.

Steps in Communication

A person who improves in all areas of communication becomes a better communicator because practice in conversational skills will promote public speaking abilities. It is helpful for public speakers to understand the communicative process. In his book, Capp also presents four steps to describe the complex process of communication. To deliver a message, a speaker must verbalize a thought to a receiver who must hear, understand, and react to what is said. Then, the listener responds verbally to the original speaker who receives the feedback from the original message. This circular process of conversation continues until the message has been communicated completely and effectively.

Capp summarized the 4-Step Process of Communication in this way:[9]

1. The sender (speaker) encodes (verbalizes) a message to a receiver.
2. The receiver (listener) decodes (hears, understands, reacts to) the message from the sender.
3. The receiver (speaker) encodes (verbalizes) a message giving feedback to the sender.
4. The sender (listener) decodes (hears, understands, reacts to) the message from the receiver.

Here is a diagram to visually depict the four-steps:

4-Step Process of Communication

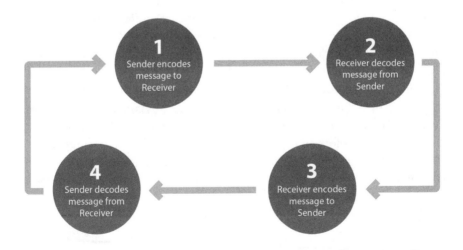

---

[9] Ibid., 6–9.

Consider this example illustrating the process of communication described. In a one-on-one dialogue, Mary is the sender (speaker) and Linda is the receiver (listener). Mary would like for her friend Linda to attend a ladies' Bible study at church. The following circular interaction might take place:

> Mary → "I would like to invite you to attend our Ladie's Bible study at church."
>   (message encoded by sender)
> Linda → "When does it meet?"
>   (message decoded by receiver then encoded back to sender)
> Mary → "We meet on Thursday mornings from 9:30 to 11:30."
>   (sender responds to the receiver)
> Linda → "I would love to attend."
>   (receiver encodes a response and continues the conversational cycle)

Throughout life, people open their mouths and speak words without really thinking about the complexity of the process. As I (Monica) experienced my infant daughter's effort to communicate by making a variety of different sounds, I thought about the challenge of this circular process that connects individuals to each other and accomplishes ministry for the glory of God.

Misunderstandings about Communication

Because the process of communication is so complex, it is often misunderstood. It would simplify matters if a person could convey thoughts telepathically to another person. If thoughts did not have to be formulated in a speaker's brain, expressed through that speaker's words, transmitted through the air, perceived through the listener's ears, understood in the listener's mind, and responded to verbally by the listener, a message would always be understood. That is not possible. Instead, God created humans to have thoughts and feelings which, to be understood by others, must be expressed in words. Overcoming the complexity of communication requires study and practice throughout the lifespan.

Many counseling books unveil the critical need for communication within marriage. For years, during premartial counseling, my (Monica) father would place three rocks before an engaged couple, signifying the three foundations of a marriage. One of those rocks stood for the critical need to communicate (connection); the others for communion (intimacy) and cooperation (marital roles). Dad wanted married couples to benefit from the mastery of communication.

While there are numerous misunderstandings about communication, Duane Litfin presents three of the most common in his book, *Public Speaking:*

A Handbook for Christians.[10] These misunderstandings can confuse both the speaker and the listener.

> *Misunderstanding 1*: Each act of communication is separate and discrete and can be studied as such. The truth is that communication is a complicated, interactive process.
> *Misunderstanding 2*: Communication is linear in the sense that a message travels one way from a source to a receiver. The truth is that human communication is circular. It begins with a spoken word and continues with further interactions.
> *Misunderstanding 3*: The speaker transfers a thought to the listeners. The truth is the listener filters information through personal perspective in order to understand the message spoken.

These misunderstandings reflect the complexity of the process of communication. Understanding these myths will improve overall communication and strengthen relationships. Though complex, communication is an essential interaction among humans. We need it to convey messages, build relationships, and serve others.

Steven Pinker and Paul Bloom declare, "Speaking is innate, writing is an invention."[11] Oral communication has several distinctive components which contrast it from written communication.[12] These differences must be considered when speaking. First, oral communication tends to be more direct than written expression. Nonverbal cues can clarify meaning while more description is necessary in writing. Second, oral communication tends to be more repetitive or redundant than written discourse. Readers can refer back to information that is written, while listeners need repetition for better understanding. Third, oral communication tends to be more fragmentary. Written language includes complete thoughts and sentences. Fourth, oral communication tends to be more personal while written communication may be more generalized. One needs to be aware of these distinctives when preparing to speak. Information needs to be delivered to be heard, not read.

Deeply desiring to share my innermost heart, I (Monica) journaled letters to my future husband as I waited for God to bring him into my life. These were

---

[10] Duane Litfin, *Public Speaking: A Handbook for Christians* (Grand Rapids: Baker, 1992), 19–21.
[11] Pinker and Bloom, "Natural Language," 707–84.
[12] Litfin, *Public Speaking*, 275–77.

bound in a leather case and given to him the night before we wed. I immensely enjoyed writing these letters, but the moments we shared as he asked me to read the letters to him out loud were even more special. My written words communicated my feelings more deeply than my spoken words. The inflection of my voice enriched the written ideas.

One of my (Monica) favorite Bible verses is Psalm 45:1, "My heart is moved by a noble theme as I recite my verses to the king; my tongue is the pen of a skillful writer." I love to write and find I am able to express on paper what is often difficult to express aloud. When I turned twelve years old, I started keeping a prayer journal. I would write out my prayers. Journaling became a daily discipline for me and helped me to articulate on paper what I was thinking about or struggling with each day. I found that I was much more detailed when I wrote out my prayers on paper than when I prayed out loud. However, when I have been asked to pray at a women's event or small group setting, I never hand out copies of a prayer to be read by everyone. I speak them out loud to the Lord on behalf of the women in the group. As women hear what is spoken out loud, there is a connection. Spoken words take on more meaning than those merely written.

According to Litfin, there are several distinct advantages of public speaking. First, important messages must often be *communicated to a large number of people*. It is much more practical and beneficial for a major thought to be shared one time to a larger group. Second, a public speech is a message which can be *organized and prepared by the speaker*. Thoughtful preparation increases the clarity and improves the effectiveness of the communication. Third, a public speech allows the ideas to be *heard by the listeners who can postpone a response* until the ideas are fully understood.[13] While spontaneous, interpersonal conversation will always be a part of daily life and church ministry, skilled public speaking can enhance a message delivery among groups and even among individuals.

---

[13] Ibid., 27.

Talking Point

Communication is a complex process
dependent on both the speaker *and* the listener.

Let's Talk about It

1. Describe the six ways author Jeff Myers suggests that communication skills can help dreams come true. What does Myers believe about people who possess strong communication skills?
2. List and define the three basic types of oral communication involved in the process of communication.
3. Identify three misunderstandings that reflect the complexity of the process of communication presented by Duane Litfin in the book, *Public Speaking: A Handbook for Christians.*
4. What are some advantages of public speaking over informal conversation?
5. Distinguish between oral communication and written communication. How do you communicate most effectively?

Chapter 3

HEARING AND
LISTENING

"The one who gives an answer before he listens—this is
foolishness and disgrace for him."
(Prov 18:13)

While talking is the most obvious part of public speaking, hearing and listening are essential to the process. An effective public speaker will be an excellent listener. Listening begins with attention and hearing. In this chapter, we will address the importance of attention and differentiate between the physiological process of hearing and the psychological process of listening. A discussion of barriers to listening and tips for good listening are included as well. A commitment to good listening will improve one's speaking ability.

Dennis the Menace discovered the difference between hearing and listening in an interaction with his neighbor. I like the comic strip in which Mr. Wilson is reading the newspaper when Dennis gives him a warm, "Hello, Mr. Wilson." No response. Dennis speaks a little louder. "Hello, Mr. Wilson." Still no response. Finally, Dennis shouts, *"Hello, Mr. Wilson!"* No answer. Dennis turns to leave and in a normal voice says, "Well, then, goodbye, Mr. Wilson." To this the neighbor replies, "Goodbye, Dennis." As he walks out the door, Dennis remarks, "There's nothing wrong with his hearing, but his listening's not so good." Mr. Wilson was not hearing-impaired but he was definitely listening-impaired!

I (Monica) have learned not to speak to my husband or brothers while they are watching television—especially when it's the Super Bowl time! It does not matter what I say or need to bring to their attention. They may hear me speaking, but they surely are not listening. They are engrossed in every aspect of the game. I can understand because I am often this way when it comes to shopping. I love to browse and find good deals. Often, when my husband speaks to me while I am shopping, I will have to ask him to repeat what he said. I hear him but definitely am not listening.

Attention

All communication begins with attention. If attention is not gained, listening cannot occur. Attention underlies hearing and listening, requiring focus on a stimulus in order to hear and receive information. Attention can only be given to one stimulus at a time and can be sustained for only a few seconds before it shifts. Therefore, attention is variable, always changing.

In *Principles of Speech Communication*, Bruce Gronbeck presents nine factors of attention: activity, reality, proximity, familiarity, novelty, suspense, conflict, humor, and the vital.[1]

- *Activity*—Attention will be gained and sustained when listeners are actively involved.
- *Reality*—References to real people, places, and events will keep a listener's attention.
- *Proximity*—When a speaker is near or close to the audience, attention will be encouraged.
- *Familiarity*—References to the familiar are attention sustaining.
- *Novelty*—Novel happenings, dramatic incidents, or unusual developments attract attention.
- *Suspense*—Surprise or hints of what will come raises the interest of the audience.
- *Conflict*—Controversy grabs attention and peaks interest.
- *Humor*—Funny comments or humorous illustrations capture and hold attention.
- *The Vital*—Information that immediately benefits the listener will gain attention. Topics which affect health, family, reputation, property, or employment are top attention-getters.

Good public speakers are aware of these factors and attempt to gain the audience's attention throughout a speech.

---

[1] Bruce E. Gronbeck, Kathleen German, Douglas Ehninger, and Alan H. Monroe, *Principles of Speech Communication*, 12th brief ed. (New York: HarperCollins, 1995), 143–48.

Some people have longer attention spans than others. Those with attention problems must consciously focus in order to hear and listen. Many people have been diagnosed with attention deficit disorders (ADD), some with hyperactivity as well. Though medication may benefit some listeners, all individuals with attention problems should learn behavioral strategies to improve attention for the purpose of listening and understanding. Attention is selective; listeners must choose to focus on specific stimuli. This selective behavior can be improved.

Attention changes throughout life. A child must learn to focus, and adults must learn to sustain attention. I (Rhonda) am learning that attention skills diminish with age. Chuck's father, our precious Papa, had dementia. In time he could not sustain attention to read his daily newspaper. My dad now has dementia and is unable to sustain attention to watch his beloved football games. When I am with him, I have learned to sit right in front of him to keep his attention on our conversation. Attention skills require lifelong learning.

There are two primary types of attention: involuntary and voluntary. Most attention is involuntary or unconscious. Responses to sound and voice are often automatic or reflexive. One cannot help but react to a smoke alarm or tornado warning. The loud, disruptive sounds demand attention. Once attention is gained, hearing and listening can begin.

Voluntary attention is more complicated. A person can choose to pay attention to a sound or voice and ignore other sounds and voices. Selective or voluntary attention is under the person's control and requires some effort and discipline. In conversation, a receiver must first choose to attend to the voice of the sender in order to hear and listen to the message.[2]

Hearing

Once attention has been obtained, hearing can occur. Hearing and listening are different. While hearing is a physiological process, listening is a psychological process. Hearing is "the special sense by which noises and tones are received as stimuli to the auditory nerves."[3] It is the perception of sound, the noises heard by the ears. It is an automatic process that occurs without noticeable effort for those who have normal hearing acuity.

Normal hearing allows an individual to perceive sound waves and voices. Hearing develops in infancy as a baby begins to recognize sounds and localize

---

[2] Duane Litfin, *Public Speaking: A Handbook for Christians* (Grand Rapids: Baker, 1992), 46–49.

[3] Merriam-Webster Online Dictionary (Merriam-Webster, Incorporated, 2013), s.v. "hearing." Accessed 18 March 2013, http://www.merriam-webster.com/dictionary/hearing.

them. Hearing acuity is necessary for the development of language and the building of human relationships. Numerous factors can interfere with hearing: distracting noises in the environment, sounds too loud or too soft for the individual's ears, or physical/medical problems. Hearing is usually beyond the speaker's control, though one might change speaking volume, seating arrangements, or conditions in the room before talking.[4]

Some people experience hearing loss. Hearing loss is most common in children and older adults. Whether temporary or permanent, hearing loss can greatly impact communication skills. According to the American Speech-Language-Hearing Association, there are three basic types of hearing loss: *conductive hearing loss, sensorineural hearing loss,* and *mixed hearing loss.*

Conductive hearing loss occurs when sound is not transmitted efficiently through the outer ear canal to the eardrum and the tiny bones of the middle ear. It usually involves a reduction in sound level or the ability to hear faint sounds, and it is often the result of fluid, infection, or allergies. This temporary type of hearing loss can often be corrected medically or surgically.[5]

As a speech pathologist, I (Rhonda) worked with many children who had speech disorders due to conductive hearing loss they experienced while speech was being developed. Their hearing loss was temporary, but the consequences were ongoing. Once the hearing problem was treated, the child had the potential for hearing clearly and correcting speech articulation errors. Speech therapy began with auditory training so the child could distinguish the difference between the correct sound and the incorrect sound. With frequent drill and practice, speech could often improve.

Sensorineural hearing loss occurs when there is damage to the inner ear (cochlea) or to the nerve pathways from the inner ear to the brain. It usually reduces the ability to hear faint sounds making them unclear or muffled. It is often the result of heredity, trauma, or aging. This permanent type of hearing loss cannot be medically or surgically corrected and most often requires a patient to wear hearing aids.[6]

I (Rhonda) worked with many high-risk children whose premature births and other neonatal complications often resulted in permanent hearing loss. Children with significant sensorineural hearing loss often required hearing aids and were typically slow to begin speaking. In the case of severe or profound hearing

---

[4] Gronbeck et al., *Principles of Speech Communication*, 35.

[5] American Speech-Language-Hearing Association (ASHA, 2013), "Conductive Hearing Loss." Accessed 18 March 2013, http://www.asha.org/public/hearing/Conductive-Hearing-Loss.

[6] American Speech-Language-Hearing Association (ASHA, 2013), "Sensorineural hearing loss." Accessed 18 March 2013, http://www.asha.org/public/hearing/Sensorineural-Hearing-Loss.

loss, the children learned sign language in order to communicate. In recent years, cochlear implants have made oral communication possible for individuals with significant, permanent hearing loss. The small device is implanted behind the ear to provide direct electrical stimulation to the auditory nerve in the inner ear. Children and adults may communicate verbally when adequate hearing is achieved.

Sometimes a conductive hearing loss occurs in combination with a sensorineural hearing loss. In other words, there may be damage in the outer or middle ear and in the inner ear or auditory nerve. When this occurs, the hearing loss is referred to as a *mixed hearing loss*. A combination of causes requires a combination of treatments for this hearing loss, which may be temporary or permanent.[7]

My (Rhonda) precious mother-in-love is ninety years of age and has been fighting a mixed hearing loss for the past few years. Her hearing has decreased due to aging, resulting in a moderate-to-severe permanent hearing loss. In addition, she has been experiencing conductive hearing loss in both of her ears due to fluid and infection. The inner ear and outer ear infections have required several rounds of antibiotics as well as frequent doctor visits to clean the eardrums and treat the ear canals. In the meantime, her hearing aids often become clogged by drainage and debris. She has received regular hearing tests as well as increased amplification in her hearing aids by the audiologist. Still, a mixed hearing loss can be very frustrating as well as difficult to treat.

Types of Hearing Loss	
Types of Hearing Loss	**Description of Hearing Loss**
Conductive Loss	sound not transmitted through the outer ear canal to the eardrum and middle ear
Sensorineural Loss	damage to the inner ear or auditory nerves from inner ear to the brain
Mixed Hearing Loss	damage to the outer or middle ear as well as the inner ear or auditory nerve

---

[7] American Speech-Language-Hearing Association (ASHA, 2013), "Mixed Hearing Loss." Accessed 18 March 2013, http://www.asha.org/public/hearing/Mixed-Hearing-Loss.

Attention and hearing are necessary prerequisites to listening. Once good attention has been gained and adequate hearing has been achieved, a person can begin to listen. Listening is one of the most important aspects of human communication.

Listening

Listening is a higher level skill than hearing. It is a psychological process that requires perception and understanding. It is reaction to sound and hearing with thoughtful attention that attaches meaning to what is heard. It is a skill one learns. People learn to "tune in" or "tune out" to listen more carefully, but most people are poor listeners. We *hear* many things but we *listen to* few.

Listening is an active process requiring attention and focus. The speaker benefits from responses that indicate the receiver is listening. In personal conversations and public speaking, listeners should respond nonverbally with facial expressions and head nods to demonstrate they are listening. Effective communicators learn to listen actively and respond appropriately to these signals.

As a teacher on a college campus, I (Monica) have the privilege of meeting with young women who come by my office to discuss specific issues they are experiencing. I find that most of them simply want someone to listen. I try to listen to everything they are saying before offering any counsel. It is imperative for me to hear *and* listen to their entire story before I offer a response or advice. Only as I listen intentionally will they begin to reveal their deep-seated struggles. One young lady revealed to me that she did not have money for a winter coat. After our conversation, I took her to the store and had her pick one out. I would have never known about her need if I was not listening intentionally. She felt free to open up and share with me because she saw that I cared about what she had to say.

There are four types of listening; (1) empathic; (2) informative; (3) evaluative; and (4) appreciative. Sometimes a listener must empathize with the speaker to understand and offer moral support and concern. Other times, a listener wants to gain information and seek knowledge for the purpose of learning. The listener may evaluate or critique a message in order to confront or challenge. Or, the listener may simply seek enjoyment or entertainment with no interest in information or evaluation. The type of listening will affect the manner of listening.

Why Listen?

Listening is important! Some people are naturally good listeners, though most are better talkers. It has been said that God gave us one mouth and two ears so that we could listen twice as much. Iconic western movie star John Wayne put our dendency to value speaking over listening this way: "You're short on ears and long on mouth." People do seem to enjoy hearing themselves speak more than they appreciate listening to others. Carpenters have a rule: measure twice and saw once. That principle could apply to listening and talking. Consider these various reasons why people should listen:

1. *Listen to acquire facts.* Sometimes people listen to gather information or gain knowledge. Students in school listen for this specific reason—especially as a test approaches. They want to gain knowledge for their scholastic success.

2. *Listen to analyze facts and ideas.* Higher level skills are involved when people listen to study or determine the nature or relationship of the information. Listening in order to respond often involves interpretation and analysis.

3. *Listen to evaluate facts and ideas.* Listening to determine the significance or worth of information by careful appraisal and study is the highest level of listening. A persuasive speech or sermon often invites evaluation and application of truth.

4. *Listen for entertainment.* Sometimes people listen simply for enjoyment, relaxation, or encouragement. An after-dinner speaker or comedian may require an audience to listen only for pleasure. Her main objective is to entertain, not inform.

5. *Listen for inspiration.* Messages that are devotional or enlightening in nature require less intense listening from the audience. Many women's events offer inspiration more than instruction. The goal is for listeners to leave reassured and hopeful.

6. *Listen to improve your communication.* People can listen to learn from others. Public speakers become more effective when they listen to others for the improvement of their own skills.

7. *Listen to show concern and interest.* There are times when more sincere listening is needed. Counselors use empathic or concerned listening as clients share their problems. Personal relationships are strengthened as listeners try to understand and reflect care.[8]

---

[8] Glenn R. Capp, Carol C. Capp, and G. Richard Capp Jr., *Basic Oral Communication*, 5th ed. (Englewood Cliffs, NJ: Prentice Hall, 1990), 60–62.

Listening is one of the greatest gifts one can give. It is also a discipline we must all develop. I (Rhonda) am a very task-driven person. As a result, I fill my days with activities and my calendars with to-do lists. When my agenda is interrupted by a visit or phone call, I can grow impatient because of the things I had planned to do. The Lord has been teaching me to be a better listener. When my mother calls, I stop multitasking and listen to her conversation. When I am grocery shopping, I pause to help a shopper or chat with the register clerk. I must discipline myself not to focus solely on my personal tasks.

What Is Listening Dependent Upon?

Listening is dependent upon a number of different variables. A person can say the same thing to a group of ten people and probably be interpreted in ten different ways. Some variables can be controlled and others cannot. However, good speakers understand the inherent biases of listeners. Listening is dependent upon attitudes, interests, motivation, emotional state, and environment.[9]

1. *Attitudes*—What do I think about the speaker? How do I feel about the topic? What are my expectations of the event? Do I have preconceived ideas or thoughts?

2. *Interests*—What level of interest do I have in this topic? What level of interest do I have in the person speaking? Do I have other more important interests right now?

3. *Motivation*—What difference is this conversation or presentation going to make in my life? Is this topic important in my life? Will what I learn make a difference in my life or in the lives of others close to me?

4. *Emotional state*—Am I tired? Am I upset or distracted? Do I feel stressed? Am I rested and relaxed?

5. *Environment*—Is this setting comfortable? Are the chairs comfortable? Is the temperature comfortable? How many people are in the room?

These variables—and others—will influence how people listen. As a listener, one must seek to understand what may impede listening. As a speaker, one must recognize the factors impacting the listener's ability to learn.

What Are Some Barriers to Good Listening?

Most Americans are poor listeners. Litfin explains that we are an EYE-oriented culture rather than EAR-oriented. Americans, especially young people who

---

[9] Ibid., 62–65.

have grown up with electronic technology, prefer visual input. The people in cultures where there is no written language or high incidences of illiteracy are EAR-oriented. In our culture, we say, "Can I have a copy of that?" or "I need to see it in writing." We prefer "reading and storage" over "listening well and remembering."[10] We must work harder on listening since it does not come as naturally to us. Attention and listening skills are better in cultures that must depend on hearing and memory for information.

Common barriers to good listening include the following:[11]

1. *Passive listening*—Many people are lazy listeners. Listening is active, involving interaction between the listener and speaker in the process.

2. *Interrupting*—Many listeners are impatient to wait for the comment to end and are eager to speak. Conversation requires give and take. Listening precedes speaking

3. *Assumptions*—People have a tendency to jump to a conclusion before a speaker finishes a thought. Making a wrong assumption is like "jumping to a confusion"!

4. *Self-focus*—In this "me-generation," people are more interested in what they have to say than what others are saying. Listening requires focus on the speaker, not on self.

5. *Past intrusion*—Previous experiences or past failures may influence a listener. A good listener must be "in the moment" in order to understand the speaker.

6. *Distraction*—Drifting thoughts and poor attention hinder good listening. Distractions can be internal or external. Listeners must focus on the words being spoken in order to listen completely and correctly.

7. *Defensiveness*—Listeners may react strongly when they disagree or have another opinion. This verbal response has been described as *duelogue vs. dialogue*. Duelogue implies two people fighting with words as their weapons.[12]

Identifying one's personal barriers to good listening is an important move in controlling these hindrances so listening may improve. Knowing personal weaknesses in listening is the first step toward improving listening skills.

Distraction is probably my biggest barrier to good listening. I (Rhonda) am highly distracted internally by thoughts of everything I must accomplish. I am distracted externally by the sights and sounds around me. When my husband and I go out to dinner, my natural desire is to face everyone and everything in the

---

[10] Litfin, *Public Speaking*, 42.

[11] Gronbeck et al., *Principles of Speech Communication*, 36–37.

[12] *Examiner.com* (Clarity Digital Group LLC, 2013), "Duelogue." Accessed 3 March 2013, http://www.examiner.com/article/monologue-dialogue-or-duelogue-how-savvy-are-you.

restaurant because of my curiosity. To give Chuck my undivided attention, I must sit facing him—and maybe the wall—to tune out the distractions around me.

The Bible teaches about the importance of listening and warns against hasty speech. In James 1:19, the apostle admonishes: "Everyone must be quick to hear, slow to speak, and slow to anger." Commentary for this verse in the *Life Application Bible* includes an exercise for overcoming barriers to good listening. "Put a mental stopwatch on your conversations and keep track of how much you talk and how much you listen. In your conversations, do others feel that their viewpoints and ideas have been valued?"[13] Effective communicators break down personal barriers to listening in order to build up people while focusing on their messages.

What Are Some Tips for Good Listening?

Since listening is a psychological behavior, it can be improved. Many people are better listeners than others. All listeners must work hard to listen well. Examine the word "listen" and notice it has the same letters as the word "silent." Silence aids good listening. Listening skills, including an appreciation for silence, are developed through hard work and training.

The practice of listening should be an intentional pursuit. In a class, I (Rhonda) attempted to illustrate the importance of listening to remembering. Five volunteers were asked to leave the room. While they were gone, the class created an unbelievable story. One by one the volunteers returned to class. Volunteer 1 entered the classroom and was told the story. Volunteer 1 then retold the story to Volunteer 2, then 2 to 3, 3 to 4, and 4 to 5. You can imagine how the story changed as it was passed along from one listener to another. Facts and feelings can get lost in translation when the quality of listening wavers. Practice listening and remembering to improve your communication skills.

Here are some helpful hints for good listening:

1. *Focus on what is being said.* Concentrate on the speaker's words, not your own thoughts.
2. *Learn what to listen for.* Listen for feelings; listen for facts; listen for direction.
3. *Listen critically or constructively.* Learn to evaluate and assess as you listen.
4. *Do not make judgments until the end.* Listen to the complete message before forming an opinion or response.

---

[13] Tyndale House, *Life Application Bible: New Testament* (Wheaton, IL: Tyndale House, 1987), 604.

5. *Do not interrupt.* Be considerate of the speaker and wait for the appropriate time to comment.
6. *Be sensitive to the speaker's body language.* Listen carefully to what is not said. Tone of voice and gestures can speak just as loudly as words.
7. *Maintain eye contact or face contact.* Look at the person who is speaking. Attend to the face and eyes for nonverbal cues.
8. *Take notes to assist listening.* Write thoughts down to improve understanding and enhance memory.

The title of this book asserts that talking is a spiritual gift. Listening can also be a spiritual gift when used to minister to another. In *Women Reaching Women: Beginning and Building a Growing Women's Ministry*, Esther Burroughs discusses spiritual gifts including "the gift of listening with the heart." She offers this challenge:

> If we would refine our gift of listening—listening with our hearts—we would have opportunity to share Christ more often. Each of us should look at the people in today's world. We'd see tired faces, stooped shoulders, tears, anger, and loneliness. But some of us have the spiritual gift of listening. We could change the kingdom of God with listening hearts.[14]

How true! In giving away the gift of listening, the sender and receiver are blessed.

To practice the spiritual gift of listening is to follow the teachings of Scripture. The writer of Proverbs 18:13 gives a warning: "The one who gives an answer before he listens—this is foolishness and disgrace for him." Jesus spoke to his disciples about restoring a brother when he said, "If he listens to you, you have won your brother" (Matt 18:15). In another encounter, Jesus questioned his disciples: "Why don't you understand what I say? Because you cannot listen to My word" (John 8:43). The Good Shepherd said: "they [My sheep] will listen to My voice" (John 10:16). The disciples also taught the importance of listening. James wrote: "My dearly loved brothers, understand this: Everyone must be quick to hear, slow to speak, and slow to anger" (Jas 1:19). In 1 John 4:6, the author wrote: "We are from God. Anyone who knows God listens to us; anyone who is not from God does not listen to us."

Listening is a biblical principle as well as a spiritual gift. One who speaks sows; one who listens reaps. Listening is as important to communication as speaking. Learning to listen more carefully will improve communication skills.

[14] Chris Adams, *Women Reaching Women: Beginning and Building a Growing Women's Ministry* (Nashville: LifeWay Christian Resources, 2005), 54.

TALKING POINT

One who speaks sows.
One who listens reaps.

LET'S TALK ABOUT IT

1. Describe the nine factors of attention as presented in *Principles of Speech Communication*.
2. What is the importance of attention to the hearing and listening process?
3. Distinguish between hearing and listening. Identify your own hearing or listening weaknesses.
4. Why is listening important? What are some barriers to listening?
5. Describe how listening can be a spiritual gift. How can you practice the gift of listening?

Part II

VERBAL COMMUNICATION

How Can I Improve My Public Speaking?

This part of the book will explore the nature of verbal communication, specifically public speaking. Sections will include preparing a speech, delivering a speech, and evaluating a speech. Specific attention will be given to work before, during, and after a public presentation.

In the fourth century BC, the Greek philosopher Aristotle wrote *On Rhetoric*, suggesting three pillars of public speaking. Since that time, his ideas have influenced all discussions about communication. Aristotle suggested that "rhetoric," or the art of persuasive speaking, is based on three foundations: *ethos, pathos, and logos.*[1]

Ethos, from the Greek word for "character," refers to the trustworthiness or credibility of the speaker. *Pathos*, from the Greek word for "suffering" or "experience," refers to the emotional appeal or passion of the speaker. *Logos*, from the Greek word for "word," refers to the reasoning or clarity of the speaker. With every opportunity to present a message, an effective public speaker should develop in each of these areas. This part of the book will address all three pillars of public speaking.

---

[1] George Kennedy, *Aristotle on Rhetoric: A Theory of Civic Discourse* (New York: Oxford University Press, 1991), 37–39.

Section I

PREPARING THE SPEECH

This section will focus on the steps involved in preparing for a speech or message. Before a message is presented, much work must be accomplished. It has been suggested that a speaker will spend ten times the length of the speech in preparation. In other words, a thirty–minute speech should have 300 minutes—or five hours—of preparation, while a one–hour speech would require 600 minutes—or ten hours—of preparation. The time and effort invested in preparation is returned in the speech delivery.

While much time and energy are required for public speaking, rarely is adequate time for preparation a reality. The investment of time should be a goal of speech preparation even when time is short. This section will focus specifically on elements important to preparing the speech: devotion and discipline, audience and occasion, topic and purpose, outlines and objectives, research and supportive material, types and parts, and exposition and exegesis. Make a commitment to always be prepared as a speaker.

Chapter 4

DEVOTION AND DISCIPLINE

*"Therefore, whether you eat or drink, or whatever you do,
do everything for God's glory."*
(1 Cor 10:31)

This chapter will consider the necessity of a Christian woman's spiritual preparation to speak. Proclaiming a word from God requires a growing relationship with God through daily devotion and personal discipline. A message from the Lord should be dedicated to him for it to bring him glory and change the lives of the listeners. First Corinthians 10:31 is a reminder that in all we do, bringing God glory should be our highest aim: "Therefore, whether you eat or drink, or whatever you do, do everything for God's glory."

The Bible includes speeches of the faithful that provide examples of powerful proclamation. The lives of the speakers and the content of the messages can instruct and instill a desire to speak from a heart of commitment. In each case, the believer's life of devotion and discipline empowered the message shared. Let us consider five women of the Bible who spoke about their devotion to God in a clear and effective way.

Miriam who was thrust into a position of leadership as a prophetess in Israel was the sister of Moses and Aaron. Her initiative was first demonstrated along the Nile River when she offered to find a wet nurse for the baby Moses, who had been hidden in a basket in the river by their mother Jochebed in an attempt to protect him from the wrath of the pharaoh. Years later, when Moses was used by God to deliver his people from bondage in Egypt, Miriam led the women in praise to God. Her enthusiastic chorus is recorded in Exodus 15:21: "Sing to the LORD, for He is highly exalted; He has thrown the horse and its rider into the sea." Her devotion to God, discipline in life, and dedication to her calling enabled her to be used by God at a critical time in history.

However, her faith faltered and she questioned the leadership of her brother Moses. The Lord disciplined her by giving her leprosy and banning her from the camp. In time, God restored her through the prayer of her brother (Numbers 12). Miriam is an example and a warning to Christian women today who would desire to speak his message: stay close to God and remain faithful to him so your testimony will not be weakened.

It is important to remain consistent in our walks with God. The moment we take our focus off of Christ and stop seeking him, we fall prey to becoming the opposite of what we desire. Miriam's story reminds us to be disciplined in our words to others. May our words be edifying to everyone with whom we share. In Col 4:6, Paul declares, "Your speech should always be gracious, seasoned with salt, so that you may know how you should answer each person."

Deborah was another woman in the Old Testament used to speak his message to his people during the period of the judges. She was the wife of Lapidoth and was faithful to the Lord. Under a palm tree within the city gates she provided wise counsel to the people. In a spiritually barren and politically weak time, Deborah was called upon by the Lord to serve her nation. God spoke through her to inspire the commander Barak to trust him to defeat the Canaanites who had been oppressing them (see Judges 4–5).

The persuasive words of Deborah to Barak are recorded in Judges 4:14: "Move on, for this is the day the LORD has handed Sisera over to you. Hasn't the LORD gone before you?" Barak immediately followed the instructions of Deborah and defeated Sisera, the commander of the Canaanite army. After the victory, she and Barak sang a song of praise to God: "When the leaders lead in Israel, when the people volunteer, praise the LORD" (Judg 5:2). Deborah obeyed God and led her people as she faithfully proclaimed his message.

Deborah is a prime example of a woman who portrayed the discipline of total obedience and surrender to God. Deborah displayed a fear of God as she rose to the occasion that was placed in front of her as a leader. She trusted in God's plan and was a confident speaker. Colossians 3:22 is a reminder to fear the Lord in all we do: "Don't work only while being watched, in order to please men, but work wholeheartedly, fearing the Lord."

Esther was a beautiful, young orphaned girl who was used by God to save her people, the Jews. She was raised by an older relative and was chosen to be queen during a time of persecution of the Jews ("for such a time as this," Esth 4:14). She spoke courageously to the king about her people, and he heeded her words. The Lord guided her as she spoke to the king: "If it pleases the king, may the Jews who are in Susa also have tomorrow to carry out today's law" (Esth 9:13). Esther is a reminder of the blessing of faithful obedience and divine proclamation as she sought to follow God's plan even if it meant her life. She is a true picture of a disciplined woman who waited on God's perfect timing to go before the king and submit her request with persuasive words.

Mary of Nazareth was a young woman who had a clear understanding of Scripture and was a faithful follower of the Lord. When chosen by God to be the mother of Jesus, she obeyed willingly and trusted God completely. She expressed her emotions in a song of praise: "My soul proclaims the greatness of the Lord, and my spirit has rejoiced in God my Savior" (Luke 1:46–47). Mary and Joseph raised Jesus in the training and instruction of the Lord, preparing him for ministry. Mary became a devoted and humble follower of Christ whose example of joyous celebration provides a pattern of praise for Christians today. In Luke 1:45, the writer describes how Mary could not help but to magnify the Lord. She most assuredly was moved in her spirit and spoke out of her heart: "A good man produces good out of the good storeroom of his heart. An evil man produces evil out of the evil storeroom, for his mouth speaks from the overflow of the heart" (Luke 6:45).

Anna was a prophetess in the time of Jesus' birth. She was an elderly widow who had faithfully served the Lord with fasting and prayers night and day (Luke 2:37). When Jesus was brought by his parents to the temple, she gave praise for the promised Messiah and spoke of him to all who would listen. Anna was a witness to the fulfillment of prophecy who glorified the Lord through her words and actions.

These five women of the Bible remind modern Christian women of the importance of devotion and discipline to prophecy and proclamation. Their speech flowed from their lives of dedication. Psalm 40:5 declares, "LORD my God, You have done many things—Your wonderful works and Your plans for us; none can compare with You. If I were to report and speak of them, they are more than can be told." Our lives should reflect the truth these words proclaim.

Devotion

As a Christian woman and as a speaker, you must evaluate your relationship with God. The depth of your devotion to God will be reflected as you prepare and deliver a speech, especially a biblical message from the Lord. Are you strong in your faith? Are you growing in him? Are you becoming the woman God created you to be? If you desire your life to count for his glory, you must walk with the Lord faithfully as you engage in Bible study, spend time in prayer, serve the Lord in ministry, and speak as a witness of his redeeming love as revealed in 1 Corinthians 3:11–13 we will be judged on the motives behind our service to the Lord: "For no other foundation can anyone lay than that which is laid, which is Jesus Christ. Now if anyone builds on this foundation *with* gold, silver, precious stones, wood, hay, straw, each one's work will become clear; for the Day will declare it, because it will be revealed by fire; and the fire will test each one's work, of what sort it is" (NKJV).

Bible Study

Bible study is essential for spiritual growth, and it is also an important source of information for preparing to speak a word from the Lord. Personal Bible study reveals not only the nature of God; it also teaches truths of the faith that can be shared with others. Devotional reading of the Bible, as well as systematic study of the Word, provide a biblical foundation for speeches and supportive material for points of the message.

Years ago, I (Rhonda) began a personal study of the fruit of the Holy Spirit as found in Galatians 5. As the Lord taught me about the virtues of the Christian life, I wanted to share what I had learned with others. I taught a Bible study to the ladies of my church on the fruit of the Spirit. Then, I wrote a book entitled, *Divine Discipline: How to Develop and Maintain Self-Control* because God convicted me about my own need for personal discipline. God has given me many opportunities to speak about "Divine Discipline" in academic classes and women's conferences. My Bible study not only taught me personally and helped me grow spiritually; it prepared me to speak and write a word from the Lord to others.

Almost all of the Bible studies and poetry I (Monica) have written have come out of my private time with the Lord. My book, *Marvelously Made: Unveil Your True Identity and Purpose as a Woman* originated from what the Lord taught me in my personal Bible study. Rarely have I sat down merely to prepare a teaching outline. Most all my writings were birthed in my heart as I sat at the feet of my Savior. Time with Jesus is of utmost necessity for an effective Bible teacher.

Consider the story of Mary and Martha found in Luke 10:38–42:

> While they were traveling, [Jesus] entered a village, and a woman named
> Martha welcomed Him into her home. She had a sister named Mary, who

also sat at the Lord's feet and was listening to what He said. But Martha was distracted by her many tasks, and she came up and asked, "Lord, don't You care that my sister has left me to serve alone? So tell her to give me a hand." The Lord answered her, "Martha, Martha, you are worried and upset about many things, but one thing is necessary. Mary has made the right choice, and it will not be taken away from her."

What is so interesting about these verses is that Martha felt it necessary to communicate with Jesus and even ordered him to rebuke her sister. If we are not spending devotional time in the Word, we are in great danger of not hearing what the Lord would have us communicate with others.

Prayer

Prayer is another vital element of spiritual growth the Christian teacher must embrace daily. Prayer draws a believer closer to the Lord. God speaks to his children during times of prayer, and his children have the opportunity to speak their hearts to him. Prayer also guides and directs a Christian who is preparing to speak, and prayer empowers the Christian during speech. It is integral to the Christian life and essential for the Christian speaker.

I (Rhonda) am always amazed how God reveals himself to me and directs me as I prayerfully prepare to speak or teach. Beginning the process in prayer and continuing to pray as I work gives me the confidence that I will be sharing what the listeners need to hear. Still, God often redirects my message as I am speaking because he knows the hearts of the ladies listening. As I speak words that I have not prepared, I am reminded of the power of prayer and the indwelling work of the Holy Spirit.

After I (Monica) spend time studying for an upcoming speaking engagement and then spend time in prayer, I am always led to surrender the message and the entire event over to the Lord. Although I study and do all I know to do in order to be spiritually prepared, I know God is the only One who knows what he desires to see accomplished. Prayers of surrender are scary at times and sometimes even frustrating. Numerous times I have had all of my notes prepared and know what I have planned to say for each minute of the Bible study, and then the Lord leads my heart in a different direction. Although it is unsettling to stray away from my notes, the Lord gives me confidence that he is declaring exactly what he desires to be said to the specific group of women placed before me.

Christian speakers must realize the need for Spirit-filled teaching. It is up to us to prepare by studying and being spiritually fit, but we must release all of the message and ourselves to the Lord. We must invite and allow him to work in and through us. What an adventure it is being used of him and submitting to his will as a useful vessel!

Service

Service is also a spiritual responsibility. God calls his children not only to grow but to serve. We are to learn from him so that we may share with others. He calls all believers to minister to others in his name. As Christians minister, they learn about the needs of others as well as the reactions of others. Christian speakers can learn topics for talks as well as illustrations and stories as they serve others in the name of the Lord.

Like many Christian women today, I (Rhonda) am very busy; my schedule is full. However, I have made a deliberate decision not only to teach at a seminary and speak in churches but also to serve the Lord through my own home church. I have served as the director of our women's ministry for more than twenty years and also serve in the welcome ministry on Sunday mornings. While I cannot do everything, I must do something in service to my Lord through my own church. As I serve him, I grow in my personal faith and receive tremendous blessings. I also learn about people and ministry so that I can teach and speak more effectively. Teaching Bible passages about service and sharing examples of personal service provide inspiration and application in my speaking.

Witnessing

Christians who are growing in their faith naturally witness about Christ. Christians are to speak a good word about Jesus as well as share with others what God has done and is doing in their lives. A godly lifestyle and sharing a word of testimony are characteristics of the Christian life. Witnessing offers the opportunity to speak out for Jesus and to practice clearly sharing words of faith.

I (Rhonda) have been challenged to speak out as a witness ever since I was saved as a young child. My dad is an evangelist and my husband is an evangelism professor, so I hear a lot about the topic. But I have also had to discipline myself to be a personal witness. Each time I speak to someone about the Lord, my faith is strengthened as each heart is opened. As I witness, I learn how to clearly communicate the truths of the Bible and explain the plan of salvation. Then, when I teach and speak, I have the platform to speak about Jesus more confidently. Witnessing and speaking go hand in hand.

Growing up as a pastor's daughter, I (Monica) continually heard messages on the importance of sharing faith and saw my parents witness to people constantly.

Both my father and mother would share with me the importance of loving Jesus and being his witness. My father recalls an occasion when I was around three or four years of age. My parents had taken me to my favorite restaurant, McDonald's. We were standing in the line to order a Happy Meal when my father saw me pull on a very sophisticated, older woman's coat. As she turned around, I boldly asked her, "Do you love Jesus?" The lady nervously answered, "Well . . . uh . . . I hope so." Although both my father and mother were turning different shades of red, my boldness pointed to the fact that they were serious about sharing their faith and it was already having an impact on my life.

These disciplines of the faith are needed for the spiritual growth and speech preparation of Christians. However, these disciplines are not possible without complete devotion to the Lord. We must possess his strength to be who he has called us to be. Being devoted in seeking him is vital to the woman who is a Bible teacher, as she will be an example to many other women.

Devotion is not a word understood by or desired by the world. Most people are devoted only to themselves and their own desires. The Bible, however, teaches believers to be devoted to the Lord and to follow him wholeheartedly. In Matthew 6:24, Jesus said, "No one can be a slave of two masters, since either he will hate one and love the other, or be devoted to one and despise the other. You cannot be slaves of God and of money."

The dictionary defines *devotion* as "ardent, often selfless affection and dedication."[1] It is loyalty and enthusiasm for a person, activity, or cause. It is literally pure love, the knowledge that one would actually give up life to protect or defend another without question or hesitation. For Christians, devotion is pure love of the Lord, a sincere expression of total faith through prayer and worship.

In the third century, a young Christian woman and nursing mother named Perpetua demonstrated her devotion to the Lord even to death. She was asked by the authorities and her own father to deny her Christian faith in order to save her life, but she refused. "Could this vase or flowerpot be called by any other name?" she asked. "I cannot be called anything other than I am, a Christian."[2] In an amphitheater before crowds of mockers, Perpetua and others were scourged by gladiators, mutilated by wild animals, and then killed by swords. Her words continue to bear witness to her deep faith.

---

[1] *American Heritage Dictionary of the English Language*, 4th ed. (Houghton Mifflin, 2009), s.v. "devotion."

[2] Herbert Musurillo, "The Martyrdom of Perpetua and Felicitas," from *The Acts of the Christian Martyrs* (Oxford: Oxford University Press, 1972), 109.

Devotion to the Lord helps a Christian be prepared at all times to speak out for Jesus. Personal commitment to the task of public speaking will also help a Christian speaker develop skills for the task. Those who think about the process of communication, learn about public speaking, study speaking techniques, and practice specific principles will undoubtedly become much more effective witnesses. Devotion to the Lord is expressed through discipline.

Discipline

Discipline is not a pleasant topic for most people. It is difficult to discipline others, but it is even more challenging to discipline oneself. However, discipline is necessary to maintain order in life and relationships. Self-discipline is a behavior that must be learned through training. It is a lifelong process of learning that begins with parental instruction in childhood and continues through personal development into adulthood.

My (Monica) brother, Brady, is in full-time ministry and has served the Lord on the mission field, in worship ministry, and now in pastoral ministry. In one of his messages on spiritual disciplines, Brady told about the time our father presented him with a special birthday present when he was just a little boy. Brady was so excited as our father sat him down and tried to communicate with him how special the gift was. Brady opened the gift with such anticipation, only to find a book with blank pages and lines. Our father explained to him that this was his very first prayer journal and that he could write down his prayers to the Lord. At the time, my brother was wondering how a book with no words could be so important. Yet he knew our father's emphasis on the book indicated its value. Now grown, Brady looks back and sees how much he learned and continues to learn from keeping a prayer journal. He conveyed that our father taught him about spiritual discipline at a young age.

The ability to motivate oneself and exert willpower is a basic trait needed personally and professionally. In 1 Timothy 4:7–9, the apostle Paul reminds the Christian of the importance of being disciplined in godliness:

> Have nothing to do with irreverent and silly myths. Rather, train yourself
> in godliness, for the training of the body has a limited benefit, but godliness
> is beneficial in every way, since it holds promise for the present life and also
> for the life to come. This saying is trustworthy and deserves full acceptance.

For the Christian, self-discipline—or self-control—is a spiritual virtue to be developed with the help of the Holy Spirit. It is listed in Galatians 5:22–23 as one fruit of the Spirit: "love, joy, peace, patience, kindness, goodness, faith, gentleness, and self-control." These nine virtues come as a unit and are not available individually. The fruit of the Spirit *is* singular, not plural; it *is* all of these virtues. It has been said that self-control is the crowning virtue of the Holy Spirit because without self-control you cannot experience the others. How true! Without self-control, there is no love, no joy, no peace, no patience, no kindness, no goodness, no faith, and no gentleness. Self-control is a necessary spiritual discipline and evidence of the Christian faith.

Self-discipline is important in the speaker's preparation of a message. Personal willpower is needed to contemplate research, organize material, and plan a speech. Many other interests and activities are distractions when thoughts should be focused on the upcoming message to be given or lesson to be taught. Discipline yourself to work on your speech and be prepared to deliver it to the best of your ability.

I (Monica) get so excited when I am asked to share at a women's event, retreat, or conference! I praise the Lord for any open door that he gives me to proclaim his truth! I have a habit of entering into prayer specifically for the event for which I have been asked to speak. I ask the Lord for direction and leadership before I begin to do any studying. Most of the time, he leads me to a specific passage or theme. I have found that I study best when I have all of my materials out in front of me. My routine includes sitting on the floor with everything laid out, including my laptop, a cup of water, and some candy-coated chocolates. I know it may sound silly, but the chocolate helps me to focus. I have grown to look forward to my study time. It is never a duty, only a delight.

The Bible says that Jesus increased in "wisdom and stature, and in favor with God and with people" (Luke 2:52). Discipline is necessary for growth spiritually, physically, and socially. Since Jesus is the perfect example for living, Christians should be disciplined to grow in all areas of life according to his pattern. Those Christians who accept the additional responsibility of speaking the truths of God must be even more disciplined in their lives.

Discipline is needed in all areas of life in order to maintain balance and ensure healthy growth. Specific goals must be established to promote spiritual, physical, mental, emotional, and social discipline. A Christian speaker should be committed to developing the disciplines of a godly life. She needs . . .

1. A disciplined heart
2. A disciplined body
3. A disciplined mind
4. A disciplined routine[3]

---

[3] Jerry Vines and Jim Shaddix, *Power in the Pulpit* (Chicago, IL: Moody Press, 1999), 72–81.

The heart of a person must be pure and holy, focused on following the Lord and obeying his commands. The body of a person must be healthy and fit, adhering to proper nutrition and regular fitness. The mind of a person must be increasing in wisdom and knowledge, through listening and learning. The routine of a person must be systematic and balanced, including regular allotments of time to pursue growth in all areas of life. These disciplines promote balanced growth in an individual and in a God-called public speaker.

A Christian must employ personal willpower in order to develop discipline, but the added resource of the Holy Spirit's power is also necessary. A speaker who wants to proclaim a message from the Lord has an even greater responsibility to maintain a disciplined life because she hopes to convey not a personal word, but his divine word. A disciplined person will become a more disciplined speaker.

In my (Rhonda) book, *Divine Discipline*, I suggest that there are three steps necessary to developing and maintaining divine discipline: personal willpower, supernatural God–power, and people's persuasive power. Every person must first exert some personal willpower; make the decision to do it. Then, Christians can add to their own limited willpower the unlimited supernatural power of God to help them do what they cannot do themselves. Finally, all Christians benefit from the persuasive power of other people encouraging them and holding them accountable.[4] Proverbs 27:17 says, "*As* iron sharpens iron, so a man sharpens the countenance of his friend" (NKJV).

I (Monica) was sharing at a teen girl's retreat and had fifteen college students traveling with me. On the second day of the retreat, I noticed several of the college girls were getting irritated with serving and had unpleasant attitudes. They did not desire to feel this way but were really giving in to their flesh. I went over to see what was wrong, and they began to share with me their struggles. I then asked them if they had been able to sleep the night before and whether they had eaten breakfast. They answered "no" to both of those questions. It is so important to exercise discipline in taking care of ourselves, so we might better focus mentally, emotionally, and physically. After the young girls were able to eat a good meal and get some rest, they had completely different attitudes.

The combination of personal willpower, God's supernatural power, and people's persuasive power will help Christians and speakers alike develop and maintain the discipline needed for life and ministry. Divine discipline results in personal development, spiritual growth, and more effective Christian ministry. It is worth the sacrifice and pain to become who God created you to be. "No

---

[4] Rhonda H. Kelley, *Divine Discipline: How to Develop and Maintain Self–Control* (Gretna, LA: Pelican, 1992), 67–103.

discipline seems enjoyable at the time, but painful. Later on, however, it yields the fruit of peace and righteousness to those who have been trained by it" (Heb 12:11).

Dedication

Devotion and discipline are essential foundations for the Christian life and a speaking ministry. Dedication is also a critical component. Unlike devotion and discipline, dedication involves a lasting commitment. A person can be devoted to a cause momentarily and be disciplined in a behavior for a time, but dedication is needed to continue on the path of perseverance. Dedication is a lifelong commitment.

Godly Christian living and effective public speaking do not happen without some effort and intentionality. In her book, *Speak Up with Confidence*, Carol Kent shares several practical principles for Christians who feel called to speak publicly.[5] All reflect a dedication to keeping God at the center of life and activity.

1. Make knowing God your highest aim. While the message you speak is important, your ultimate goal in life should be knowing God. When your relationship with the Lord is your daily priority, the others priorities of life will work themselves out. When you focus on knowing God, your message from him will be clearer.

I (Monica) am reminded of the passage in Exodus 33:12–16 where Moses is uncertain of God's specific plan to lead the people. Moses' prayer serves as a great example of this principle to "make God your highest aim." His prayer in verse 13 says, "Now if I have indeed found favor in Your sight, please teach me Your ways, and I will know You and find favor in Your sight. Now consider that this nation is Your people." Moses desired to know God's way so he could know God in a deeper manner. As we study to speak, our number one priority should be to know God.

2. Learn to say "no." It is tempting to say "yes" to every opportunity to serve or invitation to speak. However, an opportunity is not always God's will for your life. Pray about invitations to teach and speak. Learn to say "no" when you are not confident it is God's will for your life at the time. When we say "no," God often uses others to accomplish his purposes. When we say "no" to some opportunities, we can say "yes" to his invitations.

As a young wife and seminary student, I (Rhonda) learned from JoAnn Leavell, whose husband was our seminary president at the time, to learn to say

---

[5] Carol Kent, *Speak Up with Confidence: A Step-by-Step Guide for Speakers and Leaders* (Colorado Springs: NavPress, 2007), 238–48.

"no" with my teeth showing. In other words, I learned to say "no" with confidence. A smile communicates even more than the word itself.

3. Realize that public ministry is not more important than other service for God. All ministry is equal in the eyes of the Lord. There is no such thing as more important or better spiritual gifts. Everything done by a Christian to bring glory to God can be a blessing to him. Give the same effort to smaller tasks or lesser opportunities that you would to those involving many. Whether behind the scenes or in front of a crowd, everything we do should be done to the very best of our ability not to receive glory, but to give it to the Lord, who always deserves our very best.

I (Monica) will never forget a missionary coming to our church when I was a teenager. I felt so privileged to hear him share from the Word of God and looked at him as a spiritual giant. He was a great leader to his people in the Philippines and to other nations. However, I saw a true picture of his heart for God when I awoke very early one morning and looked out of our parsonage window only to see him picking up trash on the church lawn. Although he did not realize it, he was teaching me that public ministry was not more important than other service for God. Luke 16:10 also conveys this principle: "Whoever is faithful in very little is also faithful in much, and whoever is unrighteous in very little is also unrighteous in much."

4. Expect criticism. Everyone who serves the Lord in a public ministry will be criticized by others at some time. Though negativity may surprise you, do not doubt your calling when you are under attack. Instead, stay focused on what God has called you to do and move forward in confidence. Satan is the cause of confusion and the creator of criticism. Pray before you respond to critics, and listen to any constructive comments. Let the Lord strengthen you and your ministry through even the harshest personal criticism.

When I (Monica) was a teenager, I served on the youth council at my church. The council was responsible for planning events and meetings that centered on evangelism and discipleship for all the teenagers attending our weekly youth group. I tried to invite as many of my unsaved friends as possible to church because I so desired that they be born again. My heart was broken when a deacon in our church called our home (the parsonage) and asked to speak to me. I will never forget his hateful tone as he accused me of being the reason why many of the young people were not coming to the youth meeting. I did not know what to say because it was so bizarre to me. We were having an increased attendance and many were being born again. I got off the phone and cried my eyes out, knowing that I had been criticized and falsely accused. My father (the pastor) came into my room and encouraged me to love and forgive and to walk in truth. I learned so much that day from my father concerning the strength the Lord gives and how to respond to criticism.

5. Plan for celebration and Sabbath. Though Christian service and a speaking ministry take much effort and time, every individual needs periods of physical rest and times of personal fellowship. Schedule into your life rhythms of rest and worship. Spend time with your family and friends to celebrate special occasions. Even when your task list is long, take those needed breaks to spend time with God and to refresh yourself personally. You and your ministry will benefit from your moments of meditation.

My husband and I (Rhonda) live very busy lives. The demands of ministry and meeting the needs of family members fill our days. However, we have learned the rhythm of our lives, and we strive to maintain the pace. The academic world provides some natural breaks in the intense momentum. After Chuck became president of the New Orleans Baptist Theological Seminary, we learned to schedule times together during the breaks in the school calendar. The two of us take a three-day getaway in the middle of the fall and spring semesters. We enjoy a few weeks with family during the Christmas holidays, and we go on vacation during the month of July. No matter how busy our days become or how demanding our responsibilities, we know that a time of rest and renewal is coming. Times of personal retreat, family celebration, and Sabbath worship are essential.

6. Have prayer partners. Every Christian must be committed to prayer. However, it is also meaningful to have other people praying for you. Seek the specific prayer support of your family, friends, and church. Ask them to pray specifically that the Spirit of God will anoint each word you speak with power and will personalize each example with application. God works as we train and prepare for ministry, and his work continues through his people who pray and who are covered in prayer. What a precious privilege!

I (Rhonda) am truly blessed to have a supportive husband who loves me and prays for my ministry. I also have two mothers who are faithful prayer warriors. My husband, my mother, and my mother-in-love begin each day with times of prayer. They pray for me and my ministry as well as for every family member daily. I feel the power of their prayers giving me strength, wisdom, and protection as I serve the Lord. I am also blessed by several special friends who pray for me regularly. I am confident that nothing I do is in my own power or about my own ability. Instead, it is God at work in me through the power of prayer.

7. Provide a pattern for others. When Christians live and serve, they not only do so for the purposes of God but for the example provided to others. As we teach and speak, people are watching how we live. Our actions always speak louder than our words. We are models of the Christian virtues and examples of godly speakers. Older Christians are to mentor younger Christians in life and ministry. Public speakers have the opportunity and responsibility to teach young women who are called to teach and speak how to do so with dedication and excellence.

One of my (Rhonda) greatest responsibilities and sweetest privileges as a Women's Ministry professor at a seminary is to mentor younger women in their faith and ministry. I am so grateful for the godly women in my life who have mentored me through their words and actions. As a young wife, God placed a wonderful Christian woman in my life to help me see how to follow God's pattern for marriage. When my husband entered seminary, God put a caring ministry couple in my life to illustrate for me how to serve the Lord alongside my husband. In the early years of my own speaking and writing ministry, God introduced me to several precious women who serve the Lord with excellence while loving their husbands and caring for their families. I want to be that woman for younger women today, providing a pattern for their Christian lives and ministries.

The mechanics of public speaking are not what is most important, although they are helpful. The character and commitment of the speaker are the most important elements of public speaking. Try not to focus so much on technique that you forget the importance of prayer and the power of God flowing through you as you speak. Do your homework, practice your message, but above all, *pray!* Through prayer, God can focus the message and translate it to meet the need of every individual in the audience. The words of James 5:16 say: "The urgent request of a righteous person is very powerful in its effect." Be devoted to the Lord, disciplined in your life, and dedicated to his purpose so that he can work through you as you speak to change the lives of others.

TALKING POINT

Our lives should reflect the truth
the word proclaims.

LET'S TALK ABOUT IT

1. Why is spiritual preparation a key component to becoming an effective speaker to women?
2. List and describe five women of the Bible who illustrate devotion to God.
3. What disciplines should be present in a Christian woman's life to promote her spiritual growth and speech preparation?
4. List at least three principles of Christian speaking conveyed in Carol Kent's book, *Speak Up with Confidence*, that challenge you. How might you intentionally overcome these challenges?
5. Why do you think character and commitment are the most important elements of public speaking?

Chapter 5

AUDIENCE AND OCCASION

"Of the three elements of speech making—speaker, subject, and persons addressed—it is the last one, the hearer, that determines the speech's end and object." (Aristotle)

This chapter will consider the people who will hear the message and the setting for delivery. Audiences and occasions vary widely. A public speaker may have the opportunity to speak for many different audiences at many different events. A significant part of speech preparation is analyzing the particular audience and the specific occasion. Some variables are internal and some are external, some within the control of the speaker and some outside the realm of control. Careful work beforehand can strengthen the speaker's delivery and ensure a more favorable response by the audience.

Public speakers quickly learn that "one size does not fit all" in audiences. Every audience and every occasion is unique. Therefore, every speech should be unique. In *Speak Up with Confidence*, Carol Kent suggests that a speaker answer four general questions in describing the audience: *Who? What? Why?* and *How?* Before agreeing to speak at an event ask some specific questions, such as the ones below, to gain more knowledge about the audience.[1]

Who?
- Can you describe the age, gender, background, and nationality of the group?

---

[1] Carol Kent, *Speak Up with Confidence: A Step-by-Step Guide for Speakers and Leaders* (Colorado Springs: NavPress, 2007), 52.

- What magazines or books might help me better understand the audience?

What?

- What denomination or organization unites these people?
- What topics have been addressed at their past events?
- What speakers have they had recently?
- What hopes, struggles, fears, needs, and questions do the listeners share?
- What are their common interests?

Why?

- Why did they ask *me* to speak?
- Am I an expert on the subject they want to know more about?
- Why will the listeners attend? Are they a "captive audience" (university chapel), or are they here by choice?

How?

- How will I get their attention?
- Are there recent statistics related to their needs that will help me prepare?
- What does the Bible say about the answers to the questions people ask with regard to this topic?
- Is this group geared to visual learning (data projector, videos, power point presentations, and/or handouts), lectures/discussion, or straight lecture?
- How much time do I have?

Answering these questions will help a speaker gain specific information about the audience. Background research is an essential step in speech preparation.

Before any speaking engagement, I (Monica) make it a high priority to find out specifically the types of women in the audience, their ages, and their specific struggles and issues. On one occasion, I was asked to speak to a group of teenage girls. While there are common issues teenage girls may encounter, I wondered whether there were any prevailing situations that I needed to know about the girls who would be present at the event. The teen director shared with me that the majority of the girls had been abused in one form or another. This information helped me enormously: I then knew how to pray more specifically and what Scriptures to expound on in ministering to these precious young ladies.

Audience

An effective speaker must have "audience intelligence." The ability to know the audience, read a room, and discern the spirit of the occasion will help the speaker get off to a strong start. "Speaker radar" is a skill all public speakers should develop. A speaker who can detect nuances and perceive needs in an audience has a greater likelihood of success. Audience skills improve as a person has opportunity to speak publicly.

Speakers may or may not be familiar with their audiences. Sometimes an audience will be composed of family and friends who are well-known to the speaker. Other times the audience will be unknown. Sometimes your audience will be mostly Christians and other times they will not. In every case, the speaker should get to know the audience in an effort to communicate more effectively. Doing so helps to connect the speaker to her listeners at the beginning of the message.

It is so important to try to get to know the audience as best you can before you speak because sometimes you might find yourself in a place where you feel you have nothing in common with the listeners. This was the case when I (Monica) was asked to speak to a group of women in New York. When I arrived at the conference, I realized that I was one of the only single girls, the only Southern belle, the only Southern Baptist, and the only caucasian in attendance. I did not know how the 300 ladies would respond to me and was preparing myself for rejection. The more I got to know them before speaking, the more I realized how different we were, especially in regard to my Southern accent. However, if I had not gotten to know my audience, I would have been unaware. My opening comments focused on our many differences and the fears that I had that they were not going to understand this young single girl from the South. I even shared how I had a father named "Bubba." To my surprise, they laughed at these opening comments. I shared with them that although we were different and I knew I could learn more from them than they could from me, I was confident the Lord had a specific Word for all of us. To this day, I have never had such a wonderful response and such open, attentive ears in an audience. The altar was filled with ladies after each session who cried out to the Lord to make them into the women he desired. Knowing your audience is vital to effectively communicating and connecting.

While general information is helpful, more specific information about the audience provides even more insight into the listeners' perspectives. Understanding the interests, attitudes, and backgrounds of the listeners will improve communication. It is also helpful for the speaker to respond to listener feedback. Let us examine each factor separately.

Listener Interest

A first step in audience analysis is considering the interests of the listeners. Abraham Maslow proposed a hierarchy of human needs, which can help a speaker understand the general interests or needs of the audience.[2] He identified these five basic human needs:

1. *Physiological needs*—the most basic physical needs for survival (water, air, food, and sleep)
2. *Safety needs*—the basic needs for safety and security (steady employment, health insurance, safe neighborhoods)
3. *Social needs*—the needs for belonging, love, and affection based on relationships
4. *Esteem needs*—the needs for self-esteem, personal worth, social recognition, and accomplishment
5. *Self-actualizing needs*—the needs for self awareness, personal growth, fulfilling potential

Maslow's Hierarchy of Needs

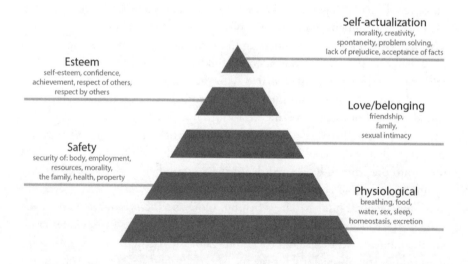

[2] Saul Mcleod, "Maslow's Hierarchy of Needs," *Simply Psychology* (Simply Psychology, 2007). Accessed 19 March 2013, http://www.simplypsychology.org/maslow.html.

While basic human needs reflect the primary interests of listeners, the secondary interests of the audience may be influenced by gender, denomination, or marital status. When a female speaker addresses a group of women, she can relate woman-to-woman to the needs and interests of her female listeners. Momentary interests may involve current events or timely subjects. Newsworthy topics are often of more interest to the audience and can be used for illustrations and examples.

I (Rhonda) am often asked to speak about stress and time management because these are two common interests among women today. Every time I speak on these topics, I vow to never do so again. It seems the week preceding my message is the most stressful week of my life as I inevitably receive new illustrations about stress to share. I am confident that these topics will always be relevant to women who juggle so many responsibilities and struggle to use their time wisely. Listener interest is a first step in audience analysis. Examining listener attitudes is also a helpful step.

Listener Attitude

Another aspect of audience analysis lies in understanding the attitude of the listeners. Listeners come with *real* attitudes and *perceived* attitudes. People in the audience may have opinions about the speaker and the subject. If the audience attitude is favorable or positive, the audience will listen more attentively. If the attitude is unfavorable or negative, the audience will be inattentive or uninterested. Neutral opinions may result in apathetic attitudes. The speaker must assess the audience as much as possible to understand interests and attitudes, encouraging more effective communication. It may also be helpful for the speaker to visit informally with audience members before speaking to get to know them better.

Many times when I (Monica) am sharing at a women's event, I try to mingle and have conversations with the individuals in the audience before they realize I am the speaker. I have found it is easier to get to know the ladies if they are unaware that I will soon address the group. When possible, I prefer sitting in the audience beside a girl who appears to feel left out or a woman who seems not to really want to be at the event. When I am called up to speak, the teen girl and/or woman looks so surprised that I am the speaker. My gesture usually connects us and opens her heart to hear God's message.

A little boy was asked to tell the difference between ignorance and apathy. When asked this perplexing question, he replied, "I don't know, and I don't care!" This illustration reflects an uninformed and uninterested listener. These negative attitudes greatly impact the listeners' response.

Listener Background

The backgrounds of listeners may influence the way they respond to a speaker. Basic facts and personal beliefs of the audience should be considered. Speakers should attempt to identify the age range, gender, ethnic background, religious beliefs, education level, marital status, social/cultural background, moral/ethical values, and group affiliation of the members of the audience. The audience may have limited knowledge of the speaker's background, so the speaker needs to quickly establish rapport and get to know the listeners.

One of my joys in ministry is speaking to women in a variety of different settings. I (Rhonda) am asked to speak in large, formal gatherings and in small, informal settings. The different venues challenge me and bless me as a speaker. I have found that my educational credentials and professional title of "Dr. Kelley" are more appropriate in the larger, more formal gatherings. However, when speaking in a smaller, less formal setting, especially to a rural, less educated group, I prefer not to use my curriculum vitae or doctoral title. I want to connect with my audience and not erect barriers between us. Knowing the background of the audience helps me guide my host in knowing how to introduce me and address me before I speak.

Listener Feedback

While speaking, a presenter should be receiving feedback from the listeners. In personal conversation, feedback can be provided verbally or nonverbally. However, in group settings, listener feedback is primarily nonverbal. An effective communicator will read facial expressions and posture as well as any audible responses from the audience. Smiles may indicate understanding and agreement. Frowns may suggest confusion or disagreement. Laughter usually means delightful support and wholehearted appreciation. Listener feedback helps a speaker determine clarity in communication and personal connection.

A teacher must observe the responses of the students in class. When teaching, I (Rhonda) pay careful attention to nodding heads, smiling faces, and attentive eyes. Students who take notes also reflect comprehension and interest. On the other hand, if the audience demonstrates curious or passive expressions and little responsive nodding or writing, I must attempt to clarify my message to regain listener attention. Audience feedback is helpful to the speaker who must make adjustments and adaptations to communicate effectively.

Also remember that at times negative feedback may be due to spiritual conviction someone is experiencing as the speaker elaborates on the Word of God. Teaching Scripture does not always guarantee a happy response. Even negative feedback can be helpful to the teacher and may assist her in determining what needs to be elaborated on in the next session or communicated with the leaders of the church. Female Bible teachers must be obedient to teach the Word and remain aware of the audience. However, it is not up to the teacher to force anyone to receive the message being communicated. Matthew 10:14 addresses this principle: "If anyone will not welcome you or listen to your words, shake the dust off your feet when you leave that house or town."

Factors in Audience Analysis	
Factor	Description
Listener Interest	general or specific interest/ needs of the audience
Listener Attitude	real or perceived feelings about the topic, occasion, or speaker
Listener Background	biographical facts or personal beliefs of the audience
Listener Feedback	verbal or nonverbal responses by members of the audience

Occasion

A speaker should also analyze the occasion while preparing to give a speech. Every event or speaking opportunity is influenced by expectations from the host and participants. The more information gathered before the event, the fewer surprises a speaker encounters during the speech.

I (Monica) experienced a major surprise at a women's event several years ago. One of the women helping to organize the women's conference told me to pack dressy clothes to wear when speaking. Since that event, I have learned to ask what "dressy" means to the particular audience and occasion. I defined dressy as a skirt, very nice blouse, and heels. When I arrived at the women's event, I discovered that I was sharing at an actual campground. Everyone had on jeans and hiking shoes. Needless to say, I had to make a quick run to the closest store possible to purchase some different attire.

It is important to be as specific as possible when gathering information about the occasion and setting of an event. Attempt to answer the following questions to better understand to whom you are speaking:

What is the purpose of the meeting? The focus of a speech will vary depending on the nature of the event. Is the purpose to evangelize or disciple? To reach out our encourage? Is it a graduation ceremony or a funeral, a dedication service or a memorial? The content of a message will be different for Christian groups as compared to those comprised of unchurched people. Be careful to speak within the boundaries of the event.

Each year the women's ministry of our (Rhonda) church hosts an afternoon tea. This event is evangelistic in nature. We encourage the ladies of our church to invite unsaved family members and friends. Typically, about half of the ladies in attendance are unchurched. It is essential for the guest speaker to understand that many in the audience are nonbelievers. We hope she will develop her material, prepare her illustrations, and deliver her message with evangelistic outreach in mind. We want her to present the gospel and offer a commitment time to allow the Holy Spirit to work in the lives of the ladies present.

Are any regular rituals planned? Some special events have specific rituals or common components such as greetings, recognition of guests, or an offering. Some events include multiple speakers, music, drama, or other features. It is important for a speaker to know if the occasion will end with a commitment time or invitation. Event planners often assume that these rituals are known. A public speaker must investigate to understand the unexpected.

My (Rhonda) husband's preaching professor in seminary told about his awkward experience when speaking for a Methodist church one Sunday morning. During his message, he became thirsty and drank water from the glass on the pulpit. As the service concluded, the pastor nervously announced that the sprinkling on an infant would not take place that morning since the guest preacher unknowingly drank the holy water. How embarrassing! Had the guest speaker inquired about the order of service, he could have discovered the scheduled baptism and requested his own glass of water.

What physical conditions will prevail? The setting for a service will often influence preparation. Will the event be in a formal setting like a sanctuary or an informal setting like a fellowship hall? Will it be scheduled in the morning, afternoon, or night? Will it be inside a building or outside? How many will attend the service? The possibility of outside disturbances like sirens, street noise, and crying babies may impact a speaker's preparation as well. Platform setup including the sound and media equipment as well as decorations should be considered. Location, seating, lighting, and temperature are factors the speaker will need to accomodate.

I (Rhonda) have had some surprising experiences while speaking in outdoor pavilions. Retreats for women are often set in remote, natural settings to provide rest and reflection. I have learned to be prepared for speaking outside. On one occasion, I swallowed a flying bug. I swallowed; I did not chew! On another outdoor occasion a roach slowly crawled up the microphone and stared at me. His antennae were very distracting, but I focused on my message and ignored the bug until it turned around and crawled away. After my message concluded, a lady who had been sitting on the front row ran up to me and asked excitedly, "Did you see the roach on the microphone while you were speaking?" When I answered "yes," she marveled that I was able to ignore the uncomfortable distraction and continue speaking. So that God's Word can be proclaimed faithfully, Speakers must focus on the message, not physical conditions.

Decorations can provide challenges to a speaker, too. When speaking for a ladies' retreat, I (Rhonda) noticed that the platform was narrow and elaborately decorated. Colorful balloons were strung across the back wall behind the stage, hanging down very low. As I waited to begin my speech, I tried to determine if I could stand behind the podium without my head touching the balloons. Unfortunately, as I stood up to speak, the balloons hovered over my head and my hair stuck straight out due to static electricity. I must have been a sight! The decorations committee should have checked the level of the balloons, and I should have tried out the stage ahead of time. Every occasion comes with its own set of challenges.

Connection

Another preparation task of the speaker is to establish and maintain a personal connection with the audience. In his book, *The Empowered Communicator*, Calvin Miller discusses seven keys to unlocking an audience. He suggests that a speaker follow specific steps to better understand the audience and encourage connection.[3]

1. *Build a speaker-listener relationship.* It is the speaker's responsibility to connect with the audience.
2. *Step over the ego barrier.* The speaker must be transparent and put aside focus on self.
3. *Promise your hearers usable information and keep your promise with content.* A speech must actually contain the relevant material promised by the speaker.

---

[3] Calvin Miller, *The Empowered Communicator: 7 Keys to Unlocking an Audience* (Nashville: B&H, 1994), 11–206.

4. *Create tension and resolution.* Attention must be gained then released when information has been presented.

5. *Construct a pyramid of priorities.* Listeners prioritize truth, interest, and inspiration. Speakers should be sensitive to these desires and respond intentionally.

6. *Make sure they hear through a "trinity of audio values."* Three vocal dynamics impact presentation: projection, dynamic, and pause.

7. *Kill interest-lag through six values of mobility or movement.* Six values should be considered:

   - *Change everything on the spot.* Spontaneous editing is often needed during a speech to adjust timing and content.
   - *Change what is not working.* Adjustments and revisions may improve understanding by the listeners.
   - *Pull from accessible back file.* Past knowledge or experience may assist a speaker in the moment.
   - *Casually ask for attention.* A speaker may need to call for attention from the audience if minds seem to be wandering or distractions occur.
   - *Heighten projection.* Increased volume or stress may refocus listeners.
   - *Quit early.* Stop speaking before the audience stops listening. A short sermon or message is okay.

I (Rhonda) am constantly in awe of the work of the Holy Spirit in my life as I stand to speak his truth. Though I carefully prepare my material and plan specific illustrations or personal examples, the Lord often brings to my mind an experience or story while I am speaking that I have not considered in a long time. I share the God-given illustration and often discover later that someone in the audience made a powerful connection with that account. The Holy Spirit, who always knows the audience, can pull from your past experience or previous knowledge to speak his Word directly to each person in the audience.

The most effective public speakers will exert effort ahead of in time getting to know the audience and the occasion as well as preparing material. During the message, an excellent speaker responds to feedback from the audience, often editing and adjusting the speech in mid-message. When speaker-listener connection is maintained from the opening comment to the closing word, the outcome of the message will be positive.

Preparation for a speech is a challenging task. No two audiences are alike. No two occasions are alike. No two speakers are alike. In addition, the same speaker is different every time she speaks. Diligent work and dependence on the Holy Spirit are essential for a public speaker preparing to give a message. Face the challenge as you focus on your audience *before* you stand up to speak for them.

TALKING POINT

The more information gathered before the event,
the fewer surprises encountered during the speech.

LET'S TALK ABOUT IT

1. Name and discuss the four general questions Carol Kent suggests in describing an audience in the book, *Speak Up with Confidence*.
2. What is "audience intelligence," and why is it so important for speakers?
3. Describe the factors a speaker should seek to identify in order to understand the listener background.
4. Discuss three questions a speaker should ask to better understand the audience and the occasion.
5. Describe the seven steps to unlocking an audience that Calvin Miller discusses in his book, *The Empowered Communicator*. How do these steps help the speaker to connect with her audience?

Chapter 6

TOPIC AND PURPOSE

Talk about your convictions.

Dale Carnegie, an expert in corporate training and public speaking, wrote *How to Win Friends and Influence People* in 1936. His bestseller has sold more than fifteen million copies and is still popular today. Carnegie believed in the importance of a speaker's topic and a speech's purpose. He often taught his students: "You cannot help but succeed, if you choose the right topic for *you*. Therefore, when preparing a speech, talk about your convictions!"

This chapter will consider the specific subject of the speech and the intended response of the audience. Each event and every occasion must have a theme or topic whether determined by the host planner or the guest speaker. The ideal theme will be determined early in the process to enable adequate preparation. The best topic will be one that the speaker considers passionately, and the purpose should be stated as the desired outcome.

About ten years ago, I (Monica) was approached by a campus pastor. He wanted me to speak on the topic of modesty to a large group of female college students who were all in leadership positions. I was surprised that a topic such as modesty would need discussion among Christian leaders. The college pastor went on to elaborate that the problem was with the student leaders who were influencing other female students. I was so burdened in my heart for these precious young women. I remember going home and crying out to the Lord for help to deliver this very important message. God stirred my heart to the conviction that every Christian woman needs modesty and propriety. Many of the female students thanked me afterward for sharing so passionately. Again, I am reminded of what Dale Carnegie wrote, "Talk about your convictions!"

In their book, *Turn Boring Orations into Standing Ovations: The Ultimate Guide to Dynamic Public Speaking*, Pat and Ruth Williams recommended that all speakers give FINE speeches. They used the acronym F-I-N-E to give the following four rules for selecting the best topic for a speech.[1]

1. *Make it **Fit***. A topic must be appropriate for the assignment and the audience.
2. *Make it **Interesting***. A topic must pique the interest and maintain the attention of the audience.
3. *Make it **Narrow***. A topic must be streamlined, simplified, and slenderized for the audience.
4. *Make it **Encouraging***. A topic must leave the audience more enlightened and uplifted than when they arrived. Season, sweeten, and spice up your speech.

A topic that fits the occasion, is interesting to the audience, is narrow in scope and focus, and is uplifting to the listeners will provide the springboard for a successful speech.

This chapter on speech preparation will address the topic and purpose of the speech. A general theme directs the topic. The theme and topic should flow out of the purpose. Each component must be considered separately and together when developing a speech.

A FINE Topic
Fit—appropriate for the assignment and audience
Interesting—gains and maintains interest of audience
Narrow—streamlined, simplified, and slenderized
Encouraging—enlightens and uplifts the audience

---

[1] Pat and Ruth Williams, *Turning Boring Orations into Standing Ovations: The Ultimate Guide to Dynamic Public Speaking* (Altamonte Springs, FL: Advantage Books, 2008), 54–55.

Theme

Most events will have a theme which is helpful in promoting and planning the event. The dictionary defines *theme* as "a topic of discourse or discussion; a subject of artistic representation; and implicit or recurrent idea."[2] A theme should guide the planning committee's selection of graphics for publicity, motif for decorations, topic for sessions, and songs for worship. In addition, the theme should be the central concept of the speech. The content of the message develops the specific subject and supports the basic premise.

A speaker's challenge is to develop a new message to fit the event's theme or adapt a familiar message to relate to the theme. With creativity, just about any topic can fit into a theme! The speaker should choose a topic about which she has a degree of knowledge or one that is intriguing enough to research.

A well-chosen theme for an event will be communicated clearly and succinctly and will provide an umbrella to cover all related materials and activities. Themes are often related to trends and current interests, titles or slogans, seasons or celebrations. Christian themes can flow from the text of Scripture. A logo can often communicate the theme visually. A theme unifies focus and efforts.

I (Rhonda) am often asked to speak about the topic of one of my books. Therefore, a Ladies Night Out theme might be "Joyful Living" or "True Contentment." The theme for a women's retreat might be "Divine Discipline" or "Personal Holiness." I may lead a workshop on "Raising Moms." Sometimes, a theme is determined by the planning team and provided to me. I was the guest speaker for a statewide women's conference that built its annual theme around Philippians 4:8: "Whatsoever things are true, whatsoever things are honest, whatsoever things are pure, whatsoever things are lovely, whatsoever things are of good report . . . think on these things" (NKJV). This Scripture provided the theme for six years with a focus on one virtue each year.

I (Monica) am often asked to share at teen girl events. At a recent conference, I was asked to speak on the theme of purity. The director had things so planned out and well organized that in support of purity, they closed the event with a "white-out brunch," where everyone wore white. The brunch helped to reinforce the message and provide specific application for the attendees.

---

[2] *American Heritage Dictionary of the English Language*, 4th ed. (Houghton Mifflin, 2009), s.v. "theme."

Topic

The topic of a speech will give it direction and focus. A topic should also appeal to the audience and be memorable. Once a theme has been determined for the event, the speaker can begin praying about the topic or topics for her presentation(s). If the speaker has multiple sessions, the topics should be related.

Pastor Andy Stanley shares insight about how he determines the topic for a sermon series. He tries to answer five questions in order to provide *information, motivation, application, inspiration,* and *reiteration* for his congregation.[3]

1. What do they need to know? *(information)*
2. Why do they need to know it? *(motivation)*
3. What do they need to do? *(application)*
4. Why do they need to do it? *(inspiration)*
5. How can I help them remember? *(reiteration)*

Selecting a topic is the most important decision a speaker will make. In *Speak Up with Confidence,* Carol Kent emphasizes the importance of choosing the best topic for a speech. Speakers should ask specific questions about potential topics. How you answer the questions will help you select the topic that is right for your event.[4]

What do I know a lot about? Your hobbies and pastimes may also be of interest to others. The subjects you read about and the topics you study may be relevant to your audience. Personal testimonies and Bible lessons will be appealing to a Christian group.

Do I have an urgency to speak about it? Do I feel enthusiastic about sharing my ideas with someone else? Select a topic that you want to study and a subject the audience will want to learn about. Be persuasive as you speak, communicating conviction and passion. The speaker and the listener should respond with interest to the topic.

Does anyone want to hear it? A scintillating speech will be ineffective if it is about a topic of no interest to the audience. Your area of expertise may only be stimulating to you. Find a topic that will appeal to a majority of the listeners.

Ideas for topics are everywhere! Keep your eyes open. Notice billboards and bumper stickers for relevant phrases. Skim magazine covers for catchy titles for

---

[3] Andy Stanley (North Point Ministries), *Andy Stanley Leadership Podcast* [Audio podcast]. Accessed 26 March 2013, https://itunes.apple.com/podcast/andy-stanley-leadership-podcast/id290055666?i=51172805&mt=2.

[4] Carol Kent, *Speak Up with Confidence: A Step-by-Step Guide for Speakers and Leaders* (Colorado Springs: NavPress, 2007), 46–51.

speeches. Advertisements on television and in print material often reflect audience interest and would be appropriate topics for talks. Keep a file or folder of possible topics for future talks. Tear out the article or page from the magazine to keep for future reference. The millions of dollars spent each year by marketing firms could help determine an appropriate topic for a speech.

As you read your Bible, make notes in the margins and in a journal as the Lord speaks to you. Study the passage and outline some major points. Note a topic or theme that you could share. Ask the Lord to reveal his Word to you, and pray for an opportunity to share it with others. Many Bible lessons begin with personal study which is life changing. Keeping a journal develops the discipline of writing and provides topics for speaking opportunities.

The Christian Leaders, Authors, and Speakers Seminar (CLASS) was founded by Florence Littauer in 1981 to provide training for public speakers and writers (www.classeminars.org).[5] Later, services were added for personality assessment and career coaching. In the speaking seminars and in their book, *Communication Plus: How to Speak So People Will Listen*, Florence and Marita Littauer provide a checklist to stimulate exploration of topics for talks.[6]

The following areas should be considered to determine if you have personal experiences that could help you select relevant topics for audiences. Begin by asking yourself these two questions: *What do I have to say about the topic? Does anyone want to hear about the topic?* Circle or underline any area below that you have experienced. I then consider that topic for a talk.

I. Personal Interests
    A. Mental Health
        1. Depression
        2. Stress
        3. Emotional problems
        4. Phobias
        5. Suicide
        6. Compulsions
    B. Physical Fitness
        1. Weight control
        2. Exercise
        3. Diet and nutrition

---

[5] *Christian Leaders, Authors and Speaker Services* (CLASSEMINARS, 2013), CLASSeminars. Accessed 19 March 2013, http://classeminars.org/about-us/team-members.

[6] Marita and Florence Littauer, *Communication Plus: How to Speak So People Will Listen* (Ventura, CA: Regal Books, 2006), 71–87.

C. Spiritual Renewal
   1. Bible study
   2. Teaching
   3. Lay counseling
   4. Spiritual gifts
   5. Prayer
   6. Emotional healing
   7. Spiritual warfare
   8. Evangelism/discipleship

II. Personal Relationships
   A. Friendship
      1. Being a friend
      2. Singleness
      3. Loneliness
      4. Estrangement
   B. Marriage
      1. Meaning of love
      2. Marriage enrichment
      3. Infertility
      4. The art of marriage
   C. Children
      1. Discipline
      2. Preschool children
      3. Teen morality and pregnancy
      4. Older and adult children
      5. Empty nest
      6. Grandparenting families
      7. Blended families
      8. Adoption and foster care
   D. Family
      1. Dealing with in-laws
      2. Overcoming divorce
      3. Single parenting
   E. Suffering
      1. Coping with tragedy
      2. Sickness and pain
      3. Death and dying
      4. Other issues of loss
      5. Abuse
      6. Recovery

III. Personal Goals
   A. Self-Improvement
      1. Self-image
      2. Communication
      3. Self-control
      4. Identity
      5. Color, clothes, fashion
      6. Beauty, makeup, hair
      7. Goals in life
   B. Leadership
      1. Qualities of a leader
      2. Leadership models
      3. Leadership issues
   C. Organization
      1. Household
      2. Personal
      3. Home decorating
      4. Workplace
      5. Time management
      6. Hospitality

Topics vary widely, connecting with speakers and audiences in different ways. Careful consideration will help the speaker match a topic to the audience and occasion so the message will be successfully communicated.

On a mission trip to India several years ago, I (Monica) was asked to speak to a group of widows. To my surprise, the majority of the widows were very young. Many of their husbands had passed away due to tribal warfare. Knowing this about my audience beforehand enabled me to pray more specifically and to prepare a message that would be relevant and helpful.

Purpose

In his book, *The Seven Habits of Highly Successful People*, Steven Covey states: "Begin with the end in mind."[7] Keeping the end clearly in mind encourages each step toward the ultimate goal. A speaker should know how to conclude before introducing the speech. A speaker should consider the aim or purpose as the speech is being developed and delivered. A purpose includes the actual goals you

---

[7] Steven R. Covey, *The Seven Habits of Highly Successful People* (New York: Fireside, 1989), 98.

want to achieve in a speech. Goals may be private (known only to the speaker), or public (known to the audience as well). The goals can be short-term (to be accomplished immediately), or long-term (to be developed over time). Every speech needs a purpose; a talk without a purpose is like a compass without a needle!

Duane Litfin defines a central idea as a "thesis statement or summary of ideas."[8] After deciding the topic, a speaker should ask the question: *What is the precise response you are looking for from the listeners as a result of your message?* Write a sentence to summarize your purpose. Carol Kent suggests that a speaker simply fill in the blank in the following statement: "As a result of this message, I want to cause my audience to _____."[9] Be as specific as possible in order to communicate the aim.

Florence and Marita Littauer emphasize the importance of the purpose in their Christian Leaders, Authors, and Speakers Seminars (CLASS). The message needs to stick out in the minds of the audience like a pier sticks out in the ocean! The acronym PIER is used to organize the information and clarify the point.[10]

P—POINT

I—INSTRUCTION

E—EXAMPLE

R—REFERENCE

In other words, every message should have a point or points; instruction which applies the points; examples including personal illustrations, stories, or quotes to explain the points; and references to validate the points. All elements should be included within a speech, though the order may vary.

I (Rhonda) have used the PIER model to develop my messages for many years now. The P encourages me to clearly identify the single point or multiple points of my message first. Then the remainder of the message can be developed in a sequential and balanced way. I literally write each point on a separate sheet of paper. In the margin of each page, I write P–I–E–R. Then, as I build my points, I make sure that each Point has Instruction, Examples, and References. The longer the message, the more each point must be expanded.

Pat and Ruth Williams explained the connection of the topic and purpose in a clear way: "Your purpose and topic are like two halves of a wishbone, and

---

[8] Duane Litfin, *Public Speaking: A Handbook for Christians* (Grand Rapids: Baker, 1992), 96.
[9] Kent, *Speak Up with Confidence*, 53.
[10] Littauer, *Communication Plus*, 106–9.

a sensible, stimulating title emerges at their fusion point."[11] Can you visualize this explanation? When the topic and purpose come together, a clear title will surface. Though interrelated, each part is separate from each other and essential to the whole.

The point or points of the speech should be clearly stated. Fletcher Dean reported in his article, "When Churchill Comes Alive," that Winston Churchill once said in a speech: "If you have an important point to make, don't try to be subtle or clever. Use a pile driver. Hit the point once. Then come back and hit it again. Then hit it a third time."[12]

TALKING POINT

A talk without a purpose
is like a compass without a needle!

LET'S TALK ABOUT IT

1. Dale Carnegie said, "You cannot help but succeed, if you choose the right topic for YOU. Talk about your convictions!" What is the *right* topic is for you? Why?
2. What are the four rules for giving a FINE speech, according to *Turn Boring Orations into Standing Ovations: The Ultimate Guide to Dynamic Public Speaking*?
3. Define *theme*. How is choosing a theme beneficial to event planning?
4. Explain the importance of selecting a topic.
5. What is PIER? How can PIER help a speaker better communicate the purpose of her message to an audience?

---

[11] Williams, *Turning Boring Orations into Standing Ovations*, 54.
[12] Fletcher Dean, "When Churchill Comes Alive," in Speech Writing 2.0, accessed 8 October 2013, http://thespeechwriter.typepad.com/onspeechwriting/2011/01/when-churchill-comes-alive.html.

Chapter 7

OBJECTIVES AND OUTLINES

Without specific, measureable objectives,
your speech will probably accomplish nothing.

S ome people are more systematic in their thinking and organized in their presentation than others. This chapter will consider the targeted objectives and
organizational structure of the speech. While the mechanical development of the
speech may not be an enjoyable part of preparation, it is necessary for an effective speech. When objectives for the speech are clearly defined and an outline is
thoroughly developed, the outcome will be desirable.

If you are naturally a more linear thinker, you may have less difficulty defin-
ing objectives and developing outlines for your speeches. If you are a more
free-floating thinker, you may need to expend more energy in organizing your
thoughts and information. The speaker's learning style will influence the method
of preparation.

The varied learning styles of the people in the audience will affect how they
listen and learn. All students/listeners do not learn in the same way. Although
there are many different learning theories, the most commonly used categorization system of learning styles includes three types of learners: visual, auditory, or
tactile/kinesthetic. While each learner is unique, visual learners typically profit
most by seeing or visualizing information. They may benefit from visual aids,
handouts, or thorough descriptions. Auditory learners are best reached through
lectures, discussions, or audiotapes. Tactile/kinesthetic learners prefer absorbing

information through experiences. Their learning is enhanced through the senses of touch, taste, and feel. Since an audience most often includes all types of learners, a public speaker should attempt to include all modes of learning when possible.

When the objectives of the speech are clear, visual learners can associate a picture with each point, auditory learners can listen to points for recall, and tactile/kinesthetic learners can raise fingers to keep up with the points. When the outline is organized, the visual learner can take careful notes, the auditory learner can recite the points aloud, and the tactile/kinesthetic learner can draw a diagram of the points.

The outcomes of the speech will also differ. The visual learner may recall a word or object associated with the speech; the auditory learner may remember a descriptive illustration; and the tactile/kinesthetic learner may demonstrate the function of an object mentioned. While there are many other differences in the ways people learn, a general knowledge of these styles will help a speaker connect the information with the audience more effectively. The different learning styles should be considered by the speaker when determining the objectives, outline, and outcome of a speech or lesson.

Discussion on different learning styles was a hot topic of education in the 1980s. I (Monica) remember having a very difficult time learning when I was in the fourth grade. I would study for my tests but did not do well. A series of tests on learning styles were conducted for the students attending my elementary school. The teachers were encouraged to teach to all different types of learners, and when they learned that my learning style was visual, I was encouraged to study for my tests by drawing pictures and using flashcards. My test scores improved instantly! To this day, I have to write down important things that I need to memorize. I have to see it as well as hear it to understand it.

Objectives

With the general topic determined and the overall purpose decided, it is time to delineate the objectives. The dictionary defines an *objective* as "something toward which effort is directed; an aim, goal, or end of action; a position to be attained or a purpose to be achieved."[1] Objectives in a speech are specific learning goals to be accomplished by the speaker. They indicate knowledge, skills, or attitudes a learner should exhibit following instruction. Objectives should flow out of the

---

[1] *American Heritage Dictionary of the English Language*, 4th ed. (Houghton Mifflin, 2009), s.v. "objective."

purpose and be described in specific, measurable terms. They should guide the presentation of information and the application of material.

In a public speaking class for women, the purpose of the course might be to provide information, observation, and application of public speaking techniques to enhance the communication skills of women in life and ministry. The objectives could include the following:

1. The student will understand basic principles of the total communication process.
2. The student will learn public speaking techniques for a variety of contexts.
3. The student will practice various aspects of public speaking.
4. The student will assess the public speaking of others in order to improve personal communication.

Specific objectives guide the course of instruction.

These four objectives flow directly out of the purpose statement. Information will be presented by the teacher and from the textbook about the basic principles of communication. Observation will occur during classroom presentations and outside speech evaluations. Application of speech principles will be offered through student presentations in class.

The four objectives are specific and measurable. Students will be graded on their knowledge of the basic communication process through a book review of the required textbook as well as a final examination. They will learn about different types of presentations in classroom discussion and in the presentations of their classmates. They will practice various types of public speeches when they read a Scripture aloud, make announcements in class, introduce a student speaker, and give a personal devotional. These four public presentations will be evaluated by the professor and all class members. The students will submit their assessment of classroom presentations and complete a speech evaluation outside of class. These course requirements will help the student fulfill the course objectives.

In a biblical message, the objectives should also flow out of the purpose and be related to the topic. I (Rhonda) have a message entitled "Mary, Martha, and Me." It focuses on the narrative account in Luke 10:38–42. The purpose of the message is to challenge Christian women to worship and work. The three objectives are to inspire the listeners to . . .

1. worship like Mary,
2. work like Martha, and
3. worship and work like Me (Jesus Christ).

When a message flows from Scripture, the objectives can be connected to the purpose with greater ease.

Outlines

The outline is the mechanism that helps accomplish the objectives. Once the destination is determined, a route is needed. The outline is like the MapQuest of a message. It helps the speaker know where to start and finish. It also helps the listener understand and remember what is said. The outline helps the speaker and listener think in a logical sequence. It should flow naturally and not be forced.

I (Rhonda) am a "map person." I love to have a map in my hand when going on a trip. When I know where I am and where I am going, I can always chart the course. Sometimes I do so with a yellow highlighter on a printed map. Other times, I follow the recommended route of a maps program. And, often, I use an electronic GPS for my navigational system. But, I always need a map or a visual route for the trip. For me, an outline is the navigational system for a speech. I may use different outline forms, but I always need a system. Otherwise, I will get lost along the road or among the words!

A message needs key points that are easy to remember. When an outline is developed, the main ideas of the speech are arranged in a clear, orderly fashion. The outline creates order, ensures proportions, and organizes divisions of the speech. It is literally the tool to help you accomplish the task. Carol Kent says, "Don't make a tool into a task."[2] In other words, the outline does not have to be complex to be effective.

Duane Litfin suggests several rules for effective outlining because many speakers do not know how to use outlines correctly.[3] These guidelines should be kept in mind as the outline is being developed:

1. Limit each of the points to a single idea.
2. Each point in the outline should be a discrete entity, distinct from its coordinates.
3. Always use a consistent set of symbols.
4. Be sure that the logical relationships between the points are accurately represented by their placement in the outline.

---

[2] Carol Kent, *Speak Up with Confidence: A Step-by-Step Guide for Speakers and Leaders* (Colorado Springs: NavPress, 2007), 55.

[3] Duane Litfin, *Public Speaking: A Handbook for Christians* (Grand Rapids: Baker, 1992), 178–83.

Several other important facts should be considered in outlining a speech. Tailor the outline to the audience. Think in outlines, and then speak from them. Make a list of points, then organize them into an outline. Keep outlines brief and simple. Also, try not to "get stuck in a rut" by using the same outline form for every speech.

Outlines help me (Monica) so much in getting ready to teach a Bible lesson. I actually write out my notes word-for-word and try to memorize them as best I can, and then I write an outline consisting of the key points of the Bible lesson. Next I write the outline on a sticky note and adhere it to the margin of my Bible to help me if I lose my place or find myself needing a reminder to stay on course. All I have to do is glance down at the outline, and I find my place again.

Pat and Ruth Williams present several general approaches to organizing information in their book, *Turning Boring Orations into Standing Ovations: The Ultimate Guide to Dynamic Public Speaking*. They suggest that information be gathered in sequences: chronological, spatial, cause/effect, topical, problem/solution, and motivational sequence.[4] While some material lends itself best to organization based on time or sequence, other information flows spatially, using visual or geographic organization. Some material is clearer when contrasting cause-and-effect, while other information is best explained topically, following a categorization or classification system. Some material presents a problem then a solution, and other information follows a motivational sequence of attention, need, satisfaction, visualization, and action. A speech may use one or more of these methods for general organization of information and specific development of the outline.[5]

There is no right way or best way to outline a speech. A speaker will have a natural method of outlining. Many preachers prefer the three-point alliterative outline, using points that begin with the same letter. Some double-alliterate the points and subpoints. Alliteration does help with comprehension and recall. However, after awhile, the congregation gets familiar with the style and can even predict the next alliterated point. It is best to vary the outline format for more effective presentation and delivery.

Once the outline is determined, the most important principle is consistency throughout the speech. Numerous different types of outlines are listed below with an example for each from personal presentations. For practice, try to develop an outline of your own for each type as it is discussed.

---

[4] Pat and Ruth Williams, *Turning Boring Orations into Standing Ovations: The Ultimate Guide to Dynamic Public Speaking* (Altamonte Springs, FL: Advantage Books, 2008), 59–61.
[5] Ibid., 62.

1. **Sentence**: Use a complete sentence to describe each point.
   Example: "A Lifestyle of Holiness" (Isa 6:1–8)
   - *Reverence* is a holy habit.
   - *Humility* is a holy habit.
   - *Service* is a holy habit.
2. **Question**: Ask a question to illustrate each point.
   Example: "Prune to Produce" (John 15:1–8)
   - Who needs to be pruned?
   - What should you prune?
   - How will you be pruned?
3. **Word**: Select one word for each point, staying with the same part of speech.
   Example: "Total Wellness" (Luke 2:52)
   - Mental (wisdom)
   - Physical (stature)
   - Spiritual (God)
   - Social (man)
4. **Visual**: Find an object or picture that illustrates each point of the outline.
   Example: "True Growth (Tree)" (Ps 1:3)
   - Be rooted (roots)
   - Be nourished (trunk)
   - Be productive (branches)
   - Be prosperous (leaves)
5. **Chart**: Use a graph or chart to depict the points of the outline.
   Example: "Who am I? My DISC Personality"
   - **Dominance**

D	**I**
C	**S**

   - **Influence**
   - **Compliance**
   - **Steadiness**

6. **Lists**: Develop a list for each point of the outline.
   Example: "The Fruit of the Spirit" (Gal 5:22–23)
   - love
   - joy
   - peace
   - patience
   - kindness
   - goodness
   - faith
   - gentleness
   - self-control

7. **Action Verbs**: Select verbs that denote action for each point.
   Example: "Lydia: A Life with Purpose" (Acts 16:11–15)
   - hear
   - worship
   - receive
   - testify
   - witness

8. **Alliteration**: Determine points of the outline beginning with the same letter.
   Example: "Mary and Martha" (Luke 10:38–42)
   - The Content
   - The Complaint
   - The Comeback
   - The Challenge

9. **How to**: Describe how to accomplish a task with each point of the outline.
   Example: "Dress for Success" (Col 3:12–17)
   - Put on *Compassion.*
   - Put on *Kindness.*
   - Put on *Humility.*
   - Put on *Gentleness.*
   - Put on *Patience.*
   - Put on *Acceptance.*
   - Put on *Forgiveness.*
   - Put on *Love.*

10. **Comparison**: Use points of the outline to describe similarities.
    Example: "Call for Help" (Jer 33:3)

    Call a Friend
    - No answer
    - Unlisted number
    - Busy line

    Call God
    - Always home
    - Does not hide
    - Always available

11. **Contrasts**: Select words for the outline to describe differences.
    Example: "Gullible or Godly?" (2 Tim 3:1–11)

    Gullible Women of the World
    - Loaded with Sins
    - Led by Lusts
    - Seek Knowledge
    - Settle for Lies

    Godly Women of the Word
    - Follow True Doctrine
    - Live Christ-like Lives
    - Seek God's Purposes
    - Grow in Faith

12. **Scripture**: Use sections of the verse to outline the message.
    Example: "Trust him" (Prov 3:5–6)
    - Trust in the Lord
    - With all your heart
    - Lean not on your own understanding
    - In all your ways acknowledge him
    - And he will direct your path
13. **Rhyme**: Choose words that rhyme for each point of the outline.
    Example. "The Christian Life" (Matt 28:18–20)
    - Know
    - Grow
    - Go
14. **Repetition**: Select the same word(s) in each point of the message.
    Example: "Trust and Obey" (Matthew 3)
    - Follow the Leader's Attitude.
    - Follow the Leader's Actions.
    - Follow the Leader's Affirmation.
15. **Acrostic**: Use the letters of the key word to give the points of the message.
    Example: "Salvation by Faith" (John 3:16)
    Forgiveness
    Available
    Impossible
    Turn
    Heaven
16. **Theme**: Follow the theme of the event in the outline.
    Example: "Tea Talk: The Art of Godly Gossip" (Acts 1:8)
    - Talk about *His Word*.
    - Talk about *His Work*.
    - Talk about *His Forgiveness*.
17. **Character**: Find a Bible character and let the outline profile the person's life.
    Example: "Rhoda—A Young Woman of Righteousness" (Acts 12:12–17)
    - She was *called* to righteousness.
    - She was *committed* to righteousness.
    - She *communicated* her righteousness.
18. **Numbers**: Determine a specific number of points and include the number in the title.
    Example: "Ten Keys to Keeping on in Marriage"

1. Keep on *dating*.	6. Keep on *forgiving*.
2. Keep on *touching*.	7. Keep on *affirming*.
3. Keep on *talking*.	8. Keep on *sharing*.
4. Keep on *understanding*.	9. Keep on *growing*.
5. Keep on *supporting*.	10. Keep on *praying*.

19. **Alphabet**: Select words that follow the alphabet in sequence.
    Example: "The ABCs of Salvation"
    - **A**dmit you are a sinner (Rom 6:23).
    - **B**elieve in Jesus (John 3:16).
    - **C**onfess that Jesus is Lord (Rom 10:9).
20. **Cause/Effect**: Identify the specific cause and the subsequent effect. (Scripture lends itself to this type of outline.)
    Example: "*If* you . . . , *then* he . . ." (2 Chr 7:12–22)

If my people . . .
- humble themselves
- pray
- seek my face
- turn from wickedness

Then I will . . .
- hear from heaven
- forgive their sin
- heal their land

Specific objectives and a clear outline will help the speaker accomplish the desired outcomes. Both the speaker and the listener can learn when the intent of the message is clearly communicated within a well-crafted speech.

Outcomes

A good speaker will always be concerned about the overall outcome or result of the message communicated. An outcome is what the speaker wants the listener to learn. For the Bible teacher, outcomes would include the truths that the teacher would want the learner to gain in the message. The outcome can be determined by an evaluation from the class itself or through testing, if the information has been taught in a classroom setting.

As a professor, I (Monica) am constantly evaluating my courses and the learning outcomes of my students. We actually have a day each semester to assess student learning. The learning outcome is sometimes difficult to measure when you are sharing at a one-day women's event or conference. However, there are creative ways to go about gaining the outcome of a message or speech. For example, I am always interested in getting feedback from the women's ministry leader on the specific decisions that were made after the message. Another method of evaluation that I have seen is a brief survey that each woman is given at the end of a women's event that helps the speaker and women's ministry team understand what was learned and what could have been communicated better.

Every speech must have objectives and an outline. It is important to focus a message around one specific theme and then develop a few measurable objectives. An outline then becomes the skeleton for the body of the speech. Learn to create outlines for your speeches. Clarity and accuracy flow naturally from a clear, concise outline. The intended outcomes will be accomplished as a result of specific objectives and clear outlines.

Talking Point

The outline is like the MapQuest of a message.
It helps the speaker know where to start and finish.

Let's Talk about It

1. What impact do different learning styles have on the way people listen and learn?
2. Why is it necessary for the objectives in a speech to be clear?
3. Describe what a learning objective is and its importance in speech preparation.
4. What are the four rules Duane Litfin suggests for effective outlining?
5. What are the outcomes of a well-crafted speech?

Chapter 8

RESEARCH AND SUPPORTIVE MATERIAL

Research is shopping for information.

Today more than ever before, public speakers must be discerning in their research. This chapter will consider available data and additional resources to support the premises of the speech. An abundance of material is available in this Internet/Information Age. However, available information is not always accurate information. An effective public speaker will find reliable sources and verify facts before presenting information as truth. The Bible should be a Christian speaker's primary source of information. The absolute truths of Scripture will always stand! We can have confidence in the Word of God. Isaiah 55:11 is a reminder to every speaker of the power of God's Word and how it does stand alone: "So My word that comes from My mouth will not return to Me empty, but it will accomplish what I please and will prosper in what I send it to do."

Seeking Information

If the outline is the skeleton of a speech, the supportive material is the flesh. Once the outline has been developed, it is time to put some meat on the bones. The longer the presentation, the further the outline must be developed. Development of the supportive material begins with research. First, research your own personal experience and knowledge as you think about lessons you have learned from the Lord and from your life. Then begin exploring the expertise of others to support your message.

Before discussing specific sources of information, consider some guidelines for research. These principles, like the Beatitudes in the Bible (Matt 5:1–12), provide guidance. While the Beatitudes of Jesus provide instruction for Christian living, the following Be-Attitudes can aid in preparing a speech.

The Be-Attitudes of Research

1. Be an expert in the area you are researching. It is very important to speak about topics you are interested in because you will need to invest a lot of time and energy becoming an expert on the topic. Knowledge and understanding in research are essential to a well-supported speech.

2. Be thorough. Time and determination are needed for complete research on a topic. Thoroughness provides depth for a stimulating speech.

3. Be accurate. A respected speaker will examine only valid, proven resources. Careful, solid research is important to establish the worth of a speech.

4. Be careful. Mistakes are easily made—especially when research is done in a hurry. Attention to detail and focus on facts is necessary for a thoughtful researcher.

5. Be honest. Research must be reported correctly and stories must be told truthfully. It is tempting for a speaker to fabricate facts to support a thesis. Trustworthiness and honesty are valuable traits in a public speaker.

6. Be a lifelong reader. Books are the source of great knowledge and information. An effective speaker is well-read because reading not only increases knowledge; it also models communication of thoughts and ideas.

The Be-Attitudes of Research
Be an expert.
Be thorough.
Be accurate.
Be careful.
Be honest.
Be a lifelong reader.

Reading is essential for research and effective communication. At times I (Monica) have found myself walking away from a source and asking myself,

"What did I just read?" The following tips for effective reading have helped me and my students to process written information.

Helpful Tips for Effective Reading

1. Pray before you read. Prayer is a necessity in the life of every believer. In 1 Thessalonians 5:17 we are instructed to pray without ceasing. Pray before you read anything! Ask the Lord for guidance as you set your thoughts on material that may or may not align with his Word. The content of what you read may be informational, instructional, enlightening, or contradictory to what you believe. Ask the Lord to teach you through what you read. Ask him to use the exercise of reading to draw you closer to him and to give you insight regarding what he wants you to know.

2. Exercise spiritual discernment. As you open your mind to the thoughts of another person, do not readily accept those thoughts as truth. Approach a secular work and an evangelical work with caution. The author of Hebrews reminds us of the exercise of spiritual discernment: "Solid food is for the mature—for those whose senses have been trained to distinguish between good and evil" (Heb 5:14). Do not overlook an uneasiness as you read a statement. An author's thoughts, recorded and published in a book, are not always biblically sound. Books should supplement our thinking and awareness of what we already know as truth. The Bible is the only infallible, inspired, and inerrant source of truth.

3. Interpret and test with Scripture. As God gives you the spiritual discernment to know the difference between good and evil in what you read, he will also enable you to take what you have read and test it with the Scriptures to see if it is true. Believers were instructed in 1 Thessalonians 5:21 to "test all things." As we learn and are taught in God's Word, we have the opportunity to model the practice of the Christians in Berea who were known as "more open-minded than those in Thessalonica, since they welcomed the message with eagerness and examined the Scriptures daily to see if these things were so" (Acts 17:11).

4. Underline, highlight, mark. Always have a pen or highlighter in your hand as you read. When you encounter something that is noteworthy, make sure to highlight or underline it, so you can go back and read it again.

5. Create a method to record key elements. Come up with a way to notate important information within a book. For example, when you read a statement you know you will use in a Bible study or speaking engagement, circle its page number. You may want to place a double ring around a page number that contains two quotes to help you find your way back to key ideas after you complete your reading.

6. Record comments. Record your agreements and disagreements with the author in the margins of the book. Dialogue with the author on what you are reading. Tracking your thoughts will help you know which pages to revisit.

7. Journal Important Content. Often there will be content in a book that you want to make sure you do not forget. Write down a quote to use in a Bible study or an illustration to share as you speak. For reference record the important content in a journal to use when you are preparing to teach, speak, or write on a given subject.

8. Read additional comments about the book. Whether she knows it or not, a reader loses important information when she fails to read the material that supplements the actual content of the book. Read the table of contents, preface, about-the-author page, publisher details, and additional data about the book to learn its background.

9. Evaluate the book. After you read, evaluate what your mind has been processing. Ask yourself: What was the author's overall theme/point of the book? Was the message of the book understandable? What did I learn from the reading? Would I suggest this book to someone else to read? If so, to whom?

10. Add to your personal bibliography. After you read any type of material, add it to your personal bibliography. A list of sources helps you enormously as you write on various topics or prepare different Bible studies.

11. Summarize the main point. After adding the source to your personal bibliography, summarize in one paragraph the main message of the book. This annotated bibliography can also be included in your journal or files.

12. Enjoy! Approach reading and research with a positive outlook.

At the beginning of the book, I (Rhonda) shared my three spiritual gifts that are not in the Bible, according to my husband Chuck. Do you remember them? My gift of talking provided the title of this book. Sleeping gave me the energy to write the book. Shopping, the third of these gifts, connected me to the value of research. I like to think that research is shopping for information! While researching could be boring and mundane, thinking of it as shopping makes it exciting and challenging. Research like you shop. Look for the bargains. Get the most for your money. Shop until you drop. Have fun as you hunt for information!

Sources of Information

There are many sources of information available. While information in the past was limited to oral tradition and printed manuscripts, information is available now in unlimited forms. Many new sources are electronic and can change on a daily basis. The greatest challenge for contemporary researchers is learning to validate information. Because information is so readily available, it has not always been verified by reliable sources. An astute researcher knows where to find trustworthy information and how to ensure the accuracy of research.

Investigation may begin in the following places:

1. The Bible. A Bible lesson must begin with the Bible as its primary source. All Christian speakers should seek to include Scripture in messages in an effort to disciple believers and witness to unbelievers.

I (Monica) have been to women's conferences and youth gatherings where no attention was given to the unchanging truths of Scripture. While life examples and witty stories may help with getting attention or making application, I strive to make the Bible my primary source when I teach. It is a necessity for any believer and most assuredly for the Bible teacher. I am reminded of the passage in 1 Timothy 4:1–5 of the exhortation given from Paul to Timothy in regard to communicating the Word of God:

> Now the Spirit explicitly says that in later times some will depart from the faith, paying attention to deceitful spirits and the teachings of demons, through the hypocrisy of liars whose consciences are seared. They forbid marriage and demand abstinence from foods that God created to be received with gratitude by those who believe and know the truth. For everything created by God is good, and nothing should be rejected if it is received with thanksgiving, since it is sanctified by the word of God and by prayer.

2. Other Bible Resources. Many additional biblical resources are available including commentaries, dictionaries, and concordances. These sources should be secondary to the inspiration of the Holy Spirit through personal Bible study. Most Bible reference materials are available online as well. Consider the *Women's Evangelical Commentary: Old Testament* [1] and the *Women's Evangelical Commentary: New Testament* [2] when preparing to teach or speak.

3. Reference Materials. Helpful information can be obtained from a variety of secular sources including dictionaries, encyclopedias, maps, charts, tables, almanacs, and *Roget's Thesaurus.* Many of these reference materials are also available online.

---

[1] Dorothy Kelley Patterson and Rhonda Harrington Kelley, eds., *Woman's Evangelical Commentary: Old Testament* (Nashville: Holman Reference, 2011).

[2] Dorothy Kelley Patterson and Rhonda Harrington Kelley, eds., *Woman's Evangelical Commentary: New Testament* (Nashville: Holman Reference, 2006).

4. Internet. Computerized searches can provide a seemingly infinite amount of information. A search engine such as Google, Yahoo, Bing, AOL Search, or MSN provides a gateway into the Web and its extensive database. A more specific description will provide more specific references. Remember that careful research requires more than a mouse click on the computer.

In this technology age, it is essential for Christian speakers to carefully consider public information and urban legend. Just because something is stated online does not mean it is true. I (Rhonda) learned so much about research while working on a master's degree and then a doctorate. Documentation was a cardinal rule for research papers. I try to utilize those same research skills when preparing a message, writing a book, or teaching a class. A fact may seem true, but it must be verified with multiple sources. Guard against easy access to information, and speak only true facts.

5. Blogs. A blog is a discussion forum or information site published online. It may be produced by an individual or group and consists of discrete entries or "posts" entered chronologically. Blogs can provide interesting information and illustrations as well as personal narrative. Facts are often not authenticated.

6. Libraries. Schools, communities, and churches maintain libraries to provide books and resources to people. The Internet Public Library also offers a reference desk with a wide variety of materials available to the general population. Information about many different topics is available through public and private libraries.

7. Bookstores. Secular and Christian bookstores are available in many communities as well as online. Books, magazines, and digital sources are sold that discuss a wide range of topics. Nonfiction, reference books, historical, and biographical books provide valuable information to researchers.

8. Newspapers and Magazines. Regular newspapers and periodicals present information about current events and popular issues. Many local newspapers and national magazines are now available online. Again, the information needs to be verified before citing the research.

9. Personal Interviews. Face-to-face discussions with experts or personal interviews with first-hand witnesses can provide helpful information and relevant illustrations for speeches. Permission should be granted before a person's example is shared in a public arena.

10. Personal Experiences. Speakers should not forget to research their own life experiences for information. Hearing a personal encounter or personal testimony can often help listeners understand and apply the points of the message. Care should be given to reveal only essential details. Beware of breech of confidentiality or becoming too revealing.

11. Nature and Science. God truly reveals himself in nature and in science, often providing insights for a speaker to convey to the audience. Observing nature as well as reading about science can add supportive material to a speech.

12. The Arts. Human creativity is expressed through cultural mediums including performing arts (music, theater, dance, film), the visual arts (painting, sculpture, photography, crafts), and the literary arts (novels, poetry, creative writing). These and other art forms provide valuable inspiration and information for a speaker.

13. Radio and TV Broadcasts. Audio and video mass communication provide extensive information programming. Reliable information is presented but needs verification before being shared in a speech.

New sources of information are being developed every day. A researcher should have no trouble finding information. The task is finding good information that is accurate, relevant, and true. Develop skills in research as God opens the doors for you to speak and teach his truth.

Supportive Material

Supportive material is any information that will strengthen the points of the speech. It comes from many different sources and could include Scripture, illustrations, examples, research facts, transitional statements, and more. A variety of knowledge is a great benefit to a speaker. Therefore, thorough and diverse research is recommended.

In *Principles of Speech Communication*, the authors suggest that there are six pillars of supporting material.[3] These are sources of data that can be used to clarify, amplify, or justify the central ideas of the speech. They support the central theme or main idea. These different types of supporting materials include:

1. **Explanations**—descriptions that make a term, concept, process, or proposal clear or acceptable. Example: To clarify a message about bearing spiritual fruit (John 15:1–8), describe the process of a gardener pruning her plants.
2. **Comparisons and Contrasts**—verbal devices that point out similarities and differences. Example: Galatians 5:19–21 and 5:22–23 may be used to distinguish between the "works of the flesh" and the "fruit of the Spirit."

---

[3] Bruce E. Gronbeck, Kathleen German, Douglas Ehninger, and Alan H. Monroe, *Principles of Speech Communication*, 12th brief ed. (New York: HarperCollins, 1995), 73–83.

3. **Illustrations and Narratives**—detailed examples that describe a concept, condition, or circumstance. Example: The biblical account of the Samaritan woman who met Jesus at the well may be used to illustrate the concept of forgiveness (John 4:1–26).

4. **Specific Instances**—undeveloped illustrations or examples usually grouped into a list to drive the point home. Example: To emphasize the biblical truth that Jesus Christ is Lord, build on the biblical descriptors he is Savior, Redeemer, Sustainer, Master, and King. He is Lord.

5. **Statistics**—numbers that show relationships between or among different information that emphasize size, magnitude, or trends. Example: To support the statement that more than half of all women work outside the home, reference a documented report such as this finding of the U.S. Congress Joint Economic Committee, showing 59.2 percent of women in the United States are in the labor force.[4]

6. **Testimonies**—citations of the opinions or conclusions of others that add weight or impressiveness to an idea. Example: To strengthen the message that prayer has power, cite author Jennifer Kennedy Dean in her book, *Power Praying: Prayer That Produces Results*: "God's specific and intervening power is released into circumstances and lives by prayer."[5]

Illustrations from real life are ideal supportive material. L. P. Lehman discussed the nature of illustrations in his book, *How to Find and Develop Effective Illustrations*. He stated, "An illustration is a basic, identifiable, everyday idea in which a listener may find himself related to the speaker and to the message."[6] It is literally a slice of life, which connects an audience and speaker. He compares a speech to a house and an illustration to a door: "A message without an illustration is like a house without a door."[7] Descriptive examples are not simply extra features of a speech; they are literally the access to a speech. The audience has no way to enter the house or understand the speech without an entryway. Illustrations are essential supportive material.

---

[4] *Joint Economic Committee United States Congress* (Joint Economic Committee, 2010), "Women and the Economy 2010: 25 Years of Progress But Challenges Remain." Accessed 3 March 2013, http://www.jec.senate.gov/public//index.cfm?a=Files.Serve&File_id=f9f3a9b8-2f54-4e83-9029-477a3fc73cd5.

[5] Jennifer Kennedy Dean, *Power Praying: Prayer That Produces Power* (Mukilteo, WA: WinePress, 1997), 14.

[6] L. P. Lehman, *How to Find and Develop Effective Illustrations* (Grand Rapids, MI: Kregel, 1985), 27.

[7] Ibid, 9.

The following illustration depicts how these different sources support the ideas of the speech.

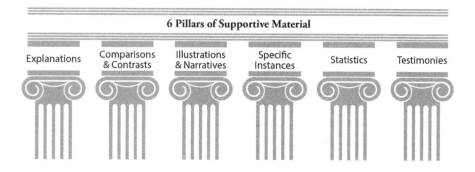

Documentation

Information that is included as supportive material must be accurately reported and documented. Carol Kent provides these guidelines in *Speak Up with Confidence*:[8]

- *Be sure of the facts.* Verify your numbers and details before speaking them aloud.
- *Do not present a fictional story as if it were true.* When you share another person's story, give them credit.
- *Be certain the story fits your aim.* Avoid using a story simply to have a story unless it is serving as an icebreaker at the beginning of your speech. The story should enhance the overall point being conveyed to the audience.
- *Get permission from family members or friends before sharing an illustration about them.* It is important to ask permission before talking about someone else—permission not forgiveness. I (Rhonda) love talking about my husband when I teach or speak. Because I love him, I want others to get to know him. Chuck knows when I tell stories about him in my student wives' class because when the ladies see him on campus, they giggle.
- *When possible, give credit to the originator of the story or cite the source.* It is best to give credit where credit is due and protect yourself in the

---

[8] Carol Kent, *Speak Up with Confidence: A Step-by-Step Guide for Speakers and Leaders* (Colorado Springs: NavPress, 2007), 80–83.

meantime. Listeners will often pay more attention when you include an outside source. I (Rhonda) love to share Chuck's insights when I write because he is so wise and perceptive. I have tried to convince him that marriage means what is his is mine. So, I share his stories and write his insights, but I always give him credit.

- *Never use another speaker's story if you are speaking in his or her territory.* Be considerate of your sources. Using another person's story in an area where she lives may cause confusion to those who know her or undermine the spirit of surprise when she tells it.

- *Adjust the length of the illustration to fit the time you have to speak.* Include an introduction, body, and conclusion in your speech. Try not to let the illustration become the entire message. Connect it with the main theme and make application, but do not let it be the only memorable thing about your presentation.

- *Write out your illustration word-for-word when developing a new story.* Practice will help in clearly communicating the illustration to the audience. Present it spontaneously for maximum effectiveness.

- *Carefully work out your transitional statement so it leads into the application of your story.* What point are you making? Work toward smooth transitions. You can say "first, second, and last." Try to make transitions obvious.

Plagiarism is stealing the creative thoughts or ideas of another person and is a major ethical issue in this information age. Because it is very easy to find information through internet search engines, it is also much easier to identify plagiarism with electronic programs designed to crosscheck sources. Though some thoughts and ideas are general knowledge, specific concepts must be credited to the original source. Plagiarism is easy to avoid as long as a speaker shares personal ideas and cites any others.

Research is a timely investment in public speaking. Many hours are needed to find valuable supportive material and to document information carefully. However, the research and documentation pay off when a speaker produces breadth and depth in material. This process in preparation should be enjoyable to the speaker and listener alike.

TALKING POINT

Available information is not always
accurate information.

LET'S TALK ABOUT IT

1. Why is it important for a speaker to find reliable sources and verify facts before presenting information as truth?
2. List and describe the six "Be-Attitudes of Research."
3. What are several sources of information where investigation may begin? Why is it important to find trustworthy information?
4. Describe the six pillars of supporting material suggest in the book, *Principles of Speech Communication*.
5. What are Carol Kent's guidelines for reporting and documenting source material?

Chapter 9

TYPES AND PARTS

"Every speech should be put together like a living thing . . .
[having] both a middle and extremities,
composed proportionately to each other and to the whole."
(Socrates)

During speech preparation, a speaker must consider the audience and occasion, responding with the appropriate type of speech containing the necessary parts. Each step in the process works together to ensure a more effective speech. A cook must follow similar steps in preparation of a meal and delivery of the delicious food. First, she considers the guests who will be eating and the occasion of the meal. Once the guest list and venue are determined, the cook can select the menu and find specific recipes. Time and effort are expended in meal preparation before the guests arrive. All elements of entertaining are important to the overall experience.

It is my (Rhonda) joy to host many meals in our home. During the summer, I enjoy reading cookbooks, gathering recipes, and developing menus. When a chapel lunch is scheduled for a guest speaker, I carefully evaluate the occasion to determine the type of menu, before selecting the appropriate recipes for the guests and occasion. I finalize the menu, shop for the ingredients, and prepare the food. My careful preparation paves the way for a successful delivery and a delicious meal enjoyed by all.

This chapter will discuss the three basic types of speeches as well as the three parts within the speech. Speeches can be given to inform, persuade, or entertain. Each speech must include an introduction, body, and conclusion. Speech delivery will be more successful when the speaker understands these basics.

Types of Speeches

Though there are many different settings for speeches, there are only three basic types of speeches: informative, persuasive, and entertaining. The content of each speech will vary as will the style of delivery. Some public speakers deliver one type of speech most often because of their communication personality or their ministry context. However, in general, speakers may give each type of speech at different times. Special occasions and unique settings call for specific types of speeches.

Informative Speech

The most common type of speech is the informative speech. Its focus is to inform the audience about a particular topic. In his book, *Public Speaking: A Handbook for Christians*, Duane Litfin writes, "The sole purpose of the informative speech is to clarify, explain, describe, define, report, or otherwise broaden the audience's knowledge about some concept, term, process, relationship, or other subject."[1] Because there is an abundance of information in the world, there is always a great need for informative speeches.

Various types of informative speeches are discussed in *Principles of Speech Communication*.[2] Informative speeches include:

1. *Speeches of Definition*: a speech to define concepts or processes in a relevant way to the audience.
2. *Instructions and Demonstrations*: a speech to explain processes or illustrate usage.
3. *Oral Reports*: a speech that arranges or interprets information for a group or class.
4. *Lectures*: a speech that provides understanding of a particular field of study.

---

[1] Duane Litfin, *Public Speaking: A Handbook for Christians* (Grand Rapids: Baker, 1992), 135.
[2] Bruce Gronbeck et al., *Principles of Speech Communication*, 12th brief ed. (New York: HarperCollins, 1995), 213–14.

I (Rhonda) am a teacher by calling, so I give many different informative speeches. While most teaching is in the form of lectures, I also offer definitions, demonstrations, and oral reports. In every instance, I try to the best of my ability to present the information clearly and with interest. Years ago, I attended a training session titled "Lectures Don't Have to Be Boring." It was a two-hour session late on a Friday afternoon, and it was absolutely the most boring seminar I have ever attended! I made a promise to myself then to make my lectures interesting.

Speakers should keep the following suggestions in mind when giving informative speeches.

1. Have a good personal understanding of the topic.
2. Organize the information in a clear and orderly manner.
3. Explain the information carefully, giving illustrations when possible.
4. Summarize the information so you do not overwhelm with too many points.
5. Use demonstrations and visual devices when appropriate.
6. Define terms completely and try not to be too technical.
7. Provide handouts for extensive data.
8. Motivate the audience to listen and make the information memorable.

Persuasive Speech

Public speakers also give persuasive speeches. The purpose of a persuasive speech is to encourage the audience "to believe, to accept, to yield to some particular point of view."[3] It utilizes ethical appeal, emotional appeal, or logical appeal. Persuasion may also be used for sales presentations, debates, campaign speeches, or even eulogies. The persuasive speaker tries to move the audience to action. Christian speakers often use persuasion when preaching or teaching a Bible lesson. The objective of the message is for listeners to believe the truth presented from God's Word.

I (Monica) was tasked with delivering a persuasive speech on a topic about which I felt passionate in a college speech course. I had recently returned from a mission trip to India and had a great desire for the Indian people to hear the gospel. I also wanted to encourage believers to share their faith in Jesus with others. So I delivered my speech on India and reaching people there with the gospel, truly urging my listeners to take the good news to the ends of the earth. After the speech, several friends and my professor expressed deep conviction to share their faith. My own passion for the subject was a key component in persuading others.

---

[3] Litfin, *Public Speaking*, 137.

In their book, *Power in the Pulpit: How to Prepare and Deliver Expository Sermons*, Vines and Shaddix acknowledge the role of persuasion in preaching and caution against manipulation.[4] They recommend the use of legitimate techniques of persuasion including the Word of God, personal character, logical reasoning, emotional appeal, and fresh imagination. When used effectively, persuasion can lead the audience to accept ideas and follow recommended behaviors.

Monroe's Motivational Sequence has often been used to structure a persuasive speech. These steps organize thoughts based on people's natural psychological tendencies.[5]

Step 1: *Get Attention.* Immediately gain attention so the audience wants to listen.

Step 2: *Show the Need or Describe the Problem.* Explain that a problem exists so the audience understands that something needs to be done.

Step 3: *Satisfy the Need or Present the Solution.* Encourage agreement with the proposed solution to the problem so the audience follows the plan.

Step 4: *Visualize the Results.* Intensify desire so the audience wants to enjoy the benefits of the action.

Step 5: *Request Action.* Call for explicit response so the audience will agree to do it.

Implementation of these steps in a speech will help persuade an audience toward action.

Entertaining Speech

The third type is an entertaining speech. While the term implies humor and laughter, in its broader sense, an entertaining speech can inspire and enlighten as well. There is definitely a need for entertainment in this serious, challenging world. Some settings lend themselves to humor and some occasions need light-hearted programs. However, some speakers can speak for entertainment while others cannot.

Duane Litfin makes four observations about entertaining speeches in *Public Speaking: A Handbook for Christians*.[6] First, not everyone can produce an effective humorous speech. Second, few speeches that are solely comedic are effective. Third, humorous speeches must have a central idea. Fourth, the goal is not

---

[4] Jerry Vines and Jim Shaddix, *Power in the Pulpit: How to Prepare and Deliver Expository Sermons* (Chicago: Moody Press, 1999), 249–55.

[5] Gronbeck, *Principles of Speech Communication*, 244–51.

[6] Litfin, *Public Speaking*, 142.

developing comedians but enhancing the use of humor. Undoubtedly, everyone has heard a genuinely funny speaker as well as someone who should leave humor to others.

I (Rhonda) had a delightful experience attending a hospitality conference for women several years ago. After a long day of travel, I quickly changed clothes for the kick-off banquet. The huge ballroom was beautifully decorated, and the four-course meal was delicious. The speaker was Jeanne Robertson, one of the most entertaining speakers I have ever heard. In her southern drawl the tall, slender beauty queen told humorous stories about life. Her quick wit and down-home style kept us laughing until we cried. Her positive message of encouragement gave us hope and affirmation. An entertaining speech can always enlighten and inspire, but late on a Friday night, it can refresh and renew.

Parts of the Speech

Every speech, no matter how long or short, should have three distinct parts—the introduction, the body, and the conclusion. In about 370 BC the Greek philosopher Plato recorded this dialogue between Socrates and Phaedrus: "Every speech should be put together like a living thing . . . [having] both a middle and extremities, composed proportionately to each other and to the whole." A message should have opening comments, the major points, and closing comments. As someone once said, "Tell them what you're going to say, say it, then tell them what you said."

The first part of a speech is the *introduction*. The purposes of an introduction are to capture the attention of the audience, build rapport with the audience, show the audience why they should listen, and orient the audience to the subject matter. A well-developed and well-delivered introduction will connect the speaker and listener and set the tone for a dynamic speech.

An introduction could include one or more of the following components:

1. reference to subject or occasion,
2. personal reference or greeting,
3. interesting description of topic,
4. a thought-provoking or rhetorical question,
5. startling statement of fact or opinion,
6. quotation from another source or list of statistics,
7. humorous anecdote, and/or,
8. illustration or visual aid related to the topic.

The second and major part of a speech is the *body*. The purpose of the body is to develop the main ideas of the speech. The body of the speech should include the main points, the subpoints, the supportive material, and the connectives. According to Litfin, the body of the speech should develop unity, order, and progress. It should communicate units of thought and clear relationships. It should expand ideas in a logical sequence.[7]

The body of a speech provides "the meat" or the main content in a thorough discussion of the topic. In *Basic Oral Communication*, the authors suggest three steps in the development of the body of a speech:

1. *Disclose a central idea.* Describe a philosophy underlying or justifying the speech.
2. *Divide the central idea into an organizational pattern.* Arrange the points and subpoints in a specific order, outlining the content.
3. *Support ideas with explanation, reasoning, and evidence.* Develop the flesh on the skeletal outline, expanding ideas through explanations, statistics, examples, analogies, testimony, and restatement.[8]

In developing the body of the speech, identify main points, explore any specific subpoints, establish an outline for the material, provide supportive information, include relevant illustrations and examples, and transition between points. A longer speech requires more points and subpoints as well as illustrations and supportive material.

The last part of a speech is the *conclusion*. The purpose of the conclusion is to end the talk in a meaningful way. Carol Kent suggests several effective methods for ending a speech:

1. a quotable quote,
2. a dynamic challenge,
3. a plan of action,
4. a thought-provoking question,
5. a summary of main points,
6. a statement of personal intention, or
7. a key story.[9]

---

[7] Ibid., 151–62.

[8] Glenn R. Capp, Carol C. Capp, and G. Richard Capp Jr., *Basic Oral Communication*, 5th ed. (Englewood Cliffs, NJ: Prentice Hall, 1990), 127.

[9] Carol Kent, *Speak Up with Confidence: A Step-by-Step Guide for Speakers and Leaders* (Colorado Springs: NavPress, 2007), 103–9.

There are several general guidelines concerning conclusions. Do not include new information in your conclusion; instead, return the audience to the introduction and the main idea. Try to make your conclusion vivid, working on clarity and conciseness. The conclusion should be long enough to accomplish the purpose but not so long as to drag the speech out. Rehearse the conclusion before your presentation to avoid rambling or fading away. Keep track of time so that you have enough for the conclusion.

When delivering your conclusion, refrain from saying, "in conclusion." These words often cue the audience to stop listening. Avoid a false conclusion, which is continuing to speak after saying you were finished. Deliver your final sentence with confidence and finality, and then stop! A little boy once said about a sermon, "My favorite thing the preacher said was 'and finally.'"

Balance in the Speech

A well-prepared and well-delivered speech will be balanced in its parts. Because each part of the speech has a purpose, each part must be presented. Keep this formula in mind for balancing the parts: a speech consists of 25 percent introduction, 50 percent body, and 25 percent conclusion. Speeches of different lengths might be timed like this:

Length	5 Minutes	30 Minutes	1 hour
Introduction	1 minute	5 minutes	10 minutes
Body	3 minutes	20 minutes	40 minutes
Conclusion	1 minute	5 minutes	10 minutes

The purpose and outline for your speech will remain the same no matter the length. In a brief speech, open with an attention-getting statement that introduces the subject. Make your points, and then close with a challenge. For a longer message, expand the introduction to clarify the purpose. Develop the major points and subpoints by adding supportive material and personal illustrations. Close with a summary of points as well as a challenge.

I (Rhonda) love to share my personal testimony. I use Proverbs 3:5–6 as my outline and can speak about my story for five minutes, thirty minutes, or an hour. For a shorter period, I make a strong statement about trust, highlight the major points of the Scripture as they connect to my story, and close with a challenge to trust the Lord. For a longer presentation, I can share more details of my story, give several related Bible verses, and teach the biblical principles from the text. Learn to use the time allotted for your speech wisely to accomplish the purpose you choose.

TALKING POINT

A well-prepared and well-delivered speech
will be balanced in its parts.

LET'S TALK ABOUT IT

1. What are the three basic types of speeches? Which one do you enjoy delivering the most? Why?
2. What are eight suggestions for giving an informative speech?
3. What is the purpose of a persuasive speech?
4. List and describe the three distinct parts to every speech.
5. Describe what an introduction could include. Describe what the conclusion could include. How can a well-prepared and well-delivered speech be balanced?

Chapter 10

EXEGESIS AND EXPOSITION

The Bible is the best primary source for a message.

Christians in leadership will often be called on to speak or teach. A Bible lesson will frequently be the focus of a Sunday school class, Bible study group, or special event. While some principles of delivering a lesson based on Scripture are the same as a general speech, a Bible lesson differs in significant ways.

The Bible is the best starting place for a Bible lesson or inspirational message. While there are many other excellent resources, the text of Scripture should always be considered first. A speaker can confidently proclaim truth from God's Word because the Bible is a trustworthy source of information. A speaker can have complete confidence while proclaiming truth from God's Word because it has nothing to do with one's own capability or strength. The Bible can stand alone based on its inerrancy, infallibility, and divine inspiration. Second Timothy 3:16–17 says, "All Scripture is inspired by God and is profitable for teaching, for rebuking, for correcting, for training in righteousness, so that the man of God may be complete, equipped for every good work."

Something that has helped me (Monica) personally is the prophet's words in Isaiah 55:11: "So My word that comes from My mouth will not return to Me empty, but it will accomplish what I please and will prosper in what I send it to do." When a speaker relies on Scripture as her primary source, she has the promise from Scripture that her message will indeed minister to people.

The Baptist Faith and Message describes the doctrine of the Bible and reinforces its role as the primary source of truth:

> The Holy Bible was written by men divinely inspired and is God's revelation of Himself to man. It is a perfect treasure of divine instruction. It has God for its author, salvation for its end, and truth, without any mixture of error, for its matter. Therefore, all Scripture is totally true and trustworthy. It reveals the principles by which God judges us, and therefore is, and will remain to the end of the world, the true center of Christian union, and the supreme standard by which all human conduct, creeds, and religious opinions should be tried. All Scripture is a testimony to Christ, who is Himself the focus of divine revelation.[1]

Though many Christians in leadership teach the Bible, few have a systematic approach for studying and teaching it. In this chapter, we will define several related terms and suggest an approach to Bible teaching. It is a great privilege and responsibility to teach the Bible. James 3:1–2 gives a warning about the seriousness of doing so: "Not many should become teachers, my brothers, knowing that we will receive a stricter judgment, for we all stumble in many ways. If anyone does not stumble in what he says, he is a mature man who is also able to control his whole body." A speaker should approach study time in Scripture with the utmost importance because it conveys truth that will change lives.

The Process of Exposition

In *Power in the Pulpit: How to Prepare and Deliver Expository Sermons*, Jerry Vines and Jim Shaddix define several terms related to Bible study and proclamation. Consider the definitions below before preparing and delivering a biblical message.

> *exegesis*—"the procedure one follows for discovering the Holy Spirit's intent in a Bible passage"
> *hermeneutics*—"the science of interpreting what a passage of Scripture means, hearing and correctly understanding what God says"
> *homiletics*—"the art and science of saying the same thing that the text of Scripture says"

---

[1] *Baptist Faith and Message*, accessed 21 March 2013, http://www.sbc.net/bfm/bfm2000.asp#i.

exposition—"the process of laying open a biblical text in such a way that its original meaning is clearly understood by others"[2]

Exegesis and hermeneutics are the processes used to study Scripture and understand its truth. Homiletics and exposition are the procedures used to communicate truth from God's Word to others. These processes and procedures allow the Scripture itself to speak meaning instead of the reader imposing meaning on the text of Scripture. Careful study of the biblical text prepares a speaker for accurate proclamation of truth.

Exegesis of a text of Scripture requires numerous Bible study skills. Students must learn to read the text carefully and pursue answers to the right questions. In *How to Read the Bible for All Its Worth*, Gordon D. Fee and Douglas Stuart suggest the importance of exploring context and content during the process of exegesis.[3]

A serious student of Scripture will search for answers to the following questions while studying the text:

1. *What is the **historical context** of the passage?* Consider time, location, culture, occasion, political climate.
2. *What is the **literary context** of the passage?* Consider the point of the teaching as well as the genre of the writing.
3. *What is the **content** of the passage?* Consider the meaning of the passage, its words, phrases, and sentences.

Thorough, systematic exegesis leads to good hermeneutics. The expositor should carefully read and study the text of Scripture before turning to secondary sources. The Bible in several translations is the primary source for exegesis. Secondary sources may include a Bible dictionary, a commentary, and a general concordance.

The next step is hermeneutics, finding the contemporary relevance of ancient Bible texts.[4] In this process, the correct interpretation of Scripture is related to the "here and now." These guidelines may be helpful during the process of hermeneutics:

1. *Study from a reliable translation.* Consider the New King James (NKJV), the New American Standard (NASB), the Holman Christian Standard

---

[2] Jerry Vines and Jim Shaddix, *Power in the Pulpit: How to Prepare and Deliver Expository Sermons* (Chicago: Moody Press, 1999), 27–28.

[3] Gordon D. Fee and Douglas Stuart, *How to Read the Bible for All Its Worth* (Grand Rapids: Zondervan, 2003), 26–29.

[4] Ibid., 29.

Bible (HCSB), or the English Standard Version (ESV) for accuracy in translation from the original languages.

2. *Learn to think critically.* Read the words, and then carefully consider their context and content.

3. *Ask important hermeneutical questions to understand meaning and make application.* What does the text say? What does it mean in its context? How does it apply to me and others today?

4. *Recognize the different genres or literary forms of the text in an effort to interpret the meaning accurately.* (See *Biblical Hermeneutics: A Comprehensive Approach to Interpreting Scripture.*)[5]

5. *Seek the help of the Holy Spirit to better understand and apply truth.*

I (Rhonda) love to systematically study a passage of Scripture. I begin by reading and rereading the text, usually in the Holman Christian Standard Bible or New King James. As I read, I underline key words and phrases. I actually diagram the sentences to understand the meaning and identify the important points. Then, I examine the context: what comes before and after the passage of the text; what is the historical context; and what is the literary context? It is always amazing to see the meaning emerge from Scripture as I commit to careful exegesis and hermeneutics.

The Principles of Exposition

Interpretation of Scripture for personal study and preparation to speak continue with the procedures of homiletics and exposition. Bible teachers must learn to say what the Scripture says correctly and clearly. Vines and Shaddix recommend these steps to analyze and proclaim the text:[6]

1. *Minimize subjectivity*: stick to correct interpretation, not personal opinion.

2. *Examine the structure*: know that different genres communicate meaning in different ways.

3. *Conduct word studies*: Explore the meaning of key words from the passage.

4. *Check out cross-references*: Find other Scriptures that address the same truths.

---

[5] Bryce Corley, Steve W. Lemke, and Grant I. Lovejoy, eds., *Biblical Hermeneutics: A Comprehensive Introduction to Interpreting Scripture* (Nashville: B&H, 2002), 378–82.

[6] Vines and Shaddix, *Power in the Pulpit*, 106–25.

5. *Consider principles of revelation*: Identify how God reveals himself in each passage.
6. *Consult commentaries and other biblical references*: Verify and support the textual meaning that you have discovered.
7. *Internalize the text before presenting it*: Meditate on the meaning of the message before sharing it with others.

I (Monica) remember my first time attempt to apply the principles of exegesis and exposition as I prepared for a speaking engagement. I wanted to do my best at studying God's Word so I could effectively communicate truth. The principles of exegesis aided me in discovering more fully the unchanging principles that the passage I studied contained. I made it my aim to apply God's truth to my own life and to teach his truth to others. I remember feeling so overwhelmed as I first learned the principles of exegesis and exposition. However, the more I applied those tools in my everyday study of God's Word, the easier and less overwhelming it became. Now it has become so natural that I cannot imagine studying Scripture and preparing to teach or speak without applying these important principles.

Several points should be remembered during biblical exposition. Always approach the text as the authoritative Word of God. Acknowledge any personal presuppositions, and let Scripture interpret Scripture. Remember that God's Word never contradicts itself. Consider didactic or teachable passages. Identify timeless biblical truths, and ask the Holy Spirit to help you understand the meaning of the text.

The Practice of Exposition

Exposition of Scripture is a serious task. Time and energy are involved in interpreting the meaning of Scripture correctly and then teaching the truth to others clearly. An expository preacher needs to spend hours each week studying the text in preparation to deliver a biblical message each Sunday. (Be grateful for a pastor who faithfully teaches the Word week after week!) Practice these principles of biblical exposition when teaching or speaking. Teach the Bible, not your personal opinions or the opinions of others. Speculation or the sharing of personal thoughts as "gospel" should be avoided. Teach the meaning of the text more than your own experiences or feelings. Teach the Bible clearly, including accurate interpretation and relevant application.

When I (Rhonda) stand up to teach the Bible or share an inspirational message, I do so after hours of prayer and study. As I begin speaking, I give my message to the Lord. I focus on the text and biblical truths, limiting my personal opinions until the application part. Women respond positively when a passage of Scripture is interpreted and then applied. The practice of exposition is always worth the effort.

The five F's below should be helpful practices as you teach a Bible lesson to a group.

1. *Focus* on a specific passage of Scripture.
2. *Find* the central idea or biblical principle of the passage.
3. *Feel* the need of your audience for the biblical principle.
4. *Fashion* your message for the audience.
5. *Faith* your delivery, allowing God to speak through you.

As a Bible study teacher or Christian speaker, begin the preparation process with exegesis and hermeneutics. Continue the delivery process with homiletics and exposition. Remember to turn first to the Bible then to other sources. Speak truth from the Bible, citing references. Teach the Bible systematically for the purpose of life change.

Talking Point

Teach the Bible systematically for the
purpose of life change.

Let's Talk about It

1. Define the following terms: exegesis, hermeneutics, homiletics, and exposition.
2. Explain the process of exegesis in a way that you can practice it.
3. What are the five guidelines that are helpful during the process of hermeneutics?
4. What principles should a Bible student/speaker apply during biblical exposition?
5. What seems most difficult for you in the exegesis process? What do you think will help you as you seek to study the Bible effectively?

Section 2

DELIVERING THE SPEECH

Giving a speech involves the whole person—heart, soul, mind, and strength. The speaker's passion must be communicated; the speaker's spiritual maturity and perception must be conveyed; and the speaker's physical condition will contribute to how well the message is shared. The best public speakers take care of their bodies, minds, and spirits.

This section will focus on the steps involved in the delivery of a speech or message. While preparation requires more time than delivery, it is delivery that conveys the message. Skill and experience enhance public speaking.

There are many aspects to the delivery of a speech. The following chapters will address anxiety and fear, presentation and style, microphones and media, articulation and voice, delivery and details, questions and answers, heart and humor, prayer and power. Practice techniques in delivery intentionally. Let the Holy Spirit work through you, maturing you as a his spokesperson. While the message is most important, the methods convey the message. Your mechanics can enhance his message! Try not to let yourself get in the way of the movement of His Spirit.

Chapter 11

ANXIETY AND FEAR

"The person who knows no fear is not only a gross exaggeration,
he or she is a biological impossibility." (Anonymous)

Public speaking is the greatest fear of many people. Standing before a crowd to give a speech paralyzes many individuals. Several surveys report 41 percent of Americans identified public speaking as their worst fear.[1] Even snakes are not as scary to some people as public speaking. Fear and anxiety are real challenges for many speakers.

Fear is "an unpleasant, often strong emotion caused by anticipation or awareness of danger."[2] Speakers can fear inadequacy, failure, rejection, or embarrassment. Fear and anxiety are similar but different. Anxiety is "a state of uneasiness and apprehension about future uncertainties."[3] Anxiety or stage fright often affects a speaker physically as well as emotionally. *Glossophobia* is the term used specifically for the fear of public speaking or speaking in general.

[1] Stephen E. Lucas, *The Art of Public Speaking* (New York: McGraw-Hill, 2004), 21.
[2] Merriam-Webster Online Dictionary (Merriam-Webster, Incorporated, 2013), s.v. "fear." Accessed 22 March 2013, http://www.merriam-webster.com/dictionary/fear.
[3] *American Heritage Dictionary of the English Language*, 4th ed. (Houghton Mifflin, 2009), s.v. "anxiety."

In this chapter, the common experiences of anxiety and fear that accompany public speaking will be discussed. The nature of fear will be described, suggestions for managing fear will be offered, and strategies for utilizing fear will be recommended. Speakers who understand stage fright, overcome stage fright, and utilize stage fright will become excellent communicators.

Understanding Stage Fright

It is important for speakers to understand that stage fright is inevitable. Almost everyone experiences some degree of anxiety or nervousness before speaking. "The person who knows no fear is not only a gross exaggeration, he or she is a biological impossibility."[4] The presence of fear is real in the life of a public speaker.

If you accept its reality, stage fright can be used for good. Without some anxiety, speakers may become arrogant experts or over-polished performers. When anxiety takes over, a speaker lacking confidence can be overwhelmed and unable to take the stage. A balance of fear and confidence serves a speaker well.

When the mind encounters fear, the body responds. Anxious feelings are typically expressed through sweaty palms, rapid heart rate, dry mouth, trembling hands, and/or knocking knees. The adrenal glands shoot energy throughout the body, and the mind often goes blank. A public speaker must quickly get control of any anxious thoughts or distracting behaviors before they take over. Reportedly 80 percent of all speakers experience stage fright.[5] A Christian speaker has the truth of God's Word to withstand stage fright and the power of the Holy Spirit to overcome fear.

The Bible speaks about fear and anxiety. Neither of these feelings are included in the fruit of the Spirit or indicated as traits of the Christian faith. In other words, neither are to be pursued. Instead, they are to be avoided or overcome in personal life and speaking ministry.

The psalmist David acknowledged that God delivered him from all his fears (Ps 34:4). God commanded the prophet Isaiah to fear not because God commanded the prophet Isaiah to fear not because "I am with you; do not be afraid, for I am your God. I will strengthen you; I will help you; I will hold on to you with My righteous right hand" (Isa 41:10). Belief in God's presence and strength helps a Christian speaker acknowledge anxiety and manage stage fright.

---

[4] Steve Brown, *How to Talk So People Will Listen* (Grand Rapids: Baker, 1993), 35.
[5] Carol Kent, *Speak Up with Confidence: A Step-by-Step Guide for Speakers and Leaders* (Colorado Springs: NavPress, 2007), 139.

In the New Testament, Jesus encouraged his disciples to speak, despite their fear of inadequacy. When commissioning his disciples, Jesus assured them with these words: "Don't worry about how or what you should speak. For you will be given what to say at that hour, because you are not speaking, but the Spirit of your Father is speaking through you" (Matt 10:19–20). Christian speakers today can claim that promise and triumph over fear when proclaiming a message from the Lord. In 2 Timothy 1:7, Paul reminded Christians then and now that "God has not given us a spirit of fearfulness, but one of power, love, and sound judgment."

The television commentator Charles Osgood encouraged public speakers to overcome fear with practice. "Public speaking is no more difficult than using chopsticks or tying a bow tie. The mysterious becomes simple once you know how to do it."[6] The more you speak in public, the less debilitating your stage fright. Specific strategies can help a speaker deal with anxiety and speak confidently.

Overcoming Stage Fright

It is easy to acknowledge the reality of stage fright but harder to overcome it. A number of mental exercises and physical practices have been helpful to other public speakers. Follow these pointers next time you become anxious when you are invited to speak.

1. Remember that the goal is not perfection. Do your best every time you are invited to speak. However, you should also accept your imperfections. Acknowledge your nervousness and move ahead.

2. Do not let your self-doubt keep you from speaking. Start slowly by accepting a shorter talk in a less formal setting. Gradually agree to teach a longer Bible study or share a testimony for a larger gathering.

3. Relax and take a deep breath. Let your body be loose, arms dangling to your side, and hands extended fully. Breathe slowly and rhythmically from your diaphragm. Develop a warm-up routine or pre-speech workout. Relaxation helps the speaker and the audience. Unfortunately, a speaker's nervousness is contagious.

4. Face your fears and look at the audience. When anxious, speakers often avoid eye contact. Do your best to look into the eyes of the group to engage their attention and reduce your fear.

---

[6] Duane Liftin, *Public Speaking: A Handbook for Christians* (Grand Rapids: Baker, 1992), 331.

5. Position your body comfortably. Try not to tense your neck and shoulders. Stand upright without slouching. Position yourself behind the podium or at the center of the stage.

6. Use body language naturally. Do not let your nervousness produce stiff movements or rigid gestures. Let your facial expressions be pleasant and natural.

7. Slow down your rate of speech. Anxiety usually increases rate of speech. When you hear rushed speech or imprecise pronunciation, slow down and speak distinctly.

8. Correct mispronunciations and clarify misstatements calmly. Speakers will make mistakes. Do not let yours confuse or disarm you. Casually correct yourself and keep speaking.

9. Stay focused on your outline, and do not let your anxious mind wander. Speakers can lose their place or forget what they are saying when they panic or their minds go blank.

10. Close confidently and leave the results to Jesus. Stop talking before your audience stops listening. Summarize your main ideas, and then conclude your message memorably. Ask God to bless what you have presented.

Stage fright is a personal matter. It affects each speaker differently. Try to speak on topics within your field of expertise. Be prepared and organized. Understand your own signs of stage fright and how to calm your fears. Have water available for a dry mouth or a scratchy throat. Be positive and confident. Enjoy yourself, and your audience will be more likely to enjoy your message.

A young student wife agreed to give her testimony for a Women's Auxiliary scholarship meeting, but the morning of the meeting, she called to say she was sick and could not share. Fortunately, another student wife readily agreed to step in and speak in her place. Later, the first young woman confessed to me (Rhonda) that her anxiety had made her sick. Now I know how to pray for her as she and her husband prepare to be church planters.

Empowering Stage Fright

Fear of public speaking can work for the good of the communicator. It encourages speakers to be prepared, accelerating the body's adrenaline and increasing energy and vitality. For Christian speakers, fear causes dependence on the power and work of the Holy Spirit. Only when a person fears inadequacy does she become totally dependent upon God. Empower stage fright as you speak instead of letting it overpower you.

The Bible includes a second definition of *fear*. While fear is the feeling of uneasiness or dread, it is also profound reverence and awe of the Lord. In

Deuteronomy 6:13, the writer commands followers of God to "fear Yahweh your God, worship Him, and take your oaths in His name." In Psalm 96:4 we read that "the Lord is great. . . . He is to be feared above all gods" (NKJV). In Psalm 96:4, we read that "the Lord is great and is feared above all gods." Job, the man of God who faced many trials, was described as a man who "fears God and turns away from evil" (Job 1:8). The Old Testament further highlights fear: "the fear of the LORD is the beginning of wisdom" (Ps 111:10). The virtuous woman in Proverbs 31 is praised because she "fears the Lord" (v. 30). Proper respect of the Lord is essential to the Christian life and can help a believer face fears.

The New Testament challenges followers of Christ to fear the Lord. It also acknowledges the feelings of fear. In Luke 12:29, Jesus instructs his disciples not to be anxious about what they will eat or drink. In 1 John 4:18, the apostle says, "The one who fears has not reached perfection in love." Paul also warned Christians about worry and fear. He wisely counseled believers: "Don't worry about anything, but in everything, through prayer and petition with thanksgiving, let your requests be made known to God" (Phil 4:6–7). Prayer enables peace to replace fear.

Another Scripture by the apostle Paul can help Christian speakers be empowered by the Holy Spirit to overcome stage fright. Paul was not an eloquent speaker. He was fearful as he testified and taught. However, he was obedient and spoke out with the help of the Holy Spirit. Read his account from 1 Corinthians 2:1–5:

> When I came to you, brothers, announcing the testimony of God to you,
> I did not come with brilliance of speech or wisdom. For I didn't think it
> was a good idea to know anything among you except Jesus Christ and Him
> crucified. I came to you in weakness, in fear, and in much trembling. My
> speech and my proclamation were not with persuasive words of wisdom but
> with a powerful demonstration by the Spirit, so that your faith might not be
> based on men's wisdom but on God's power.

Paul acknowledged his fear of speaking and accepted a truth of Scripture. God can speak through our inadequate human lips. In fact, when we speak out through our fear, it is truly the Lord speaking through us. His message, which is always much more eloquent than ours, has the power to transform lives.

Each time I (Rhonda) speak, I experience some anxiety as well as great excitement. It was not unusual for my dad, a prominent evangelist, to call my sister or me to a platform in front of hundreds of people to share our testimonies without any time for preparation. I learned to be ready to speak, if called upon, when sitting in his revival meetings. Though I have spoken in public to large gatherings since my childhood, certain settings and topics cause me to become fearful.

The first time I (Rhonda) spoke at Ridgecrest Baptist Assembly for a women's conference, I experienced unusual panic. While dressing for the day, I was gripped with fear. I began to breathe rapidly, turn red, and sweat profusely. During my sudden attack of anxiety, I stopped all that I was doing, knelt down on the floor, and began to pray. The Lord began to give me supernatural peace and confidence in those moments. After some time, I stood up and continued to dress. The Lord seemed to balance my panic with a bit of humor as I walked out of the room to speak. My silk skirt instantly clung to my legs due to the dry air. In that moment of surprise and embarrassment, I began to laugh uncontrollably! Since that experience, I have learned to trust the Lord through my anxiety and fear in public speaking.

TALKING POINT

God can use your fear
of speaking for his good.

LET'S TALK ABOUT IT

1. Describe the difference between anxiety and fear.
2. What are some specific principles and Scripture passages concerning anxiety and fear?
3. List several pointers to help you overcome stage fright.
4. How can stage fright enable a speaker to become better equipped for a speech?
5. Distinguish between the two types of fear written about in Scripture. In what ways have you struggled with fear? How has God's Word enabled you to overcome it?

Chapter 12

PRESENTATION AND STYLE

"Personalities are the filter, or colored glasses, through which we view life. They affect the way we communicate."[1]

There is not one perfect type of speaker or presentation style. Effective speakers come in all shapes and sizes. No two public speakers are exactly alike. In fact, the most successful speakers are those who develop their own speaking styles to a level of excellence. They resist the temptation to imitate a favorite speaker or teacher. God created each individual, and the goal is to master one's own speaking style.

Years ago, I (Rhonda) had an epiphany about my speaking style that had quite an impact on me. I was asked to be one of three keynote speakers for a women's conference involving hundreds of ladies. I was the last speaker of the opening session. The first speaker was hysterically funny, and the audience laughed until they cried. I panicked because I am not funny! The second speaker was humble and sweet, and the audience cried as they heard her tender stories. I panicked because I am not sweet! The Lord clearly spoke to me as I stood up to speak: "Be Rhonda. Be yourself, and speak from your heart." I spoke with the confidence of the Lord. My counsel to you is the same: Be yourself; be the speaker God created you to be.

---

[1] Florence and Marita Littauer, *Communication Plus: How to Speak So People Will Listen* (Ventura, CA: Regal, 2006), 25.

In fashion, there are four basic styles. Each person tends to prefer one specific style over the others. The *romantic* style is feminine, soft, and delicate. The *sporty* style is casual, natural, and neutral. The *trendy* style is contemporary, fashionable, and faddish. The *classic* style is traditional, conservative, and functional. All four fashion styles appeal to some women. In the same way, speaking styles vary. Each style will connect with different listeners and should be a true reflection of the speaker.

A few years ago, I (Monica) was sharing at a two-day women's conference. The women's ministry director had asked me and another lady, whom I had not met to be the keynote speakers. Before I was introduced to the audience, the other speaker came up to me and introduced herself. She was so full of energy that I became nervous inside. At the last minute, she asked me what I thought about adding a funny joke to my notes to get the ladies to laugh or even participate with her in a funny drama. I did not feel comfortable making last minute changes to what I felt the Lord had laid on my heart to share. I noticed immediately that we had two opposite personalities. I was more concerned with the content of my message than trying to entertain. The other speaker, who was a dear lady, had a desire to make the women feel comfortable and laugh. There was nothing wrong with her idea; it was just different than mine. As she asked me to participate with her, I declined by sharing with her that I was not gifted or talented enough to make changes just a few minutes before I was to speak. I assured her that what she had on her heart to share would be great for the women. As I pondered our differences, I realized that although we were opposites in our personalities, we complemented each other for a women's conference because our different presentation styles brought balance. As you teach others, it is so important to understand who God created you to be and the unique style he has given you.

This chapter will discuss presentation formats and speaker styles. The goal is to identify your own speaking style in order to enhance your skills. Ask yourself who you are as a public speaker. What is your public style, your private style, and your ideal style?

Your Public Style

What is your public speaking style? How do other people think you communicate? Public speakers are categorized by the audience. In general, speakers are perceived to be one of the four following types of speakers:

    1. *The Apologizer* lacks confidence, makes excuses, over explains, and repeats herself.

2. *The Performer* has too much confidence, is too showy or flashy, her actions and words are too perfect, and she talks at the audience, not to them.
3. *The Computer* has a dry delivery, fills her time with details and statistics, and does not interact with the audience.
4. *The Effective Speaker* balances self, audience, and message, is spontaneous, open, well-prepared, and interacts with the audience.

Women often begin speaking with an apology. Lack of confidence, extreme humility, or intimidation cause many women to make excuses when they speak. Hesitancy and nervousness not only distract the speaker; they also influence the listener. The apologizer rarely inspires interest or encourages listening.

Recently, I (Rhonda) was introduced by a precious lady who was a classic apologizer. She stood behind the podium nervously. Her complexion was pale, her voice trembled, and her hands shook. She began to speak hesitantly by saying, "I don't know why they asked me to do this. I'm so nervous. I've never done this before." Immediately, we all felt so sorry for her. She did not motivate me to listen—and I was the speaker! However, when she actually began the introduction from her prepared notes, she did a good job. She would have been much more effective if she had started her introduction without the apologies.

Professional speakers are at risk of becoming the performer. When someone speaks often, especially on the same topic, the speech can become rote. Excessive confidence or perfect execution may distance the speaker from her audience. A professional speaker must work to connect with the audience and to keep the flow spontaneous to avoid the appearance of stiffness or over preparation.

I (Rhonda) have been fortunate to hear many well-known speakers and published authors. Most are very effective public speakers. However, one well-known speaker came across as a performer when she spoke for a women's conference I coordinated. When she walked out on the platform, she was overdressed for the occasion. She carried no Bible or notes. Her words were memorized and seemed canned. Her movements also seemed mechanical and choreographed. She did not seem to connect with the audience personally. My own opinions were verified by the participant evaluations. The majority responded with disappointment, commenting about her lack of warmth and mechanical presentation.

A speaker has a tendency to sound like a computer when the speech is filled with information and instruction. Excessive data and minute details can be difficult to deliver with interest and can be overwhelming to the listener. Handouts and overhead slides are useful in documenting the extensive data. Informational speeches should include illustrations and examples to break up the flood of facts.

I (Rhonda) love to teach the Bible. I learn so much in my personal study that I want to share it all with my class. I must realize that not everyone enjoys the details and background that I enjoy. Excessive information can be overwhelming. I equate it to a dump truck driver who backs up, drops the hatch, and unloads everything all at once. I must learn how to balance my content with the interests of my audience so I will not come across as a computer spouting off too much information.

When I (Monica) first started to teach, I was a combination of an apologizer and a computer. If I felt inadequate, I immediately apologized rather than focusing on the delivery of the message. I also emphasized content so much I failed to connect with my audience. My mother was kind enough to be honest with me after one speaking engagement. She knew my heart was warm to the ladies, though it was not evident in my voice. She encouraged me to infuse more warmth in my tone while speaking. I took her advice and began to think of different ways I could connect with the women as well as the content of the Word of God. I realized I could be a more effective communicator by allowing my personality to be expressed in my teaching.

All public speakers should desire to be effective. Adequate preparation and comfortable delivery help the speaker relate to the audience. Though styles of speaking may vary, effective speakers communicate spontaneously, interacting naturally with listeners. The content of the message must be relevant, and the presentation must be confident. Practice can help all public speakers improve in the eyes of the public.

Your Private Style

What is your private speaking style? How do you think you communicate? People tend to communicate like their personality types. Years ago, the Greek philosophers determined there are four basic personalities. While no one reflects a particular personality exactly, everyone has a dominant personality trait. That trait will determine an individual's style of communication. There is no perfect personality and no perfect style of speaking.

The four basic personalities introduced first by Hippocrates, the ancient Greek philosopher, are Sanguines, Cholerics, Melancholies, and Phlegmatics. In their book, *Communication Plus: How to Speak So People Will Listen*, Florence and Marita Littauer discuss how the different personalities tend to communicate.

- *The Popular Sanguines* are the talkers of life, who live for audience response. They tend to have loud speech, easy laughter, and expressive body language.

- *The Perfect Melancholies* are the thinkers of life who avoid frivolous conversations. They tend to speak only when they have something significant to contribute and share their feelings rarely.
- *The Powerful Cholerics* are the workers of life who rarely engage in chitchat. They tend to speak in commands and use very directed body language.
- *The Peaceful Phlegmatics* are the watchers of life who speak only when they have something of value to say. They tend to speak softly and use relaxed body language.[2]

What is your communication personality? Which personality type described above best describes you? I (Rhonda) am definitely a Popular Sanguine communicator. I love to talk! Remember, talking is my spiritual gift! I live to talk and do so with a loud voice and expressive body language. My husband Chuck is a Perfect Melancholy personality who thinks deep thoughts and speaks only when he thinks he has something profound to say. God does have a great sense of humor in uniting two different personalities in marriage. Though I must patiently wait for my husband to verbalize his thoughts, I always have his listening ear for my incessant chatter. Different speaking personalities communicate more naturally with different personalities in an audience.

Littauer and Littauer not only identified the different communication personalities, but they also made suggestions to help each personality to communicate more effectively. These suggestions will help interpersonal communication as well as public speaking.

The Popular Sanguine Communicator should . . .

1. Limit conversation
2. Tone down voice
3. Learn to listen

The Perfect Melancholy Communicator should . . .

1. Add humor
2. Enter into the conversation
3. Think positively

The Powerful Choleric Communicator should . . .

1. Be interested in others
2. Lighten up
3. Ask rather than demand

---

[2] Ibid., 26–28.

The Peaceful Phlegmatic Personality should . . .

1. Get enthused
2. Express opinions
3. Open up[3]

My (Rhonda) husband, Chuck, works diligently to improve his communication. When he was called to preach, he realized that his shy, introverted personality would be challenged. He consciously attempts to initiate conversation with others. Chuck has become an excellent conversationalist during meals at our dining room table. He asks interesting questions and engages everyone in the conversation. When he preaches, Chuck speaks so powerfully under the leadership of the Holy Spirit that people would never imagine he has a melancholy personality type. God can empower every personality style to communicate more effectively.

Your Ideal Style

What is your ideal speaking style? How do you wish to communicate? Remember that your goal is not to become someone else. You should seek to be your best self, the best possible communicator God intends you to be. Keep these tips in mind as you develop your public speaking skills.

1. *Be true to your personality.* Speak naturally as in public as you do in private.
2. *Be unique.* Do not try to imitate other speakers.
3. *Be interested in your topic.* Speak about subjects that are of interest to you as well as the audience.
4. *Be as prepared as possible when you speak.* Invest time and effort into your message.
5. *Be confident and comfortable as you stand to speak.* Learn to handle any nervousness or fear.
6. *Be willing to speak often.* Volunteer to speak so you have opportunities to practice.
7. *Be aware of bad habits.* Work to eliminate weaknesses like fillers (uh, er, um), pauses, smacks, rocking, and rapid rate of speech.
8. *Be a student of communication.* Learn from outstanding public speakers.
9. *Be honest and open as you communicate from your heart.* Authenticity can naturally connect you to your audience.

---

[3] Ibid., 28–30.

10. *Be passionate and persuasive as you communicate a message from the Lord.* Let your love for Jesus come across powerfully in your speaking and teaching.

God created everyone in his image and gave each person a unique personality. Always do your best to communicate in your style and manner. Remember the truth found in Psalm 139:13–14, "For it was You who created my inward parts; You knit me together in my mother's womb. I will praise You because I have been remarkably and wonderfully made. Your works are wonderful, and I know this very well." God created you uniquely. Pray before speaking or teaching: "Lord, help me to simply be 'me,' filled with your Holy Spirit."

TALKING POINT

Master your own speaking style.

LET'S TALK ABOUT IT

1. List and describe the four types of public speakers. What type of public speaker do you think you are at this time? What type of speaker would you like to become?
2. List and describe the four basic personalities and explain how they communicate, as indicated by Florence and Marita Littauer, in their book, *Communication Plus: How to Speak So People Will Listen.* What is your communication personality?
3. What are some helpful tips given by Florence and Marita Littauer concerning your communication personality?
4. List ten tips that will help you understand your ideal speaking style. With which do you most struggle?
5. Why do you think people have the tendency to imitate others more than being themselves? Why do you think speakers do this? What truths should we remember from Scripture in order to be who God has called us to be as speakers?

Chapter 13

MICROPHONES
AND MEDIA

Murphy's Law:
"Anything that can go wrong will go wrong"
(especially with microphones and media).

Public speaking today can be enhanced by amplification and visual aids. While the message must have meaning, it cannot connect with the audience if it is not heard and understood. Technology has improved sound systems and media and will continue to do so into the future. A dynamic public speaker knows how to use microphones and media well and learns to make the sound technician her best friend.

The marquee of a church in the New Orleans area regularly posts the pastor's sermon title. One week the sermon was "The Devil Is in the Sound System." I am sure there was a story behind that message. Most speakers can tell their own stories about problems with the sound system and visual aids. There is no need to fabricate stories involving technology since they happen naturally. Speakers must be prepared for the unexpected.

I (Rhonda) enjoy teaching this topic in my public speaking class because I have so many stories to tell. On one occasion, I was speaking for a women's conference at a church across the street from a funeral home. The sound technician warned me that occasionally the frequencies between the two buildings connected and the ambulance service broadcasted into the sanctuary. Later, while I was speaking, I opened my mouth and a deep male voice called for an ambulance to pick up a dead body. I was stunned, though the church members chuckled at this familiar interruption. Another time I was teaching a seminar that included a video clip. When I moved my slides ahead, an aerobics video abruptly began. We all laughed as the technician hurriedly tried to find the correct video. I have learned to expect the unexpected and go with the flow when using microphones and media.

Something that has helped me (Monica) be more at ease when the unexpected happens is to lay it all in the Lord's hands before the actual speaking engagement. Years ago I spoke to a large group of women at a conference in India. As I was making a main point, the power turned off. I was told to just keep speaking because it was common in that area for the power to randomly turn off throughout the day. I could have become frustrated, but I had to trust in the Lord and his sovereignty. I am so thankful he gave me the words to say as I no longer could read my notes!

This chapter will discuss the effective use of microphones for amplification and media for visualization in public presentations. Though content is key, the message will not be communicated if it is not heard or understood. In larger gatherings and more formal settings, amplification is necessary. In teaching or training with informative speeches, visual aids are often helpful. A public speaker must learn skills for using both effectively.

Amplification

Microphones and amplifiers are often necessary when speaking to a large audience or in a large area. The equipment varies as do the technicians who run the systems. No two are exactly alike. The type, size, and quality of microphones vary and impact the audibility of the speech. As technology expands, sound systems improve, helping public speakers immensely. One who often speaks publicly must be aware of microphone usage.

Several different types of microphones are available. Some are stationary while others are mobile. A *podium or stand microphone* is most typical—especially when multiple speakers are on the platform. *Handheld microphones* are often used by musicians and may also be used by speakers. They may be wired or wireless, have long cords or no cords. A *lavaliere or lapel microphone* clips on the speaker's clothing and allows mobility while speaking. *Headset or over-the-ear microphones* have become popular in recent years. They offer flexibility and mobility as well as good voice quality and minimal extraneous noise. A guest speaker typically uses the amplification system provided by the host church or company. Professional speakers and musicians may travel with their personal sound systems.

I (Rhonda) have experienced numerous microphone challenges, but my husband had a memorable one that was both embarrassing and fairly dangerous. Chuck was asked to speak for a chapel service in a Baptist college where our friend is president. He gave Chuck a glowing introduction while using a wired handheld microphone. In an attempt to get the long cord out of the way, he jerked the microphone just as Chuck walked up to the podium. The cord tripped Chuck, causing him to fall to his knees on the platform in front of the student body. As the audience gasped and our friend turned red, Chuck popped to his feet thanks to his football training. The story still reminds us to be careful with a microphone cord.

While many people may be fearful of microphones, they should see them as a speaker's friend. Microphones can be intimidating, and a speaker must remember their purpose. On several occasions, I (Monica) have had difficulty hearing women speak due to low voice volume projected into the microphone. Microphones and sound systems are tools to be used and not objects to be feared, but we must understand how to use them. Practice and experience help a speaker use microphones with confidence. The following suggestions should also be kept in mind.

Placement: The sound technician may help the speaker with microphone placement to properly balance voice and ambient noise. Generally, a podium or stand microphone should be pointed toward the speaker's mouth about six to eight inches way. A lapel microphone should be six to eight inches below the chin, clipped to the lapel. It should face the screen if slides are utilized. Headset microphones should rest comfortably along the chin-line. If popping or whistling sounds are heard, the microphone may be too close to the speaker's mouth.

Projection: Since a microphone provides volume, it is not necessary to speak loudly or shout. Speak clearly in a normal range. Increase volume for emphasis and decrease volume to gain attention. A microphone projects the sound and protects the voice.

Practice: Whenever possible, arrive early for a sound check. Test the microphone with the technician before the audience arrives. Adjustments can be made to microphone placement and equipment levels. Speak normally into the microphone when testing. Never blow into it or tap it or even say, "test-test-test." Instead, deliver a few lines of speech at a normal speaking level. A thorough microphone check will verify that sound is audible in every area of the room.

Consider a few other do's and don'ts when using a microphone.

1. *Do* dress with a microphone in mind. *Don't* forget to wear an outfit with a lapel and a belt or waistband.
2. *Do* wear minimal jewelry and accessories. *Don't* let jingling or scratching distract from the speech.
3. *Do* consider hand gestures. *Don't* knock a stand microphone or cover a lapel microphone with your hand.
4. *Do* check the echo effect. *Don't* be distracted if speech reverberates in the room.
5. *Do* keep on speaking. *Don't* let microphone problems or sound system issues disrupt the flow of the message. When sound problems occur, continue your message and let the technician work out the problem.
6. *Do* remember a microphone amplifies anything you say. *Don't* make embarrassing comments or potentially inappropriate statements while wearing one.

I (Rhonda) have developed some routines for checking the sound system. I try to arrive early for sound checks, and I typically repeat my key Scripture into the microphone. When he tests the microphone, my husband always quotes the opening lines of a famous sermon by a favorite African American preacher. I listen carefully to my speech during the sound check since I have a tendency to whistle "s" sounds. "Sibilancy" (the whistling of s, z, sh, ch, and j sounds) is common in speaking and is, more noticeable with amplification. I have found it helpful to go to the ladies room to attach the microphone and battery pack before turning it on. The technician should mute your microphone until you begin speaking.

Microphones are helpful tools in public speaking. Visual aids can also enhance a speech when used effectively. While some people process information presented verbally, others learn best visually. As a result, public speakers must learn to engage all available modalities or senses in an effort to communicate the message clearly.

Visualization

Visual and media aids include any nonverbal aspect of a speech presentation. They include objects, handouts, slides, or movie clips. Speeches, lectures, and sermons today utilize visual aids more often due to the development of software presentation programs. Slides can involve lists, graphs, diagrams, maps, and other visual representations that can be helpful but are not always recommended. Every speaker must determine when visual aids are appropriate and how to use them expertly. They can increase clarity, improve persuasion, and enhance memory. However, any type of medim must be used effectively.

Consider visual aids to present information, enhance mental retention, and clarify complex ideas. Make the visuals relevant to the content, appropriate for the audience, and clearly visible. Colors should be bright, and graphics should be clear. Try not to overwhelm or confuse with too much information. Visuals should enhance the message not detract from it.

Often when I (Monica) share at teen girl retreats or women's conferences, I speak on the topic of living life without a masquerade, approaching the Lord in authenticity. Several times while speaking I have displayed an actual mask to simply serve as a visual aid. It is amazing the effect one small prop can have on the audience. Without fail, women have approached me afterward to say how powerful the visual aid was in helping them understand the issues in their lives.

Graphic presentations are frequently utilized in educational instruction and are even required in classroom assignments. Christian speakers often use slides and other visuals when teaching conferences or leading seminars. Development of slide presentations has become easier with the numerous templates provided.

These principles should be considered when developing and delivering graphic presentations.

1. *Wording:* Limit the number of words on each slide and the number of slides in a presentation. Clear, simple slides are better than those that are congested.

2. *Font:* Choose a clear, legible font in a large size. Make it easy to read from a distance. Stand five feet away from the computer screen to judge adequate font size. Always save the font with the file on the CD or flashdrive to ensure exact conversion. Also, place text in the center of the slide.

3. *Color and Graphics:* Select bright background colors with distinct font contrast as well as clear, visible graphics. Use light fonts on dark backgrounds or dark fonts on light backgrounds. Avoid extreme visuals or distracting color schemes. Use complementary images and visual variety.

4. *Data:* Minimize information on the slides. Outline major points and verbalize the explanation. Supplement with handouts when extensive information is necessary. Limit the bullet points and numbers on each slide to avoid confusion.

5. *Spell Check:* Always use the software's checking program to eliminate spelling and grammatical errors. Proof slides and handouts carefully. Have another person objectively proof the slides to limit typographical and grammatical mistakes.

6. *Animation:* Avoid too many bells and whistles. While animation can make graphic presentations dynamic, it can also be distracting and

difficult. Movement and sounds are confusing to some people especially those with attention deficit disorders. Animation can also cause technical challenges. Carefully consider digital images, audio clips, and video clips before including them. Practice the presentation to promote smooth performance.

Many musicians travel with sound systems and technicians because of the importance of amplification and video projection. In an ideal world, all public speakers would own personal equipment including microphones and media. When possible, speakers should provide a personal laptop or tablet computer as well as adaptive cables to facilitate exact presentation.

Always confirm the projection equipment provided and arrive in time to set up and test the presentation. Always carry a backup medium for your media (CD, flashdrive, etc.). Determine whether or not to turn the overhead lighting off, and communicate carefully with the building personnel.

In my early years of teaching, I (Rhonda) became known as the Queen of Overheads. Long before computerized presentations, I understood the importance of visual cues to reinforce verbal communication. I used overhead slides to present definitions, lists, charts, and maps. When software programs were developed for presentations, the content of my overheads became the basis for my classroom slideshows. I am grateful that I am a linear thinker who visualizes in points. It has helped my utilization of technology. For nonlinear thinkers, extra effort must be expended to place information in graphic presentations.

When utilizing microphones and media, remember Murphy's Law: "Anything that can go wrong will go wrong." This statement seems to be true in life and particularly true in public speaking. Be prepared for surprises when speaking, and be flexible when challenges occur. Always have a Plan B in mind when things go wrong, and remember that content—not media—is the key.

Talking Point

Always have a Plan B when using
microphones and media.

Let's Talk about It

1. List and describe three suggestions to keep in mind that will help a speaker to be confident while using a microphone.
2. Describe a time when you as a speaker have personally witnessed Murphy's Law.
3. What are six do's and don'ts regarding microphone use.
4. Describe the importance of visual aids in a speech.
5. List six principles that should be considered when developing and delivering computerized presentations.

Chapter 14

ARTICULATION AND VOICE

"The voice is the most underused and overlooked tool."[1]

Articulation of sounds and projection of voice are important aspects of public speaking. Words can be spoken but if not understood by the listeners, the message is not communicated. Voice can be produced but if not audible and clear, the message is not communicated. The speech mechanism must work properly for speech to be articulated clearly. The vocal mechanism must be healthy for voice to be produced and resonate normally. God created humans with the ability to speak. Humans must learn to shape sounds and produce voice.

I (Rhonda) have an undergraduate and graduate degree in speech-language pathology as well as more than twenty years of clinical experience in the field. My primary professional work was with children in a medical setting. As a result, many of my patients had medical or physical causes for speech and/or voice disorders. It was my job to evaluate their skills, develop treatment plans, and provide therapy to remediate their deficits. I recognized the impact of communication disorders on the children and their families. I also shared the joys as the children learned to speak and interacted verbally with other people.

Speech and voice are important skills for children and adults alike. Interpersonal communication and public speaking require adequate articulation and

---

[1] Christine Jahnke, *The Well-Spoken Woman: A Guide to Looking and Sounding Your Best* (Amherst, NY: Prometheus Books, 2011), 79.

projection. Without clarity, a person cannot communicate thoughts or interact effectively. In this chapter, we will discuss speech enunciation and vocal projection in public speaking as well as offer suggestions to improve overall speech articulation and vocal hygiene.

Articulation

The mechanics of public speaking include articulation and voice. Speech is the way sounds are shaped to communicate thoughts verbally. For clarification, the following speech terms should be defined before the discussion begins. Several of the terms are similar though each is distinct. The noun and verb forms will be cited.

> *articulation (articulate)*—shaping or forming sounds when speaking vowels and consonants; to utter clearly
>
> *pronunciation (pronounce)*—the ability to utter speech which is intelligible; to produce a speech sound or word
>
> *enunciation (enunciate)*—"the crispness and precision with which you form words"[2] to pronounce with clarity
>
> *diction*—enunciation or delivery of words and phrases in speaking or singing; the speech sound quality of a speaker
>
> *elocution*—the art of public speaking; the study of formal communication dating back for centuries
>
> *accent*—the characteristic pronunciation of a particular geographical region; distinctive pronunciation of a specific nation, locality, or social class
>
> *dialect*—the local characteristics of speech that deviate from standard speech; "language use—including vocabulary, grammar and pronunciation—unique to a particular group or region"[3]

Speech intelligibility is essential to a clearly communicated message. Sounds and words must be produced clearly by the speaker so the listener can easily understand what has been said. Enunciation, pronunciation, volume, and rate all impact intelligibility of speech. A public speaker should work continually on improving intelligibility because speech is very important for at least five reasons.

1. Speech is often the first impression made by a speaker.
2. Poor speech distorts meaning and causes confusion.
3. Mispronunciations reflect poor effort and awareness.

---

[2] Bruce E. Gronbeck et al., *Principles of Speech Communication*, 12th brief ed. (New York: Harper Collins, 1995), 80.
[3] Ibid., 180.

4. Speech is a uniquely human characteristic that connects people.
5. Speech is a learned behavior that can be improved.

Children begin speaking in the first months of life. Cries are a baby's first form of communication and are followed by coos, babbling, and laughter. Speech sounds from the simple to complex are learned as a baby shapes sounds from voice.

- At about one year of age, a child begins producing words and then short phrases.
- By two to three years of age, a child should be able to clearly produce simple speech sounds including /p/, /b/, /m/, /w/, /h/, and /y/.
- By three to four years, a child should master the following speech sounds should be mastered: /t/, /d/, /k/, /g/, /f/, and /v/.
- By four to five years, a child should have developed: /l/, /sh/, /ch/, and /j/.
- By five to six years of age, the child should be able to pronounce the most complex speech sounds: /s/, /z/, /th/, /r/, and consonant blends.

The developmental sequence enables a child to speak clearly and prepares the child for reading phonetically. The sequence of complexity also reflects mispronunciations by adults in interpersonal conversation and public speaking. Adults typically mispronounce the most complex speech sounds.

Articulation errors occur in childhood development and adult speech. The most common errors are *substitutions* (wabbit/rabbit or fink/think), *omissions* (at/hat or do/dog), *distortions* (thun/sun or shue/sue), and *additions* (coerch/coach). Speech errors repeated over time become habituated and more difficult to correct. However, drill and practice can correct most speech errors in children or adults. Misarticulated sounds and words should be identified and remediated by a public speaker to ensure that her message is understood.

Articulation skills can be improved since speech is a learned behavior. Individuals with articulation disorders should be referred to speech-language pathologists (also known as speech pathologists or speech therapists) for intervention. People can work personally on less severe speech errors. The following suggestions will be helpful to improve speech intelligibility in public speaking.

1. Be aware of the correct production of consonant and vowel sounds in speech.
2. Monitor the pronunciation of personal speech.
3. Exaggerate speech sounds for clarity.
4. Practice and work out the articulation of troublesome words.
5. Avoid dialectical errors that could be a distraction.

Speech errors are often cute when spoken by a young child. I (Rhonda) remember my sister's mispronunciation of a university name when she was little. Instead of Loyola, Mitzi said, "Yoylola." We laughed lovingly and pronounced the name the same way ourselves. One of Mitzi's four sons had difficulty pronouncing the "r (er)" sound correctly as he was learning to speak. He said "bud/bird," "guhl/girl," and "thud/third." Sometimes we giggled about the mistakes, but we also repeated the words correctly. In time, he learned to pronounce the sound and words correctly. Though speech errors are delightful in young children, they are distracting when produced by adults.

Fluency problems can sometimes interfere with speech intelligibility. Normal speech flows rhythmically. Listeners are challenged when disruptions in fluency occur. Sounds may be repeated or elongated in children from about three to five years of age as they search for words to say ("I-I-I" or "I—"). This dysfluency in adults or older children is called stuttering or stammering. According to the American Speech-Language-Hearing Association, stuttering is "a disruption in the fluency of verbal expression characterized by involuntary, audible, or silent repetitions or prolongations of sounds or syllables."[4] Mild stuttering includes the repetitions, prolongations, or interjections of sounds or syllables ("uh, uh, uh"). More severe stuttering may include block, which is the inability to actually emit or produce sound, often accompanied by physical strains or movements. Another dysfluency—cluttering—is a disorder of rapid, unorganized and often unintelligible speech. Cluttering and stuttering are different speech disorders, though they may coexist. While developmental dysfluency should be ignored as the young child learns to speak, persistent disorders are best treated by speech pathologists using behavioral techniques. Dysfluencies interfere with public speaking and need remediation.

On my (Monica) third birthday, my parents wanted to make the day very special for me. In addition to caring for my one-year-old brother who needed much of their attention, my mother prepared blueberry pancakes with a candle in them for breakfast. Later, when my father came home for lunch, we all shared a special birthday time together, singing and celebrating. Then, in the late afternoon, they hosted a wonderful party for all my little friends at the local McDonald's! The next day, my parents noticed that I was stuttering and unable to talk in smooth sentences despite repeated correction. They finally took me to a doctor, who after hearing me talk and stutter, began to question my parents about our recent activities. He concluded that there had been so much excitement that it

---

[4] *American Speech-Language-Hearing Association* (American Speech-Language-Hearing Association, 2013), "stuttering." Accessed 21 March 2013, http://www.asha.org/public/speech/disorders/stuttering.

must have put me over the top! They were told to no longer correct me or bring attention to my stuttering but to speak clearly when talking to me and ignore the dysfluency. After one year, the problem went away. I am so thankful for the Lord's help in getting me through this developmental stage!

All people should work to improve speech for the purpose of communication and connection with others. Public speakers have an even greater need to improve speech in order to communicate a message clearly to a group of people. Speech articulation and fluency shape the clarity of communication.

Voice

Voice is produced from vibrations of the vocal cords. It is then shaped into sounds and words for human speech. Parameters of voice include *vocal quality* (clarity and tone), *volume* (loudness and projection), *variety* (pitch range and stress) as well as *vibrancy* (energy and enthusiasm). Effective public speakers learn to master these vocal parameters for conveying the message purposefully and passionately.

God created humans with the amazing ability to communicate. He designed a perfect vocal mechanism for the production of speech. The Bible records God's words often spoken aloud with voice. God gave voice to his children not only so they could communicate with each other but so they could speak his message of hope. John the Baptist called himself "a voice of one crying out in the wilderness: Make straight the way of the Lord" (John 1:23). Jesus spoke the message of salvation to all people: "If anyone hears My voice and opens the door, I will come in to him and have dinner with him, and he with Me" (Rev 3:20). Today, the Word of God is spoken through human vehicles. He is the message; humans are his voice. Christian speakers must take care of their voices so the Word of God may be proclaimed.

The vocal mechanism includes the lungs (source of breath), the diaphragm (controls flow of air), larynx (pronounced "lar-inks," contains vocal cords to vibrate and produce sound), oral and nasal passages (resonates sounds), and the articulators including tongue, lips, teeth, and palate (shape speech sounds). Dysfunction by or damage to any of these structures may cause speech or voice disorders.

Voice disorders are typically diagnosed by a medical specialist, specifically an otorhinolaryngologist (ENT doctor). A speech pathologist specializing in voice care may be involved in the evaluation and treatment as well. Organic voice disorders are caused by physical problems such as prolonged laryngitis, vocal lesions (nodules, polyps, ulcers, etc.), trauma, or tumors. The physical causes need medical assessment and may need medical treatment prior to therapeutic intervention.

Functional voice disorders result from misuse and abuse or stress and tension. They require vocal rest, elimination of abuse, and vocal retraining.

Common contributing medical problems include allergies, sinus congestion, mucus buildup, mouth breathing, and gastric reflux. Some foods and liquids are harmful to the voice due to their drying effect, increased risk of gastric reflux, and so on. Public speakers and singers should limit consumption of harmful substances including coffee and other caffeinated drinks, greasy or spicy food, dairy products or citrus before speaking, teaching, or performing. Other voice care strategies will be presented later in this chapter.

I (Rhonda) am predisposed to voice problems. It often seems like my "thorn in the flesh" (2 Cor 12:7). My seasonal allergies and sinus drainage frequently irritate my vocal cords. Because I teach for several hours at a time and project to speak publicly, I can experience vocal strain and laryngitis. I employ all the techniques I have learned as a speech pathologist. First, I seek medical treatment, taking antihistamines and decongestants. Then, I make behavioral changes. I reduce my talking when possible; increase my water intake; suck on cough drops or throat lozenges; and sleep with my head raised on the pillow. I do my part to preserve my voice because there is nothing more frustrating than to have a message from the Lord that cannot be communicated due to lack of voice.

Public speakers should practice good vocal hygiene. The voice, like the body, requires proper care. Good posture and upright positioning improve projection. Relaxed muscles and reduced muscular tension minimize laryngeal strain. Proper breath support increases projection and length of utterance. Appropriate rate of speech and clear enunciation reduce vocal strain. Balanced resonance, varied pitch, and controlled volume also help. Vocal warm-ups and cool downs as well as proper rest, nutrition, and exercise protect the voice.

In her book, *The Well-Spoken Woman*, Christine Jahnke highlights the distinctive voice of United States Representative Barbara Jordan from the state of Texas. Jordan is remembered as having "booming pipes that seemed heaven-sent."[5] Her voice was powerful, her diction clear, and its resonance was deep. Her gift of voice was nurtured in the Good Hope Missionary Baptist Church in Houston and was utilized in law as well as politics. In 1984, Barbara Jordan was named the "World's Greatest Living Orator." She was an extraordinary human whose vocal abilities made her even more special.

According to Jahnke, there are five P's of a vibrant voice:[6]

- Pleasing Pitch
- Picked Up Pace
- Purposeful Pauses

---

[5] Jahnke, *The Well-Spoken Woman*, 83.
[6] Ibid., 88.

- Pronounced Pronunciation
- Projection to Be Heard

The voice must be strengthened to communicate with confidence. Vocal range must be expanded and vocal variety increased. Maximize the vocal parameters and minimize damage or abuse.

Billy Graham, the world's foremost evangelist for decades, practiced good voice care. For more than forty years, he exercised daily and practiced speaking regularly. As he talked, Graham warmed his voice up like an opera singer does the scales. At a comfortable volume and with proper breath support, he said, "Yes. Yes. Yes. No. No. No."[7] If the great preacher Billy Graham faithfully practiced his voice, should you not also? All public speakers must commit to personal vocal care.

Voice Care

The following suggestions will be useful to public speakers who desire to practice good voice care.

1. Avoid excessively loud volume, especially screaming or shouting. Speak only when your conversation partner is within an arm's reach, and avoid speaking in noisy settings.
2. Avoid abrupt bursts in speaking. Use a relaxed effort.
3. Limit throat clearing and coughing. Swallow to clear mucus from the vocal cords.
4. Drink six to eight glasses of water a day, especially when taking decongestants.
5. Decrease consumption of caffeinated beverages which dry out the vocal cords.
6. Rest your voice if your throat is infected or if hoarseness persists. Avoid whispering for an extended time. Instead, use a very quiet voice.
7. Avoid eating milk products (ice cream, yogurt, cheese) before speaking. Dairy products may coat the vocal cords and disrupt vocal quality.
8. To decrease possibility of reflux of stomach acid avoid eating three hours before going to bed. Avoid eating certain foods and drinking certain beverages (i.e., spicy foods, fried foods, carbonated drinks) that may trigger reflux at any time.
9. Vary the pitch of your voice within an octave range; however, avoid extremely high pitch and extremely low pitch.

---

[7] Pat and Ruth Williams, *Turning Boring Orations into Standing Ovations: The Ultimate Guide to Dynamic Public Speaking* (Altamonte Springs, FL: Advantage Books, 2008), 146.

10. See your doctor if hoarseness or throat pain persists more than two to three weeks.

In their book, *Power in the Pulpit*, Jerry Vines and Jim Shaddix discuss "Playing the Voice." Because he developed a vocal nodule which required surgical removal, Dr. Vines learned the importance of vocal hygiene. He has found it helpful to be sensitive to weather and climate, to give attention to fit of clothing, to regulate home and office temperatures, to develop good nutritional habits, to get plenty of rest, to exercise regularly, to give attention to physical ailments, to avoid using the voice excessively before and after preaching, and to use the voice as often as possible.[8]

A public speaker, especially one with a message from the Lord, must develop distinct speech and care for the vocal mechanism. Make a commitment to improve speech skills and voice quality. Become an expert in using the vocal mechanism given by God.

Talking Point

The voice is God's instrument
of human proclamation.

Let's Talk about It

1. What are the five reasons speech intelligibility is important?
2. List five suggestions that will help improve speech intelligibility.
3. What are the five P's of a vibrant voice, according to Christine Jahnke?
4. Why is it important to commit to personal voice care? What are the ten suggestions useful to public speakers who desire to practice voice care?
5. Describe your plan for improving your speech skills and voice quality.

---

[8] Jerry Vines and Jim Shaddix, *Power in the Pulpit* (Chicago, IL: Moody Press 1999), 287–90.

Chapter 15

DELIVERY AND DETAILS

"Preplanned spontaneity will help you achieve the balance between being ready for anything versus anything goes."[1]

P ublic speaking is a challenging endeavor. Many hours and extensive effort must be invested in a speech. Speech delivery involves many details and much discipline. Good speeches do not simply happen, and great speakers are not plentiful. Though most people are born with the innate ability to communicate, few people develop the art of public speaking. This chapter will discuss the methods of speech delivery, principles of delivery, and details of delivery in an effort to reveal how to improve public speaking skills.

Steve Brown includes a relevant mandate for speech delivery in his book, *How to Talk So People Will Listen*. His second of ten commandments is, "Thou shalt not have one method of giving a speech."[2] He supports the premise that public speakers should be able to deliver speeches in a variety of ways despite a preferred delivery method. He suggests that speakers should fit the methodology to the audience. Brown's other commandment,

---

[1] Christine Jahnke, *The Well-Spoken Woman: Your Guide to Looking and Sounding Your Best* (Amherst, NY: Prometheus Books, 2011), 176.
[2] Steve Brown, *How to Speak So People Will Listen* (Grand Rapids, MI: Baker Books, 1993), 145–55.

which addresses public speaking is, "Thou shalt not make long speeches; thou shalt speak gently; and thou shalt deviate."[3] Women who are called by the Lord to speak or teach should take these commandments to heart. Make a commitment to vary your method of delivery, matching methodology with message and methodology with occasion.

Delivery Methods

Like there is not one perfect type of speaker, there is not one perfect method of delivery. Every speaker must determine what method of delivery fits the personal style of the speaker as well as the purpose of the speech and the occasion. Each speaker will probably utilize each method of delivery at some time and on specific occasions. Though most speakers have a preferred method of delivery, a versatile public speaker will be aware of the different methods and will be able to use each effectively when indicated.

The four primary methods of speech delivery are *manuscript, memorized, impromptu,* and *extemporaneous.* Each method requires similar preparation though different delivery. The style of presentation and utilization of notes is different for each. As each method is described below, consider a situation calling for each type of delivery.

The Manuscript Speech is written out word-for-word beforehand and is read word-for-word from a script or teleprompter. There are several advantages to this delivery method: words can be carefully selected, timing can be carefully managed, and content can be carefully reviewed. Several disadvantages may develop with this type of delivery method: presentation may sound forced, tone may sound monotonous, vibrancy may sound flat, and eye contact may be limited. Manuscript speeches may be appropriate when precision and accuracy are required for media speeches, political messages, or graduation charges as well as when controversial issues are discussed.

Some people may tease or torment those who speak from a manuscript. A playful preacher once took the sermon notebook of his friend who had excused himself to the men's room just before he was introduced to speak for a pastors' conference. The sermon notes were passed across the front row of the auditorium while he was gone. The preacher panicked when he returned and realized his manuscript was missing. If speaking from a manuscript, make sure to keep it in your possession.

---

[3] Ibid.

I (Rhonda) heard about a pastor who always preached from a manuscript. One Sunday a fun-loving deacon decided to play a trick on him by removing one page of his manuscript. As the pastor preached about creation from the book of Genesis, he became frustrated. He kept repeating, "And Adam said . . ." Shuffling through the pages of his manuscript, the pastor finally concluded, "There seems to be a leaf missing." The audience laughed while the speaker was embarrassed.

The Memorized Speech is written out beforehand and memorized word-for-word. It is then quoted from memory by the speaker without notes. A memorized speech allows maximum movement and audience focus. It can be a very powerful form of delivery from the audience's perspective. It requires excellent memory skills. Therefore, a lapse in memory is always a risk in this delivery method. Memorization may sound rote or stiff and can develop a sing-song rhythm if not carefully monitored. Only a few speakers will be able to speak from memory confidently.

The most effective memorized speeches are less formal and more conversational in nature. Predetermined words do not allow for audience feedback or speaker adjustment. Memorization may be indicated in character sketches and for other similar reasons as the manuscript speech. This delivery method should have an integral relationship with the content of the message.

My (Rhonda) husband, Chuck, has an excellent memory. He prepares his sermons mentally and preaches without notes. He often memorizes his Scripture text for his sermons. In a recent graduation ceremony, Chuck began quoting Scripture after Scripture in a conversational tone as he gave the charge to the graduates. The audience was mesmerized by his presentation as he wove together numerous biblical texts about the call to ministry for the class of graduating seminarians. His memorized delivery made the message even more powerful.

W. A. Criswell, a great pastor of First Baptist Church of Dallas, Texas, was an outstanding orator. He delivered most of his sermons from memory. During the 1970s, a youth band participated in the musical worship during a Sunday morning service. As Dr. Criswell's passion and persuasion increased in his sermon, the young drummer got excited and played a loud rim shot on his drums. The preacher was so startled that he lost his place in his memorized sermon and forgot his next words. He quickly closed the service in prayer to the embarrassment of the drummer and the surprise of the audience. Even seasoned public speakers must be prepared for surprises during speech delivery.

The Impromptu Speech is delivered on the spur of the moment without preparation. Ministry often calls for speaking off the cuff. Even when no time is available for preparation, thoughts must be organized and ideas must be presented clearly. Previous preparation and research as well as familiar messages are invaluable resources for those asked to speak spontaneously. In 1 Peter 3:14–16, the writer declares:

> But even if you should suffer for righteousness, you are blessed. Do not fear what they fear or be disturbed, but honor the Messiah as Lord in your hearts. Always be ready to give a defense to anyone who asks you for a reason for the hope that is in you. However, do this with gentleness and respect, keeping your conscience clear, so that when you are accused, those who denounce your Christian life will be put to shame.

Those in leadership positions must always be prepared to facilitate a meeting, give a report, or share a testimony. Unusual circumstances sometimes call for an impromptu message. A scheduled speaker may become ill or have travel delays requiring a backup speaker. Speakers must also respond to questions and handle debates spontaneously. Lack of preparation should not become habitual. This bad habit can lead to bad speeches or bad lessons.

Mission trips provide numerous occasions for impromptu speaking. Unclear details, cultural differences, changing schedules, and unexpected needs may necessitate speaking without advance notice. When Chuck and I (Rhonda) first married, we led a group of 200 college students on a mission trip to Singapore and Malaysia. During our training sessions, the long flights, and the two weeks of ministry, Chuck recited this motto repeatedly: "Flexibility is our favorite word." Each one of us was required to be flexible many times. Someone was often called on to speak or sing on the spur of the moment for Vacation Bible School, a musical concert, or a worship service. That ministry lesson has served me well through the years. I am always prepared to give an impromptu speech.

The Extemporaneous Speech is prepared in advance and presented from abbreviated notes. An outline guides the flow of points though exact words are left to the speaker at the moment of delivery. There is a logical progression of thoughts that are freely delivered. Most topics lend themselves to extemporaneous presentation. Thorough preparation and prayerful saturation ensure the material will be presented smoothly and understood clearly. Most occasions call for an extemporaneous speech, which many public speakers believe to be the preferred method of delivery.

Christine Jahnke describes extemporaneous speaking as "preplanned spontaneity" in her book, *The Well-Spoken Woman*. Preplanned spontaneity is just what it sounds like: "a balance between being excessively scripted and being unprepared."[4] It combines competence and casualness. Jahnke uses Elizabeth

---

[4] Jahnke, *The Well-Spoken Woman*, 155.

Dole as an example of a public speaker who used preplanned spontaneity with excellence. At the Republican Convention in 1996 when her husband was nominated for president, Mrs. Dole broke with traditional speech delivery. She moved away from the stationary podium and descended the staircase into the audience in the large convention center. Though less formal and seemingly spontaneous, her words and movements had been carefully rehearsed and choreographed. Thousands of people were intrigued as she walked down the aisles and talked to them warmly.

Extemporaneous speech delivery can be strengthened by preplanned spontaneity. As Jahnke points out, "Preplanned spontaneity will help you be ready for anything versus anything goes."[5] Those public speakers who master extemporaneous delivery will always be ready for anything.

Delivery Principles

When the time arrives for the well-prepared speech to be delivered, the speaker will likely experience excitement and increased adrenaline as well as some anxiety. The hard work and personal effort in preparation are the foundation for an effective speech and should give the speaker confidence. Dynamic delivery is the vehicle for success.

Most public speakers report a euphoric feeling when speaking in front of a large crowd. Energy and emotion are expended while speaking. The high of public speaking continues through the speech and typically for several hours afterward. Then the mind and body begin to relax. Some speakers experience an emotional low, almost as if hitting a wall after speaking. Public speakers must learn to manage the ebbs and flows of speech delivery.

I (Rhonda) am one of those public speakers who rides a rollercoaster during speech delivery. I invest much energy in my messages, giving my all physically and emotionally. After the speech, I am still excited as I interact with people in the crowd. An hour or two later, I literally feel the energy drain out of me. I have learned to sit down, get something to drink, and breathe deeply for a few minutes. I find it hard to go out for lunch or dinner with a group of ladies after speaking because my energy is waning. In mentoring young women who are called to teach and speak, I try to warn them about the rollercoaster experience of public speaking. Many can imagine the excitement of speaking but not the depletion. Speakers must learn the cycle of elation and deflation that may accompany public speaking.

[5] Ibid., 176.

This section will consider five principles of effective speech delivery that may increase understanding of the public speaking cycle. Though the speaker, setting, and subject will vary, these principles remain constant. Keep these general truths in mind when standing up to speak.

1. *Effective delivery involves the whole person.* Public speaking requires investment of—mind, body, and spirit. Knowledge and experience are not the only ingredients for a good speech. A speaker must involve herself physically and mentally as well as spiritually. A speaker who feels well and is in good physical condition will be able to speak with more energy. A speaker who is emotionally stable and happy will be able to speak with greater joy. A speaker who is spiritually mature will be able to speak God's Word with greater power.

Before any speaking engagement, my (Monica) goal is to remain calm and relaxed. I always try to leave time, after I get dressed for the speaking engagement, so I can sit down in a quiet place to pray alone. After I pray, I review all of my notes, and then I pray again. If I eat before I speak, I choose to have something very light. I also prefer not to have long, detailed conversations with people before I speak so that my mind can stay focused on the message the Lord has laid on my heart. This routine has helped me enormously in my message delivery. It is important for every speaker to find a routine that helps her be physically, mentally, and spiritually prepared for each speaking engagement.

2. *Effective delivery considers the total speaking situation.* The content of the message and the method of delivery must be appropriate for the setting and occasion. An excellent message shared at the wrong time, in the wrong place, and in the wrong way can be a disaster. An experienced public speaker does her homework to know the speaking situation and to prepare her speech for it.

I (Monica) will never forget a speaking experience I had when I was nineteen years old as I traveled with my father to a remote part of India. We were very excited about evangelizing and teaching these people, especially when we were told that we were the first missionaries to visit this specific tribe in 100 years! I was asked to speak to a group of women and would have an interpreter for the entire speaking engagement. The interpreter was the only one who knew English, so he was my only way to communicate with those gathered. I had everything written out ahead of time so it would be easier to speak in complete sentences and to stay focused while using an interpreter. My topic was "God's Strength in Our Weakness." To clarify the principle, I used an illustration of a vacuum cleaner, trying to convey that one must have the vacuum cleaner plugged into an outlet in order for it to have power. My point was that we needed the Holy Spirit in our lives in order to have strength. Just as the vacuum cleaner had no use without a power source, we have no strength apart from the Lord. There was nothing wrong with the illustration, but I became very embarrassed as I realized that the listeners, as well as the interpreter, had never heard of a vacuum cleaner or even electricity. I tried explaining, but the interpreter remained confused. He finally looked at me and said, "We do not know." I had to switch gears completely. I experienced a communication disaster as I sought to deliver my point in the wrong time, in the wrong place, and in the wrong way!

3. Effective delivery communicates ideas without calling attention to techniques. A skilled public speaker expresses ideas without stating them implicitly. She uses the skills and techniques in practice and does not state them aloud. Voice is projected, speech is articulated, and breath is supported as the speaker communicates the message. Eye contact is maintained, gestures are used naturally, and posture is held erect. Techniques are obviously implemented though the speaker need not mention them.

I (Rhonda) often teach classes or seminars on public speaking. In that case, it is helpful to comment about a public speaking technique utilized. The students seem to understand demonstrated techniques and principles better when I do. However, in a public speech, no mention should be made of a specific strategy. In a good speech, the ideas are communicated effectively because the techniques are incorporated fully.

4. Effective delivery establishes rapport with listeners. A message cannot be conveyed accurately or persuasively without a strong connection between the speaker and audience. Effort must be expended by both the speaker and listener for a relationship to develop and a message to be communicated. Desire for connection and rapport is as important as audience analysis.

One of the wonderful things I (Monica) love about speaking to women is that regardless of age or personality differences, I can always connect with those of the same gender! Many times before I speak, I will open with something funny about being a woman. This helps build a connection and allows the audience to see I am much like them.

In their book, *Power in the Pulpit*, Vines and Shaddix suggest several ways to connect with the audience when delivering a message or sermon.

- *Remember your calling.* The God who called you to serve him will empower you to connect with your audience to communicate his message.
- *Keep your heart warm and receptive.* Be open to the Lord as he speaks to you and to the listeners as they listen to you.
- *See each idea as you present it.* Make the ideas come alive in your mind so they can be imagined and understood by the audience.

- *Create intellectual and emotional stimuli.* Use words and feelings that will stimulate the minds and hearts of your listeners.
- *Watch the reactions of your people.* See the individuals in the audience as you speak. Notice their responses and reactions to verify their comprehension of your message.
- *Provide adequate emotional support.* Use examples and supportive material to strengthen what you say. Also, provide a means of response for listeners whose hearts and minds are stirred.[6]

5. Effective delivery uses both visual and auditory signs. God created humans not only with the ability to communicate but with the use of multiple senses. Humans have eyes for seeing, ears for hearing, a nose for smelling, and hands for touching. Ideas are communicated more completely when multiple senses are engaged. The speaker and listeners express and understand the message more clearly when visual and auditory stimuli are utilized.

In their book, *Principles of Speech Communication*, the authors discuss the importance of sensory imagery in their section on presenting a speech. They propose that people grasp their world through the senses of sight, smell, hearing, taste, and touch.[7] A speaker who incorporates the different senses to communicate a message will be much more effective. The strategic use of language and careful choice of words will stimulate the listener to recall previous experiences of sights and sounds. Imagery opens the listener's mind to experience the true meaning of the speaker's message.

Delivery Details

There is a common saying that the Devil is in the details. This statement implies that the small details can be most difficult or challenging. Most people are naturally inclined to ignore the minor matters that can ultimately become their biggest problems. As applied to public speaking, the details can be the downfall to an otherwise good speech. The little things, such as a mispronounced word or poorly researched data or rapid rate of speech, can interfere with the message being communicated. An experienced public speaker will pay attention to the small details as carefully as the main ideas of the message. Try not to let the Devil take over the details of your speech.

Remember these delivery details as you stand up to speak.

---

[6] Jerry Vines and Jim Shaddix, *Power in the Pulpit* (Chicago, IL: Moody Press, 1999), 303–4.
[7] Bruce E. Gronbeck et al., *Principles of Speech Communication*, 12th brief ed. (New York: Harper Collins, 1995), 161–65.

1. Start with a bang!
2. Speak with confidence.
3. Develop ideas thoroughly.
4. Support points with examples, illustrations, and statistics.
5. Relate directly to the audience.
6. Help the listeners make application.
7. Respect time frame and context.
8. Finish with an effective conclusion.

The delivery of a speech or teaching of a lesson involves so much more than speaking words or sharing ideas. The best delivery method must be selected; the underlying principles must be remembered; and many different details must be handled. While challenging, speech delivery can be life changing for both the speaker and the listeners. Prepare and plan, but above all else pray. When you stand up, speak up with the confidence God supplies.

TALKING POINT

Speakers must learn the principles
of speech delivery.

LET'S TALK ABOUT IT

1. List and define the four primary methods of speech delivery.
2. What are five principles of effective speech delivery?
3. List six different ways a speaker can connect to the audience according to the book, *Power in the Pulpit*.
4. What are the eight delivery details that an experienced public speaker needs to consider?
5. Describe your preferred method of delivery and why you like to speak in that way.

Chapter 16

QUESTIONS AND ANSWERS

*"Always be ready to give a defense to anyone who asks you
for a reason for the hope that is in you." (1 Pet 3:15)*

In this chapter, we will offer answers to specific questions about unique speaking opportunities. While there are three basic types of speeches (informative, persuasive, and entertaining), there are many different variations of talks and settings for speeches. Christian women, especially those in leadership, have many opportunities for speaking to groups, large and small.

On some occasions, a speaker will be asked to give a lengthier talk. Thorough research and preparation are essential to effective major speeches. Significant time must be invested before standing to speak. However, many other public speaking occasions, shorter and less formal, will arise in life and ministry. These also deserve a speaker's focused preparation time and effort.

Formal public speeches are rare. Informal types of speaking are frequent. People are asked to make announcements, give instructions, and provide introductions. Christians are often called on to read Scripture or pray aloud. Leaders must speak frequently when they facilitate a discussion session or preside over a meeting. Women's leaders must always be prepared to speak, and believers must always be ready to speak a word of witness (1 Pet 3:15). The Lord requires our best in any ministry opportunity. Experience gained in smaller tasks will prepare the Christian for greater ministry.

Unlike other chapters in this book, this one will involve interaction. Common questions about public speaking situations will be posed (Q_1), and then several responses will be provided (A_1, A_2, A_3). You may have other questions, which can be discussed through the blog: *www.talkingisagift.blogspot.com*. You ask; we answer! We will try to apply communication principles to some unique contexts.

Q_1–How Do I Introduce a Speaker?

Leaders are often asked to introduce a speaker. Christian women may be asked to introduce a weekly Bible study leader, a workshop or seminar teacher, a keynote conference speaker, or someone giving a testimony. Introductions have purpose and can be effective or ineffective. Always do your best!

A_1– **First, realize that introductions for program guests serve a purpose.** Every speaker needs an introduction whether she is familiar to the audience or not. A guest introduction serves several specific purposes. It . . .

- creates a pleasant atmosphere,
- gives the qualifications of the speaker,
- stresses the importance of the subject, and
- creates a desire to hear the speaker.

The speaker giving an introduction can smoothly transition from one aspect of the program to the next and should keep the program flowing. The content of the introduction highlights relevant qualifications of the speaker and briefly presents the topic or theme. The introducer may mention a personal connection to the speaker but should never focus the comments on herself.

I (Rhonda) have been introduced in some interesting and sometimes humorous ways. On one occasion, I was asked to speak for a senior adult luncheon at my home church. The lady assigned to introduce me said, "Since all of you know Rhonda, I thought I would use my time to update you on my recent surgery." She literally described her procedure and her recovery. Fortunately for all of us, she stopped short of showing us her scar!

Another time, I (Rhonda) was introduced to speak for several hundred ladies at a formal luncheon in a hotel ballroom. I was holding a red rose while I was escorted on the arm of a sweet lady of the church from the back of the large room. As we walked down the aisle and between the tables, all the ladies stood while my entire professional vita (biographical sketch) was read over the sound system. I felt like a blushing bride, humbled by their respect and accolades as well as embarrassed by the extensive reading of my credentials.

Several years ago, I (Monica) was asked to speak at an event focused on the launching of a church's first official women's ministry. The women's ministry director stood up to introduce me, and I assumed her introduction would be brief. However, before she introduced me she began to talk about her busy week and an upcoming mission trip. After forty-five minutes passed, I realized I had very little time left to speak if we were going to adjourn on time. I decided to share an abbreviated message, giving a word of exhortation and encouragement to the women. The pastor called me the next day to apologize and invited me back to speak again, explaining that the women's ministry director was inexperienced and had much learning to do in situations like that one.

A$_2$– **A guest introduction must be prepared carefully and prayerfully.** Background research should be gathered, and the speaker should be undergirded in prayer. When developing an introduction, remember these helpful hints:

- Make the introduction a separate speech.
- Use humor in good taste.
- Do not over-praise the speaker.
- Do not talk about yourself.
- Do not stress the speaker's speaking ability.
- Avoid trite and over-used language.

A well-prepared, well-delivered speech of introduction sets the tone for the message to come. It opens the hearts of the audience to the message and paves the way for the speaker to connect with the listeners. When an introduction is inadequately presented, the speaker must often begin by introducing herself.

My (Rhonda) typical introduction is less than stimulating. Ladies who lack experience and confidence when speaking before a crowd often begin nervously with apologies. They say too little or too much. They may be poorly prepared or unaware of the nature of an introduction. I love to be introduced by one of my women's ministry students when ministering in their own churches. Their understanding of the purpose of the introduction, their careful preparation, and their confident delivery make speaking a joy. I believe the Holy Spirit works even more powerfully through the speaker and in the hearts of the listeners when an effective introduction precedes a message.

I (Monica) will never forget being introduced by one of my former women's ministry students at a women's conference. She spoke about how she was personally touched and challenged by the women's ministry course I had taught. I was very humbled by her comments. She began to cry as she shared how she had been praying a long time for the women's conference that was finally a reality. Although her comments were brief, I remember thinking how prayerfully she must have thought through each word she so eloquently spoke and how the other ladies seemed to connect with her and with the theme for the entire conference.

A_3– **A guest introduction needs to be delivered succinctly and sensitively.** The length of an introduction should be in proportion to the length of the message. For instance, if a speech is brief (ten to fifteen minutes), the introduction should be only one or two minutes. If a speech is longer (thirty to sixty minutes), the introduction may be three to five minutes. An introduction must also be appropriate for the setting, occasion, and audience.

Keep these delivery techniques in mind when giving a speech of introduction.

- *Connect the speaker and audience.* The introduction is the connecting link between the speaker and the listeners. It should bring the two together and break down any barriers.
- *Establish credibility.* Present enough information to establish the speaker's credentials, explain why the speaker is gifted on the subject, and give the audience a reason to listen.
- *Highlight relevant accomplishments.* Do not read an endless list of degrees or credentials. Do not give away the speaker's message. Point out specifics that relate to the audience.
- *Keep comments brief.* Do not turn the introduction into a speech of your own. Keep it simple and short. Focus the attention on the speaker who is often a guest.
- *Answer questions in the minds of the audience.* Who? Where? What? Why? Give basic information about the speaker to answer unspoken questions.
- *Speak with confidence.* When it is your turn to introduce the speaker, get up quickly and try to speak without notes and without hesitation.

Remember these points when you give an introduction. Be brief. Be interesting. Be positive. And, try not to give away too much. The acronym KISS is a good reminder for introductions: Keep It Simple, Sweetie!

J. D. Grey was the beloved pastor of First Baptist New Orleans from 1937 to 1972. He was dear friends with Hershel Hobbs, a great Southern Baptist statesman, and they were both jokers. Hobbs was invited to speak for a stewardship banquet. During the meal, Grey asked Hobbs what his topic and major points would be for his message that night. When Grey stood to introduce his friend, he began by giving the exact title and points of Hobbs' upcoming message. Hobbs turned pale as Grey laughed and said, "Gotcha!" This was a mean trick to pull on a preacher before his sermon. However, the Lord spoke through him mightily.

I (Rhonda) have the privilege of attending many pastors' conferences and denominational conventions with my husband. It is typical for preachers to "preach" their speech of introduction or nomination. The podium and platform tempt them to share their own message from the Lord instead of introducing the preacher for the program. No matter the setting or occasion, a speaker must honor the assigned responsibility. When asked to introduce, make an introduction. When asked to speak, speak.

Before introducing a guest speaker, I (Monica) try to discuss with the speaker what I plan on sharing with the ladies. I then try to memorize what I am going to say in order to stay completely focused on what needs to be said and what I know the speaker is comfortable with me communicating.

Q_2– How Do I Make Announcements More Interesting and Effective?

Announcements are essential to any ministry. Information must be dispensed and attendance must be encouraged. Without announcements, the most exciting events and the most meaningful ministries lack response. The word must get out so that people may be blessed. Leaders must learn how to make necessary announcements more interesting and effective.

A_1– **There are three basic reasons for announcements of special events and ongoing programs to be made:**

1. Information needs to be disseminated.
2. Important programs need to be highlighted.
3. People need to be motivated.

Keep these reasons in mind as you prepare your announcements and deliver the reminders. Do not be embarrassed to make announcements. Understand their importance and present them with confidence.

A_2– **All announcements are not created equal.** Some announcements get attention, keep interest, and produce response. Others lack appeal. To those the audience does not pay attention, show interest, or respond positively. Keep these suggestions in mind when making announcements.

1. Present the information clearly.
2. Summarize the activities briefly.
3. Create enthusiasm about the events.
4. Highlight the ministry opportunities.
5. Give the specific details for events.

Remember to keep announcements short, sweet, and specific!

A₃– **Some announcements lend themselves to creativity.** Skits, pantomime, or dramatic interpretation may make an announcement more interesting. Videos, visuals, or handouts may clarify the specific information. Testimonials or personality highlights may stimulate curiosity. Incentives or prizes may motivate people to attend.

Publicity and promotion are essential to the success of events or programs. However, word-of-mouth continues to be the most effective advertisement. In an impersonal world—people, especially ladies—love a personal invitation. So, develop creative publicity, ensure thorough promotion, and present interesting announcements. While also encouraging ladies to inform their friends and invite their neighbors to women's events.

I (Rhonda) recently had a frustrating reminder that ministry cannot be announced enough. A new student wife emailed me to see if there was "anything for wives on campus." I wanted to scream! For one month, as the school year began, we had been aggressively promoting the classes and fellowship meetings for student wives. We made verbal announcements in chapel services, distributed brochures in the Campus Life Fair, delivered fliers door-to-door, and posted Facebook events. Where had she and her husband been? After my initial frustration, I began to feel grateful that she had emailed an inquiry. Many people remain silent and uninformed.

There is never too much publicity. There are never enough announcements. The importance of word-of-mouth promotion can never be exaggerated.

I (Monica) have found word-of-mouth communication to be more effective than any other means of publicity. However, due to the very busy lives and constant demands women have, we can never receive enough reminders. I serve as the women's ministry director of my church and once a month we have a women's Bible study before the Sunday morning service. Although our women's ministry is listed on a flier handed out each Sunday to the entire body, the women are given two special personal invitations. We also post reminders on Facebook and send emails. Announce, announce, and announce again.

Q₃– How Do I Read Scripture Clearly and with Passion?

Speakers often read through Scripture rapidly to get to their own message. Whether intentional or not, some Christian speakers take little time or effort to prepare for the public reading of Scripture. Rapid rate, unclear speech, and lack of inflection may cause confusion to the listener or reflect apathy by the speaker. Nothing is more important than the clear, careful reading of God's Word.

A$_1$– **When preparing to read Scripture aloud, give thought and prayer.** Take time to rehearse the words as well as reflect on the message. Time and effort should be invested before reading Scripture. These strategies may be beneficial as you take seriously the public reading of God's Word:

1. Select an appropriate, complete portion of Scripture.
2. Choose the best translation to communicate the meaning of the text.
3. Practice reading the passage aloud to yourself or another person. Record the reading to evaluate and improve your speech.
4. Work out difficult pronunciations. Divide long words into syllables and stress the appropriate syllable. Dictionary.com has an audio pronunciation tool that may help.
5. Practice reading interpretatively. Use emotion, expression, and feeling as you read.
6. Prayerfully read the passage, asking the Lord to connect his truth to the listeners.

Though impromptu reading of Scripture may occur in a Sunday school class or spontaneous reading may happen in a Bible study group, Scripture readings most often can be prepared in advanced. Always do your best when reading God's Word aloud.

A$_2$– **When you read Scripture aloud, speak with confidence in God and His Word.** Follow the words of the text carefully while occasionally making eye contact with the audience. Do not rush because the words of God are the most important words you will speak. Keep these points in your mind as you read Scripture aloud:

1. Hold the Bible up and your head erect so your voice will project and your facial expressions will be visible.
2. Adjust the rate of your speech for mood and emphasis.
3. Enunciate words clearly. Mild exaggeration of pronunciation is helpful.
4. Use accurate phrasing and pausing. Breathe at punctuation marks.
5. Emphasize words to stress meaning.

Take seriously the reading of God's Word, knowing Scripture has the power to transform lives.

Some years ago, I (Rhonda) learned personally the power of reading God's Word aloud. I spoke for a large gathering of charismatic women. I had carefully prepared a biblical message. Briefly into my message, I realized that the ladies responded enthusiastically to the reading or reciting of Scripture. While they seemed interested in my points and personal illustrations, those women of the

Word were most inspired by the truth of Scripture. I edited my message on the spot to emphasize Scripture and minimize my own thoughts. What a powerful truth about the public reading of Scripture!

I (Monica) remember hearing a woman speak when I was a teenager. She had so much to say and was very engaging. However, when she read Scripture, she never made eye contact. Her audience was so connected to her as she began reading but because she looked down the entire time while reading, she lost that connection.

Q₄– How Do I Facilitate a Panel Discussion?

Panel discussions are often a part of programs for women. A panel discussion is a forum to present information and to discuss personal opinions. Forty-five to sixty minutes is adequate time for the typical panel discussion.

A₁– **Several "experts" in a particular field may be asked to serve on the panel.** Questions are posed to them and each has the opportunity to respond. The questions may be gathered before the discussion begins or may be asked spontaneously by those in the crowd. A panel discussion provides several perspectives on a single topic and helps the listeners apply the information to their lives.

Every panel needs a moderator or facilitator whose role is different from the panelists. A strong moderator should have a general knowledge of the subject and the ability to communicate clearly. A speaker should remember these tips when moderating a panel discussion:

1. Introduce the panel members to the audience.
2. Clearly introduce the topic or issue of the discussion to the panelists and audience.
3. Ensure the pace of the discussion, encouraging participation by all panelists.
4. Maintain control and order—especially with more controversial topics.
5. Involve all audience participants, limiting length and number of questions.
6. Repeat questions from the audience to the panelists for clarity.
7. Summarize comments before transitioning to the next question.
8. Conclude the discussion before it fades. Thank the audience and panel for participating.

A₂– **Three-to-five panelists ideally provide a variety of viewpoints on the subject.** When serving on a panel, each participant must understand the focus and follow the guidelines. Should you be asked to serve as a panelist, begin opening comments by restating the question. Keep comments brief and relevant. Respond to the question specifically, and ask for clarification if necessary. Give examples as well as data to clarify information. Share the time for discussion with other panelists. Enjoy the interaction.

A_3– **The setting and format of a panel discussion should be carefully organized.** Attempt to position the panelists comfortably on the platform, not rigidly behind a table. To amplify volume and minimize time delays, provide microphones for each panelist. Light the platform so nonverbal cues from the panelists are visible. Raise the lights in the room so audience members can be seen by the panelists. Graphic presentation slides are rarely used since panel discussions are informal and interactive. If a panel discussion is included in a program, it should be carried out with excellence. The moderator and panelists must fulfill their specific responsibilities.

I (Rhonda) love to moderate panel discussions. Different communication skills are needed to connect the panel and audience. It stretches me personally to understand the nature of the question and encourage a thorough response. I often make brief comments to summarize and transition. Sometimes I use humor to lighten the tone or illustrate a point. My goals are to keep the discussion going and to blend into the background as I focus the attention on the expertise of the panel.

Recently, I (Monica) was asked to be on a panel about "Resolving Conflict in Ministry," and I was the only female contributor. Although we were not given the questions ahead of time, I prepared by reviewing key Scripture verses on this very important topic. My preparation time helped me have more confidence when I spoke and gave me some significant direction as I answered questions.

Q_5– How Do I Moderate a Question and Answer (Q&A) Session?

A time for questions at the end of a presentation is often helpful. As the speaker, you may need to acknowledge questions from the audience and respond appropriately. A speaker can choose to save questions until the end of the presentation or take questions throughout the speech. The role of questions is to personalize the content to the listener's life. Keep these suggestions in mind:

- Be respectful of all questions, whether they seem wise or foolish.
- Establish an atmosphere conducive to questions from the audience.
- Recognize inquiries from all participants, limiting questions from only the most talkative ones.

- Diffuse controversial questions and redirect unimportant comments.
- Be tactful, responding in love as well as truth.

The New Orleans Baptist Theological Seminary hosts a point/counterpoint conference each year, discussing relevant faith and culture issues such as the Resurrection of Jesus, intelligent design, pluralism, and life after death. Each academic presentation is followed by a question and answer period. The conference chairman establishes ground rules before the discussion. With humor and honesty, he reminds the audience of these facts: "There is such a thing as stupid questions;" "Participants have paid to hear from the experts, not from you;" and "Do not use the microphone to bash the opposing viewpoint." The Q&A time is more beneficial to all because the guidelines are followed.

While a seminary student attending a Q&A session, I (Monica) remember observing one of the participants who completely dominated the time. He was very harsh in his responses. The audience was not helped in any way, and his spirit caused more division than harmony. Questions must be posed in love. Answers must be given positively.

Q$_6$– How Do I Lead a Meeting and Guide a Discussion?

An important responsibility of leadership is guiding a meeting. Committees or groups must gather to plan and implement action. Without effective leadership, those meetings can be unproductive wastes of time. It is the president or chair who should prepare and conduct the meeting so that the purpose is accomplished. *Robert's Rules of Order* is helpful when conducting more formal business.[1] The following tips are helpful when leading a meeting.

- Send a meeting reminder and announce the agenda so members can consider the topics in advance.
- Develop a timed schedule from the agenda to ensure all topics are covered equally.
- Encourage all members to participate in discussions.
- Redirect the conversation when the focus drifts.
- Delegate responsibilities of leadership when possible.
- Adjourn the meeting on time, encouraging group members to remain for fellowship if desired.

---

[1] Henry Martyn Robert et al., *Robert's Rules of Order Newly Revised* (Cambridge, MA: Da Capo Press, 2011).

Recently, I (Rhonda) hosted a meeting of our Student Wives Council. After the meeting, the group's president asked for feedback. She wanted to know how to improve as a leader when guiding a meeting. She specifically asked about handling people who change the subject or talk too much. We discussed the importance of having an agenda and adhering to the set times. She was concerned about being too forceful as she guided the discussion. I assured her that a leader must lead the meeting to keep the agenda from being derailed. I am confident that this young woman will become an outstanding leader because she is taking seriously the responsibility of guiding a meeting a job that many people would think insignificant in comparison to public speaking.

Q_7– How Do I Serve as the MC (Master/Mistress of Ceremonies) of a Program?

Special events and some programs involve a Master or Mistress of Ceremonies (MC). An MC is the person in charge of the procedure at a public occasion; who introduces speakers, players, or entertainers. The Catholic Church has had an official position at the Vatican for a Master of Ceremonies in the Papal Court since the Middle Ages (15th century). His responsibilities include overseeing protocol for religious rituals. Royal courts in European countries often have an MC to conduct stately ceremonies such as coronations and receptions.

Though her role is less formal, an MC of a women's event serves as the hostess and presider. Knowledge of protocol or the etiquette for such occasions helps the MC fulfill her duties more completely. If asked to MC an event or program, remember the following:

- Be pleasant and create a positive mood.
- Understand the purpose of the gathering and maintain it.
- Present the program guests and interact with the audience.
- Keep the event moving smoothly.
- Maintain order and decorum.
- Conclude on an uplifting note, encouraging people to attend again.

Television award shows, including the Oscars and the Grammys, struggle to find an ideal MC every year. It is not easy for a famous actor or popular comedian to emcee well. A different set of professional skills are required. The best and worst list of award show hosts acknowledges that not even the most loved Hollywood star is guaranteed to excel as an MC. Preferred hosts balance humor and accolades well, move smoothly and sensitively through a program, emcee with the right timing and tastes. These principles of emceeing can be learned from award shows and other public programs for application to ministry.

Q₈– How Do I Share a Testimony or Brief Devotional?

Testimonies and devotionals are short speeches. While some steps of preparation are the same as those associated with longer speeches, there are differences as well. A testimony is sharing a personal experience without telling a whole life story. A brief testimony should focus on one life event or one faith lesson. A devotional is a brief inspirational thought with a Scripture reference and personal application. Both presentations should only be three to five minutes in length. Always do your best with these shorter speeches, keeping these tips in mind as you prepare:

 A₁– **First, consider *what* to share.**
- Share your own personal experiences or insights.
- Organize your thoughts logically.
- Develop the introduction, main idea, and conclusion.
- Write an outline on index cards or notepaper.
- Try not to read your speech word for word.
- End with a concluding challenge.

 A₂– **Then, consider *how* to share it.**
- Be open and transparent.
- Boldly share the message of Christ.
- Speak clearly and comfortably.
- Give hope and encouragement.

Two of the most powerful testimonies I (Rhonda) have heard were shared in a prison setting. The student testimony during a graduation ceremony from the New Orleans Baptist Theological Seminary program at Phillips State Prison in Georgia was powerful. The graduate tripped and fell down with a loud bang as he walked up the steps to the platform. He jumped up and wiped off his robe. His first words captured our attention when he said, "In life, all of us fall down. I have fallen down. We have fallen down. But, the Lord has picked us up and given us another chance." Wow!

A student in our (Rhonda's) women's prison program at the Louisiana Correctional Institute for Women gave a moving testimony in a public speaking class. She shared about "Doing Life Together." While most Christians think of living life alongside of others, the prisoner was literally talking about serving a life sentence with her classmates. It was a powerful testimony about the importance of Christian fellowship and accountability.

Q₉– How Do I Give an Effective Impromptu Speech?

An impromptu speech is one given on the spur-of-the-moment, without time for preparation. Circumstances often demand an unexpected speech. The motto "always be prepared" is a good reminder for public speakers. Ministry often involves spontaneous speaking or teaching. Christian leaders should be flexible and willing when the need arises for a last minute speaker.

Though little preparation time is provided, always do your best and try not to make excuses. Consider these suggestions when speaking off the cuff:

1. Take a deep breath and say a quick prayer.
2. Focus your thoughts on one or two ideas.
3. Write down a few points to guide your thoughts.
4. Speak about a familiar topic or share a personal insight.
5. Start with a few opening comments, quickly develop your main idea, then close up with a bang.
6. Speak clearly and confidently.

I (Rhonda) have learned to be ready and willing for an impromptu speech. It is often my privilege to travel with my husband when he is invited to preach. When the church learns of my presence, they may invite me to speak for the women's ministry or a Sunday school class. Sometimes the request comes at the last minute on Sunday morning. I always travel with an outline or two. If asked to share my testimony, I can do so in a five, thirty, or sixty minute version. If asked to teach a Sunday school class, I can share a Bible lesson I have recently prepared. I never want to miss an opportunity to share what God is doing in my life.

Q₁₀– How Do I Communicate in a Radio or Television Interview?

Media are an effective means to communicate a message. Television, radio, and social media provide forums for speakers. The two-way dialogue of media communication is different from the one-way monologue of public speaking. Unique skills are required to conduct a media interview or to be interviewed.

A₁– **An interviewer must research and prepare before conducting an interview.** Each program has a different purpose and every audience has a different personality. The following skills will be helpful to those conducting an interview.

- Focus on your guest and not yourself.
- Ask questions from the perspective of your audience.

- Express questions in fifteen seconds or less.
- Read the guest's book or research the topic.
- Prepare questions but feel free to add questions spontaneously.

A_2– **An interviewee must learn how to respond clearly and concisely to interview questions.** An author or professional expert may have extensive knowledge but not be an effective media guest. Try to relate to the audience, not speaking down to them or over their heads. Relax and enjoy your interview. Consider these reminders:

- Concentrate on the questions asked.
- Explain your thoughts in a few sentences.
- Keep answers relevant and to the point.
- Be energetic and sincere.
- Do not become defensive or emotional.
- Rephrase the questions you are asked.
- Highlight your major insights.
- Summarize your thoughts as you conclude.

I (Rhonda) had the privilege of hosting a radio/TV program called "A Word for Women" for many years. It was an awesome opportunity to encourage my female listeners and to introduce relevant ministries. I interviewed many guests with education or experience in areas of interest to women. I quickly learned that the brightest person or most published author is not always the best media guest. Experts often have difficulty summarizing thoughts briefly and simplifying more complex ideas. I always worked harder as the host to interview "A-list guests," those with credentials and publications.

I (Rhonda) gained knowledge about interviews from my years of broadcasting. I relate to the interviewer when I am being interviewed. My greatest affirmation is for a host to say "the interview flew by" or "that was such an easy interview." It means I fulfilled my role well.

The Lord will stretch you as you prepare and present in different ways. Learn to moderate panel discussions, emcee special events, facilitate meetings, respond to questions, conduct interviews, and always communicate God's work in your life in a clear and passionate way.

" **TALKING POINT**

Always do your best
in every speaking situation. "

LET'S TALK ABOUT IT

1. What purpose does the introduction serve? How can you effectively introduce a speaker?
2. What purpose do announcements serve at a women's ministry event?
3. List and describe several effective ways to read Scripture aloud.
4. What are six helpful hints to remember when serving on a panel?
5. Describe your most challenging speaking situation. How has this chapter helped you in becoming a more effective communicator?

Chapter 17

HEART AND HUMOR

"The best and most beautiful things in the world
cannot be seen or even touched.
They must be felt with the heart." (Helen Keller)

Helen Keller, deafblind pioneer in education for the disabled, once said: "The best and most beautiful things in the world cannot be seen or even touched. They must be felt with the heart." A woman's heart is her source of life, literally and figuratively. It is the vital organ of the physical body that pumps blood throughout the system. Spiritually and emotionally, the heart produces human feelings and desires. The Bible mentions the heart about 300 times, and though the heart is inclined toward evil due to sin, it can be transformed by the power of God in response to a personal faith (Jer 17:9–10; Mark 7:21–23; Rom 10:10; 2 Cor 8:16). A Christian speaker should seek to be a woman after God's own heart (Acts 13:22 NIV).

Mary, the mother of Jesus, was such a woman. The Lord first spoke to her heart before she conceived the Son of God by the Holy Spirit (Luke 1:26–38). She heard and believed in her heart that she was chosen by God to bring the Messiah into the world. She then spoke words of praise from her heart. The Lord next spoke to Mary's heart through her relative Elizabeth (Luke 1:39–45). When Mary heard and believed in her heart that she was blessed of all women, she spoke words of gratitude from her heart (Luke 1:46–55). The Lord spoke to Mary's heart again through the angels and shepherds (Luke 2:8–20). She heard and believed in her heart that her child was the Savior and Messiah who would take away the sins of the world. The Bible records that "Mary was treasuring up all these things in her heart" (Luke 2:19). She pondered or meditated on the words of God before speaking words of truth herself.

Christian speakers must maintain open hearts to hear from God and honest hearts to speak his truth faithfully. Openness and honesty are keys to effective communication. They can be developed and maintained through a dynamic personal relationship with Jesus Christ. The emotions of the heart provide the passion and joy in public speaking. Joy is one human emotion that is often experienced and expressed through humor.

In this chapter we will consider the concepts of heart and humor. Openness and honesty are reflected through one who is in right relationship with God and others. Humor and lightheartedness are experienced in life and expressed in words by a speaker who recognizes the joy of the Lord. As a public speaker, seek to be open, honest, and joyful.

Openness

An effective speaker speaks from her heart and with humor. As she speaks, she must develop an atmosphere of openness and honesty as well as enjoyment. According to the book, *Principles of Speech Communication* the speaking atmosphere is the mind-set or mental attitude that the speaker seeks to create in the audience. The desired atmosphere is based upon the speaking situation, the speech's purpose, and the listener's expectations.[1] However, a speaker must be open and transparent to connect with the audience.

Being an open and honest speaker is not always easy because of the uncertainty of the responses from people in the audience. I (Monica) struggled for years with an eating disorder that I kept secret from everyone except the Lord and my parents. As I was healed by the Lord and found absolute deliverance, opportunities to share what God was doing in my life presented themselves. My first opportunity was in high school when I was asked to meet with girls, who were struggling with eating disorders; I had a chance to offer them hope. At times through the years, I have been hesitant to share my personal story with others. However, I have felt the Lord encourage me to do so at specific times. When I have shared my personal story with others transparently, women have waited to thank me for my authenticity. Due to my openness, the ladies were

---

[1] Bruce E. Gronbeck et al., *Principles of Speech Communication*, 12th brief ed. (New York: Harper Collins College Publishers, 1995), 169.

open to the Lord for his healing touch! Authenticity from the speaker will always have a positive effect on the audience.

A Christian message from the heart must come from the heart of the Lord and the heart of the speaker. Sincerity and genuineness open the listener's heart. Any message is more powerful when the speaker is passionate and earnest. Speaking from the heart reaches the hearts of others.

To speak in this manner, a Christian communicator must first hear from God. Then, she must be concerned for others and willing to share personally. She feels a burden to help everyone hear from the Lord and respond to his gospel of hope. When Jesus spoke, his words from the heart changed the hearts of those who heard him (Luke 24:32).

I (Rhonda) recently asked a group of women, "Who is the most sincere and transparent speaker you have ever heard and why?" My interest was in the "why" more than the "who." Of course, the consensus answer was Jesus because he is perfect. Actually, we can learn a lot about openness and sincerity from his sermons and personal encounters. The Gospel of Mark alone records "they were all amazed" many times in response to the words of Jesus. Mark 6:34 reports that Jesus was moved with compassion and then spoke honestly and sincerely. The immediate and unrehearsed responses to my question underscore the importance of speaking from the heart.

When asked for descriptions of a sincere speaker, this same group's responses included the following: "She talks to me, not over my head; she listens without judgment, and speaks without condemning; and she does not hide who she is, she shares warts and all."

Florence and Marita Littauer stress the importance of speaking from the heart in their book, *Communication Plus*. They teach others how to reach the hearts of their audiences in six steps.

1. *Establish a need.* Recognize personal needs and relate to those of others.
2. *Give a personal testimony.* Real-life examples illustrate the point.
3. *Present a plan.* Once the problem is identified, propose specific steps toward a solution.
4. *Offer hope.* Always point people to Jesus and give them a way out.
5. *Call for commitment.* Give every audience a challenge for change.
6. *Expect results.* Be confident in your own response and the positive commitments of others.[2]

---

[2] Florence and Marita Littauer, *Communication Plus: How to Speak So People Will Listen* (Ventura, CA: Regal, 2006), 123–26.

These guidelines will encourage speakers to be more open and honest.

A speaker must be willing to share herself with the audience. Listeners respond to a speaker who is believable and real, willing to share about both her successes and failures. Someone whose life seems too perfect may have listeners tuning out. If every story ends with a happily-ever-after, it may seem too good to be true.

It is also necessary for the speaker to maintain personal privacy and to respect the privacy of others. A personal testimony can be shared without all the gory details. A general description without too many specifics can keep the focus on the solution, not the problem. Some Christians speak so much about their lives before Christ that they sound like they are sorry to be saved. Others speak too freely about their family members or friends. Openness and respect must be balanced. My (Rhonda's) husband says it this way: "There are windows in the house but no glass walls in the bathroom." In other words, some things need to stay private and behind closed doors.

Honesty

Honesty and trust are foundational to the relationship between the speaker and listeners. A speaker should tell the truth and not exaggerate the facts. Though a speaker's vivid imagery heightens the listener's understanding, blatant lying hurts the speaker's credibility. Complete honesty is always expected by the audience. It is imperative for a speaker to give credit where credit is due. If a speaker is not sharing an original thought, she must cite the source.

After his sermon, a well-known preacher was questioned by the pastor. The exact same sermon, including the same personal illustrations, had been preached by another person in the same pulpit. The fraudulent preacher had preached the evangelist's sermon as if it were his own. Another time, I sat through a worship service with my husband who was quietly quoting along word-for-word everything the speaker said. The pastor preached a famous sermon to his congregation as if it were his original creation. One pastor was actually exposed publicly for plagiarizing all his sermons. Dishonesty will not be tolerated.

People are smart enough to recognize a phony or fake who is speaking. Florence Littauer recalls with concern a public speaker who wrote "cry here" in red in her outline.[3] She literally planned for her tears. How artificial! To reach the hearts of people, a speaker must be sincere and honest.

A speaker must have integrity and wisdom. In their book, *Power in the Pulpit*, Vines and Shaddix suggest the following qualities for those speakers who desire to be credited with strong character and moral excellence (1 Thess 2:1–12):

---

[3] Ibid., 124.

- Authentic and endearing
- Down to earth
- Speak the same to one or one thousand people
- Gentle, loving spirit
- Give glory to God
- Relatable, believable, personal
- Inspiring, convicting, captivating, enthusiastic
- Joyful and loving
- *God-given mission*: a speaker must have a specific call from God
- *Genuine motivation*: a speaker must have a sincere desire to teach God's truth
- *Gentle manner*: a speaker must have a compassionate and loving heart[4]

Commitment, compassion, and concern in the heart of a speaker connect with the heart of the listener.

The writer of Proverbs teaches about the power of words hidden in the heart, warning the listener to "guard your heart above all else, for it is the source of life" (Prov 4:23). The heart controls the life and the lips. A heart that is godly will speak truth to the hearts of listeners.

Joy

Humor can capture the attention, change the pace, relax the audience, release tension, and help the speaker connect. However, it is not always necessary or appropriate. Humor is inappropriate when forced, in bad taste, or poorly timed. When used ineffectively, humor can hurt the message more than help it. For a Christian speaker, joy should be the tone of speech whether the topic is serious or funny.

Peggy Noonan is a political columnist and speech writer. Though she wrote specifically about politicians in her book, *On Speaking Well*, her comments about humor apply generally to all public speakers. Even the most serious people can use humor to make a point when appropriate. True wit is a happy surprise and should be used when possible. Noonan writes, "Wit from a woman standing on a bare stage and giving you her views is more surprising still."[5]

Humor is a helpful vehicle in speaking, teaching, and writing. Unexpected humor can surprise and capture the audience. It must also be used with caution. Clarity and timing are crucial. Words must be carefully selected and presented

---

[4] Jerry Vines and Jim Shaddix, *Power in the Pulpit* (Chicago, IL: Moody Press, 1999), 72–74.

[5] Peggy Noonan, *Simply Speaking: How to Communicate Your Ideas with Style, Substance, and Clarity* (New York: Harper Collins, 1998), 13–15.

with time delay for response. Humor often builds as the speaker shares one point at a time. Tension and release combine to bring about a laugh. According to Chuck Swindoll's book, *Saying It Well*, humor should be avoided in three situations: in solemn occasions, painful issues, and unfamiliar territory.[6] Humor does not always translate accurately into other languages or across different cultures.

Jokes and funny stories are only two types of humor. Life experiences are often more humorous than jokes. My (Rhonda) husband and I often say, "We do not have to make up funny stories. They just happen in our lives." However, remember your life does not have to be funny, and you do not have to be humorous to be an effective speaker.

Anita Renfroe is one of my (Rhonda) favorite Christian comedians. Her humor flows from her life as a mother and minister's wife. Her famous "Mom Song" is humorous because mothers can relate, in one way or another, to every phrase she includes. It is not what she says but how she says it that brings a smile to the listener's face. Anita's motto is, "Love God, love people, and love laughing!" This is a helpful goal for all public speakers.

Barbara Johnson was a delightful writer and humorous speaker. The titles of her books bring laughter themselves. In *Splashes of Joy in the Cesspools of Life*, she discusses the importance of humor in life and ministry. Johnson considers humor to be the sixth sense. She recognizes that humor can "help you overlook the unattractive, tolerate the unpleasant, cope with the unexpected, and smile through the unbearable."[7]

I (Rhonda) am a naturally happy person who loves to laugh. I try to see the humor in life and share ironies with joy. I do not tell jokes often. When speaking to an unfamiliar audience, I feel humor helps me build rapport. When I make fun of myself in a good-hearted way, I believe it breaks down barriers with the audience. I agree with Swindoll who said, "Humor gives us permission to be vulnerable with dignity."[8] Consider the advantages and disadvantages of humor before using it, and allow it to flow naturally.

Like my friend Rhonda, I (Monica) do not share jokes often while speaking. However, there have been several times when I have presented something funny to serve as an icebreaker for a women's conference or to highlight the point of my message. I consciously try to include humor when speaking, since it does not come naturally to me. Humor can be powerful when used effectively, in the appropriate way and at the appropriate time.

---

[6] Charles Swindoll, *Saying It Well: Touching Others with Your Words* (New York: FaithWords 2012), 192–95.

[7] Barbara Johnson, *Splashes of Joy in the Cesspools of Life* (Nashville: W Publishing Group, 1992), 109.

[8] Swindoll, *Saying It Well*, 198.

Checklist for Using Humor

Purpose

_____ 1. Is my humor in good taste or will it damage my credibility as a speaker?

_____ 2. Does my humorous story have a point?

_____ 3. Has the story been overused? Is it a cliché?

_____ 4. Does the point of my humor relate to the point I am making in my speech?

_____ 5. Am I using the humor simply for its own sake, or does it have a purpose in my speech?

_____ 6. Does the humor increase group cohesion?

_____ 7. Does the story depend upon potentially offensive ethnic, religious, or gender stereotypes? If so, can I rework the story to avoid offensiveness?

_____ 8. Is the story brief enough not to sidetrack me?

_____ 9. Where is the humor used in my speech? Can I keep it from getting in the way of the idea I am clarifying?

Delivery

_____ 1. Does the use of humor make me self-conscious?

_____ 2. Can I communicate a humorous story well? If not, what can I do to improve my delivery?

_____ 3. Is the punch line clear?

_____ 4. What will I do if my listeners do not respond appropriately to my humor?

_____ 5. Have I tested my stories on others?

_____ 6. Can I avoid copying the delivery style of someone else and use my own speaking style?

From Bruce E. Gronbeck et al., *Principles of Speech Communication,* 12th brief ed. (New York: HarperCollins College Publishers, 1995), 291.

In *Principles of Speech Communication*, the authors provide practical guidance on the use of humor in public speaking. First, they suggest three rules for telling a humorous story.

1. Be sure that the story is at least amusing if not funny; test it out on others before you actually deliver the speech.
2. Be sure that the story is relevant to your speech; if not, it will appear to be a mere gimmick.

3. Be sure that your story is in good taste; if not, adapt it or find another illustration.[9]

These same authors also provide a checklist for using humor. Questions are posed to help determine the most effective way to use humor. Each question relates to the purpose of the speech or the method of delivery.[10] See the checklist below.

Heart and humor are important elements of speech delivery. The passion of the heart flows from the speaker's mouth. Openness and honesty give credibility to the words, and humor can often open the hearts of the listeners to receive the message.

TALKING POINT

"Guard your heart above all else,
for it is the source of life."
(Prov 4:23)

LET'S TALK ABOUT IT

1. What are the two keys to effective communication, and how can they be maintained?
2. What are the six steps Florence and Marita Littauer write about in the book, *Communication Plus: How to Speak So People Will Listen* that speakers can apply in order to reach the hearts of their audiences?
3. Describe the three qualities that should characterize the life of a speaker/ preacher concerning strength of character as suggested by Vines and Shaddix in the book, *Power in the Pulpit*.
4. What are the three rules for telling a humorous story suggested in the book, *Principles of Speech Communication*?
5. Elaborate on Proverbs 4:23. How important is it to have a clean heart as a speaker? In what ways can you apply this verse to your life as a speaker?

---

[9] Gronbeck et al., *Principles of Speech Communication*, 135.
[10] Ibid., 291.

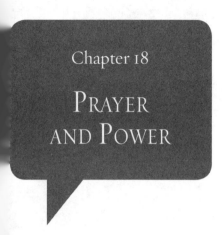

Chapter 18

PRAYER AND POWER

"If speaking is like cooking,
then prayer turns the recipe into a meal."[1]

A Christian speaker has the responsibility of preparation but also has the privilege of prayer. Before, during, and after the speech, the speaker should commit the message to the Lord in prayer. Prayer opens the heart to hear from God and directs the mind to speak to others. Without prayer, a person speaks only words. With prayer, a Christian can speak truth. Pray to speak truth from God each time you speak publicly. This chapter will discuss the role of general prayer, personal petition, and the Holy Spirit's work in the life of a Christian speaker.

Jesus illustrated the importance of prayer in His life. In John 17, he prayed specifically for himself and others. He sought God's guidance with the words of his mouth and the meditations of his heart. His prayer focus can be a pattern for Christians at all times, especially before speaking or teaching.

In the first five verses of John 17, Jesus prays for himself. He prays specifically to glorify God and expresses a desire to complete the work assigned to him. Speakers should pray for themselves personally, requesting that they glorify God and serve him through speaking. In the second section of John 17 (vv. 6–19),

---

[1] Charles Swindoll, *Saying It Well: Touching Others with Your Words* (New York: FaithWords, 2012), 155.

Jesus prays for others. He prays specifically for his disciples to hear from the Lord and be united in their message. Christian speakers should pray that their audiences will hear from the Lord and understand the proclaimed truth. In the last section of John 17 (vv. 20–26), Jesus prays for all believers to be one with the Father in taking the gospel to the world.

> Righteous Father!
> The world has not known You.
> However, I have known that You,
> and these have known that You sent Me.
> I made Your name known to them
> and will make it known,
> so the love You have loved Me with
> may be in them and I may be in them. (John 17:25–26)

Christ's words in the hour before his death are a reminder that prayer is important to life and essential to ministry. As a Christian speaker prepares to speak and stands to deliver, she must commit her words and herself to the Lord. Then the Holy Spirit will speak through her with power.

Prayer

A Christian speaker should begin praying about her message from the moment she is invited to speak. Prayer not only helps a speaker know what to say, it keeps the focus on God, not self; it opens eyes to the needs of others; and it calms the spirit with confidence to speak.

Most of the time, I (Monica) am able to write my teaching outline and notes directly after (and sometimes during) my prayer times. Many times after I pray, the Lord will lead me to the exact passage of Scripture and specific message he desires me to share for a speaking engagement scheduled many months away. The Lord leads through prayer and places within the heart of the speaker the message she needs to share with a specific audience.

In his book, *Saying It Well: Touching Others with Your Words*, Chuck Swindoll writes: "If preaching is like cooking, then prayer turns the recipe into a meal."[2] Prayer gives meaning to a speaker's words. Like a recipe, a message has many ingredients. It is not the individual ingredients, but the blending of all ingredients that gives the dish a satisfying taste. It is prayer that blends together the contents of the speech and the methods of delivery to make a powerful message.

---

[2] Ibid., 155.

This illustration comes to life for me because I (Rhonda) love to cook and do so often as president's wife at the New Orleans Baptist Theological Seminary. Before, I carefully review the recipe to secure each ingredient from the grocery store. I line up all the ingredients on the counter as I begin cooking. I read and reread the recipe to ensure nothing is omitted. Occasionally, however, I get distracted or in a hurry, forgetting to buy something at the store or forgetting to add an essential ingredient. The meal may still be edible but is not as expected or intended.

Through the years, my family (Rhonda) has laughed about my mother's first few attempts to make cornbread for Chuck. The first time, she forgot salt, so the cornbread tasted bland. The next time she forgot the baking powder, so the cornbread did not rise. The third time she baked it too long, so the cornbread was hard. Mother finally got the cornbread just right, and we have enjoyed it often. A message from the Lord is just not right without prayer.

Prayer has a way of helping everything else in life come together. In general, a speaker should pray daily, without ceasing (1 Thess 5:17). Praise to the Lord as well as personal petitions are vital aspects of prayer. Prayer should be focused on the purpose of the speech, occasion of the speech, and content of the speech. Prayer should be for the speaker and for the listeners. At all times, pray for God's will to be accomplished in the message and messenger, in the hearers and their hearts.

Through prayer, the speaker is also able to surrender the message, the delivery, and the audience to the Lord. I (Monica) remember listening to one of my mentors, Dorothy Patterson, lecture on the importance of surrendering everything to the Lord and leaving the results to him. Without prayer, a speaker can become very frustrated and discouraged. However, through prayer, a speaker is reminded that God is in control of everything and can be trusted.

E. M. Bounds' book, *Power through Prayer* has been called the greatest book on prayer ever written. Bounds believed a preacher's prayerful heart and the Holy Spirit's anointing gave power to the message. He said, "Prayer, much prayer, is the price of preaching unction. Prayer, much prayer, is the sole condition of keeping the anointing. Without unceasing prayer, the anointing never comes to the preacher. Without perseverance in prayer, the anointing, like over-kept manna, breeds worms."[3] Christian speakers must be persistent in prayer.

I (Rhonda) know, without a doubt, when I am prayed up before speaking. I feel confident. My words flow freely, and the listeners respond positively. I have great joy and energy as I speak. I also know when I have been prayed for by the

---

[3] E. M. Bounds, *Power Through Prayer* (Grand Rapids, MI: Baker, 1991), 74.

host church. Often, I receive prayer notes from church members in advance. When I arrive at the church, great anticipation and excitement is expressed by many ladies. As I speak, there is a conscious sense of the presence of the Holy Spirit, and the ladies respond to the movement of the Holy Spirit in the commitment time. Prayer by the speaker and congregation is integral to the Christian message.

Several times students have approached me (Monica) at the beginning of the semester in a Christian Life and Evangelism course I teach. They whisper in my ear, "I am praying for you as you teach us more about Jesus." Knowing they are praying for me encourages me and gives me a great confidence as I teach.

Petition

A petition is a type of prayer focused on specific requests or supplications. It is asking God for something in a more formal way. It is seeking God's intervention to provide for needs and receive strength in trials. While God hears all prayers, he desires that his children pray intentionally and frequently from the heart. Like the model prayer of Jesus, all petitions should be prayed in accordance with God's will, "Your will be done" (Matt 6:10).

In her book, *Speak Up with Confidence*, Carol Kent voices a concern for public speakers who do not pray. She says,

> I have a recurring fear that you [the speaker] will be caught up in technique and ignore that the most important part of the delivery of any message is the power of God flowing through you to the listener. Do your homework, practice your message, but above all pray! It is always my prayer that God will translate the message to meet the need of every individual in the audience.[4]

Echo Kent's commitment every time you speak publicly. Consider these specific petitions when preparing to speak:

1. *Pray for God's wisdom and for what he wants you to say.* There are many topics to discuss and many good ideas, but only God knows what the people need to hear.
2. *Pray that your message will glorify God.* Deliver your message with humility. Focus not on self but on the Savior.
3. *Pray for a teachable atmosphere.* Ask the Lord to open minds and hearts to the message and to minimize distractions and interruptions.

---

[4] Carol Kent, *Speak Up with Confidence* (Colorado Springs: NavPress, 2007), 154.

4. *Pray for the people who will attend.* Specifically ask God to break down barriers, connect the ladies present, and change lives.
5. *Pray for yourself.* Confess your sins and weaknesses. Acknowledge your need for God's strength and power.

I (Rhonda) enjoy coordinating conferences for women at the seminary and our church. I find that nothing is more important to this process than prayer for the speaker and participants. We often develop a prayer plan for those attending the conference. Over a specific number of days, ladies are directed to pray for the particular concerns for the speakers and musicians as well as the particular needs of the attendees. A conference bathed in prayer always gives glory to God and produces results. The intense prayers of righteous women are very powerful (Jas 5:16).

Power

Fervent prayer and a receptive heart pave the way for the work of the Holy Spirit. A Christian speaker will experience no greater joy or blessing than the anointing of the Spirit as she speaks. God's power flows through the speaker who is available and willing. Although a speaker will experience great joy in allowing the Holy Spirit to flow through her, she also may experience great fear in releasing the message to the Lord. True surrender in prayer does not always mean that the message will go as the speaker has planned. When the Holy Spirit is at work, he may bring to mind a different illustration or outline that the speaker did not plan. Though such instances may at first seem a bit scary, there is nothing like being used by God and experiencing the power of the Holy Spirit.

In 1 Corinthians 2:1–5 Paul the apostle wrote about the power of the Holy Spirit working through him. He spoke to people in weakness and fear, depending not on his personal ability but on the power of God. He said, "My speech and my proclamation were not with persuasive words of wisdom but with a powerful demonstration of the Spirit, so that your faith might not be based on men's wisdom but on God's power" (vv. 4–5). The Lord has reminded me (Monica) of this truth many times. I experience great weakness in many areas before any speaking engagement. Usually I lack confidence and begin to tell the Lord, "I cannot do this." He reminds me that I cannot speak and I have nothing to share in and of myself. If, however, I allow him to strengthen me, he will use me to proclaim his truth and will give me confidence.

Paul was not skilled like the Greek orators. Though well educated and professionally trained, he acknowledged that his rhetoric was a result of God's anointing and not his ability. Gifted speakers must be dependent upon the work of the Holy Spirit. Untrained speakers can trust the Lord to speak through them as well.

John Huss's biography of R. G. Lee, the great pastor of Bellevue Baptist Church in Memphis, Tennessee, includes a report about the anointing of God while preaching. Lee recalled that as he preached, "It seemed as though Someone had wrapped a warm blanket about [him]. There was a sensation as though Someone's tender fingertips were caressing up and down [his] body."[5] God spoke through Dr. Lee that morning, and 126 people responded during the invitation. That night, he baptized 52 of the new converts. The Spirit moved in a mighty way.

Have you had an awareness of the Holy Spirit while speaking? I (Rhonda) have. It is a humbling and emotional experience. Sometimes, I actually feel the Spirit's presence physically. I may tear up, tremble, or become weak. Other times, the Holy Spirit puts thoughts in my mind or words in my mouth as I speak.

As I (Rhonda) spoke for a women's conference some years ago, the Holy Spirit prompted me to share how God taught me to forgive my father when he left my mother and the ministry. I rarely speak publicly about that personal experience, and I had not planned to do so then. When God spoke to me about it clearly, I obeyed and shared honestly. During the decision time, a young woman shared with me through tears that she was struggling to forgive her abusive father. I was able to offer her biblical principles that had helped me. Obviously, the Lord spoke directly through me to that one woman.

Another time, God prompted me (Rhonda) to share openly about the struggle my husband and I faced with infertility. After my message, a precious lady came up to me crying. She and her husband had been unable to have children. It was breaking her heart. Because I listened to the Holy Spirit, I was able to encourage another person with Scripture promises and words of hope. I always ask God to anoint me as I speak, and I do my best to obey when he speaks to me.

Jerry Vines and Jim Shaddix discuss the anointing of God in their book, *Power in the Pulpit*. They acknowledge that the Christian speaker or preacher has an advantage over other public communicators. The anointing or inspiration of God is a tremendous power. They conclude:

> Anointed preaching places God into the sermon and on the preacher. When a preacher preaches in the power of God, the results are remarkable. He preaches with inspiration and fullness of thought. He has both freedom and simplicity of utterance. This element of the divine in preaching must

---

[5] John W. Huss, *Robert G. Lee* (New York: Macmillan, 1948), 196–201.

be foremost in the preacher's preparation and delivery if it is to be lastingly effective.[6]

An anointed speaker is filled with the power of God to speak truth with fervor to the hearts of the hearers.

A Christian speaker must spend time in prayer and Bible study regularly. She must live a godly life faithfully, seek God's anointing diligently, and speak His Word clearly. Then, the Christian communicator will experience the impact of prayer and the power of the Holy Spirit in her speaking.

TALKING POINT

Pray for God's will to be accomplished in the messenger and the message, and in the hearers and their hearts.

LET'S TALK ABOUT IT

1. How important is prayer in the life of a speaker?
2. List and define the three types of prayer mentioned in this chapter.
3. What are five specific petitions that should be considered when preparing to speak?
4. How can the Christian communicator experience the impact of prayer and the power of the Holy Spirit in her speaking?
5. In what ways has prayer had an impact on your speaking and teaching?

---

[6] Jerry Vines and Jim Shaddix, *Power in the Pulpit* (Chicago, IL: Moody Press, 1999), 64.

Section 3

EVALUATING THE SPEECH

Evaluation is the final step of the public speaking process. Speeches begin with preparation of the message and continue with actual presentation. However, the speech is not completed with the words "the end" or "amen." It is final only after evaluation. Speakers need to assess their own messages to determine if the purposes were accomplished and the audiences were engaged. Much can also be learned by evaluating the speeches of others—great communicators throughout history and modern times.

This section will focus on the steps involved in examination of a speech or message after it has been presented personally or by another speaker. The speaker should conduct critique and follow-up after each message in order to learn and improve. Self-expression of appreciation, self-examination of the speech, and self-improvement by the speaker culminate the speech positively. Observation and examination of other speakers is also helpful as speakers benefit from making informal observations and formal examinations of others. Though style and substance must be individualized, a speaker can learn techniques and skills from others.

Chapter 19

CRITIQUE AND FOLLOW-UP

Critique rather than criticize personal speeches or the public speaking of others.

Speaking skills can be improved incrementally one speech at a time. This chapter will discuss speech follow-up and will suggest constructive methods of self-evaluation. Recommendations will be made to improve personal public speaking skills. Because gratitude and grace are godly qualities to be developed for speech follow-up, expression of appreciation due to others, and personal evaluation of one's presentation will be considered. Speakers fall short when they do not complete the follow-up process of public speaking.

Immediately after the speech, the public speaker will be strengthened by personal evaluations and follow-up. In this important step of public speaking, a person should not be totally focused on self. Instead, recognize those who worked diligently to make the event happen and acknowledge those who invested time in attendance. Public praise encourages others and strengthens their connections with the speaker. Gratitude may also be expressed later in writing.

Self-examination should also follow the speech. Constructive critique—not destructive criticism—is helpful. The speaker should honestly reflect back on what was said and how it was said. Then energy can be focused on improving weaknesses and continuing strengths in the future.

Criticism and critique are two different words with different attitudes. A dictionary defines *criticism* as "an act of passing judgment as to the merits of anything (usually involves finding fault)."[1] *Critique* is defined as "a serious examination and judgment of something (constructive criticism is always appreciated)."[2] A criticism is typically emotional while a critique is intellectual. A criticism is usually vague and general while a critique is concrete and specific. A criticism is a harsh observation or negative comment; a critique is a thorough review or fair analysis. A criticism finds faults, condemns, and judges; a critique sees possibilities, clarifies, and questions. While a criticism states what is lacking, a critique identifies what is working. Criticizing one's own speaking or the public speaking of others is not productive. However, critiquing speeches can be very productive.

Self-Expression

The speech experience does not end with the last spoken word. Like a tennis serve, the speech process involves preparation, delivery, and follow-through. With the last word, a speaker should not emotionally and physically shut down. Relief and exhaustion after speaking need not hinder follow-up.

After the speech, the speaker should calmly and confidently gather her notes and walk from the podium. Facial expression and body language should communicate pleasure and fulfillment. While listening to other speakers and program conclusions, the speaker should pay attention and convey interest. When the program ends, the speaker should maintain connection with the audience through casual conversations and personal interactions. The audience remembers positively a speaker who invests in the people not only during but after the speech.

Common courtesies are important after speaking. A speaker should express gratitude for hospitality extended. Final farewells also bring closure to the event and strengthen new relationships. Written expressions of gratitude are appreciated as well. The speaker should take time to write a thank you note to the event host. It is also meaningful for the hostess to express appreciation.

In a day when handwritten communication is uncommon and proper etiquette is unfamiliar, take seriously the expression of thanks to your hostess. A personal note written by hand expresses sincere appreciation in a tangible way. Use quality paper and pen. Write clearly and neatly. Open the letter with a general expression of thanks followed by several specific sentences describing meaningful highlights. Close your letter with gratitude and a warm farewell (such as sincerely, gratefully, with warm regards, or blessings).

---

[1] *American Heritage Dictionary of the English Language*, 4th ed. (Houghton Mifflin, 2009), s.v. "criticism," http://www.thefreedictionary.com/Criticism (accessed 22 March 2013).

[2] *American Heritage Dictionary of the English Language*, 4th ed. (Houghton Mifflin, 2009), s.v. "critique," http://www.thefreedictionary.com/Critique (accessed 22 March 2013).

Many correspondence books have been published, providing helpful guidelines for note writing. Learn letter-writing skills from resources and from practice. Personal notes will flow more freely with practice and sincerity. Develop some phrases that express gratitude naturally. The following suggestions may help:

- "a challenging message"
- "message accomplished its purpose"
- "heartfelt words connected with the listeners"
- "relevant illustrations and examples"
- "a message directly from God's Word"
- "positive responses to presentation"

Always make the time to express appreciation to the speakers for events you host.

It is also meaningful for the hostess to write the guest speaker with appreciation and feedback. I (Rhonda) make it a practice to write a note of thanks to any guest speaker I have invited and include some participant comments. I may include a thank-you note with the check given at the event, but I also write another note later. It means so much to me as a speaker to receive a written expression of appreciation after returning home. One women's ministry leader included a summary of the event evaluations with her note to me. What a joy to know that ladies responded to my messages with decisions for Christ!

Self-Evaluation

An important part of personal growth and development is self-evaluation. It is helpful for a speaker to evaluate herself after each speech to learn from the experience. Identifying strengths and weaknesses on a regular basis promotes excellence in speaking. A speaker should also have general goals for sharpening speaking skills.

After each presentation, a speaker should ask herself if she was satisfied with her speech. What went well? What needs more work? Was she confident as she spoke or, if not, what caused nervousness? The following questions may provide more in-depth self-evaluation:

1. Did you accomplish the purpose of the speech?
2. Did you adapt to the setting of the speech?
3. Did you connect with the audience and receive positive feedback?
4. Did you witness response to the speech?
5. Did you experience any specific problems?

In addition, it may be helpful to examine each stage of the speech process. The following questions may promote more personal insights. Take time to suggest strategies for areas needing improvement.

Preparation

1. Did you spend adequate time in prayer and preparation?
2. Did you make an accurate analysis of audience and occasion?
3. Was your outline clear and were your points balanced?
4. Did you thoroughly develop your content and supportive material?
5. Did you adequately prepare presentation materials, including any hand-outs or slides?
6. Were your speaking notes effective?

Delivery

1. Did you speak confidently?
2. Did you capture attention with introductory comments?
3. Did you maintain connection with the audience?
4. Were your wardrobe, makeup, and hair appropriate for the event?
5. Did you adhere to time allotted and pace all parts of the speech?
6. Did you notice mistakes or stumbles?
7. Did you use words and language appropriately?
8. Did you use natural gestures and body language?
9. Did you employ consistent eye contact and appropriate expression?
10. Was your speech clear and well paced?
11. Did you use appropriate volume and projection?
12. Did you feel audience connection and response?
13. Did you manage challenging situations?
14. What new techniques or material might you incorporate into your next presentation?

If available, an audio or video recording offers objective feedback. Consider listening to a replay of your speech. It can help you identify strengths and weaknesses.

I (Rhonda) have a mental exercise to follow after every speech. I immediately thank God for the opportunity to share his Word, and I thank him for speaking through me. Before beginning self-evaluation, it is essential to give God the glory. I quickly evaluate my message if I am speaking to the same group again so that I can improve in delivery and add to content. I save a more thorough self-evaluation for later. I use my speaking outline to assess preparation and delivery. I often make notes on my outline to remember recommendations when presenting the message again. As I conclude my time of self-evaluation, I give God the glory again and ask him to continue using my message in the lives of the hearers.

I (Monica) remember one of the first times I heard a recording of myself speaking. I was surprised how many times I said "um." I was thankful to become aware of my mistake and made a conscious effort to avoid it in the future. Evaluating my speech in this way aided me tremendously.

A speaker should always seek to strengthen speaking skills. Speech conferences and public speaking books provide resources for growth. General reading and cultural awareness suggest relevant topics and interests. An effective speaker should always think about future speeches and should listen carefully to other public speakers. Remember to critique rather than criticize your personal speeches and the public speaking of others.

Self-Improvement

Bookstore shelves are filled with self-improvement books. Magazines and blogs publish many articles about self-improvement since everyone has room to improve. Public speakers should aspire for excellence personally as well as professionally. Thus, Christian speakers are challenged to continue learning skills and practicing techniques.

The following suggestions will promote personal development in communication and public speaking.

1. *Make a heartfelt commitment to improve communication.* The first step in self-improvement is a sincere desire to do better.
2. *Develop as a person.* Growth mentally, emotionally, and spiritually is reflected in an individual's public speaking abilities.
3. *Build a storehouse of information.* A speaker should increase knowledge through reading, listening, and learning.
4. *Observe other communicators in action.* Awareness of effective speaking strategies influences a speaker positively. Model your speaking after the strengths of others.
5. *Study the great speakers and speeches of history.* Learn from those whose speaking excellence has perpetuated itself.
6. *Practice communicating.* Accept invitations to speak whenever you can, whether for small groups or large. Experience in all settings strengthens speaking skills.
7. *Improve listening skills.* Since listening and talking are involved in the process of communication, improvement in one area naturally helps the other.
8. *Expand skills in speech preparation.* Invest as much time and energy as possible in prayer and preparation. Find new ways to be well prepared for every speech.

9. *Organize and outline speeches effectively.* Learn to arrange relevant material and create useful outlines. Content must be developed efficiently to be presented effectively.
10. *Increase skills in speech delivery.* Find new techniques to develop public speaking. Give each speech your full effort.

Though I (Rhonda) feel God gave me the gift of talking, I need to work on improving my communication skills. I should always have goals to achieve and should never be satisfied with my speaking abilities. I regularly teach classes on general communication and public speaking. While I may teach from a similar outline and use the same slides, I always add new content, new illustrations, and new resources. These updates help keep me and my material fresh. I also set a goal to read several new public speaking books and to attend a speaker's conference each year. Self-improvement is not possible without effort and planning.

For a Christian speaker, only God knows the full impact of the speech. Immediate feedback personally and from others is beneficial, but the most significant praise and most lasting rewards will be experienced in the future. In heaven, faithful Christians will be greeted by the Lord with "well done." People touched by the life and ministry of a faithful speaker will express gratitude for eternity. Rarely does a Christian understand the impact of her service to the Lord. It is important to remember that words spoken have both earthly and eternal significance.

TALKING POINT

Only God knows the full impact of the speech.

LET'S TALK ABOUT IT

1. Explain the difference between criticism and critique.
2. Compare and contrast self-expression and self-evaluation.
3. What five questions may help a speaker make a more in-depth evaluation of her speech?
4. List ten suggestions that promote personal development in communication and public speaking.
5. In what areas do you think you need to improve as a speaker?

Chapter 20

OBSERVATION AND EXAMINATION

"Vertical and horizontal listening are necessary for Christian speakers."[1]

While there is no one perfect speaker in the world, there are many excellent speakers. Much can be learned by listening to and observing a wide range of speakers in a variety of contexts. Insights can be gained from the strengths and weaknesses of public speakers, and ideas can be prayerfully incorporated into one's own speaking style.

Assessment of the public speaking of others should consider several personal characteristics or traits in addition to skills and abilities. Observe the speaker's character and integrity, sensitivity and awareness, knowledge and information, and desire and passion. Make certain the speaker is someone whom you should emulate.

This chapter will present approaches to observing other speakers and evaluating their speeches for the sake of personal improvement. Suggestions will be given for informal as well as formal observations. A speech evaluation will be presented for use when assessing the public speaking skills of others. Incorporate observation of speakers in the quest for excellence in speech giving.

---

[1] Quentin Schultze, *An Essential Guide to Public Speaking* (Grand Rapids, MI: Baker Academic, 2006), 45–49.

Informal Observations

People with a desire to improve public speaking skills can benefit from the evaluation of other speakers. Awareness and informal observations should become a natural mindset of a speaker. Without pen and paper or objective criteria, make mental notes as others speak. Learn to communicate more effectively through observation and examination as well as practice.

Some general guidelines will provide structure for informal observations. Begin noticing the speaker even before the speech starts. Continue observation during the speech and until the speaker is no longer within sight. Consider observing the following aspects of communication, incorporating them into conscious thought.

Before the Speech

Observe the setting and platform before the message begins. Is the platform conducive to comfortable positioning and movement by the speaker? Is the lighting adequate for good visibility? Are the podium and props set up properly? Is the screen visible for any slides used, and will the speaker be able to reference them easily? Will the speaker be positioned physically to connect with the audience? While some features of setting and stage are beyond a guest speaker's control, some adjustments and adaptations can be made to improve the speech.

Notice the speaker's behavior and mannerisms even before she speaks. How does she interact with people before the session begins? How does she participate in the program as a part of the audience? How does she approach the stage and position herself for speaking? Does her appearance reflect readiness for the event?

I (Rhonda) smile when remembering one speaker's entrance. She hurriedly walked out of the stage door onto the platform, obviously forgetting that she was in view of the audience. She stopped abruptly and took a deep breath. She smoothed her hair and clothes. She swung her arms to relax, took another breath, then walked slowly to the podium. She had a good pre-speech routine, but it should have been completed before she entered the auditorium. Be aware of your visibility to the audience even before you begin speaking.

During the Speech

While the speaker shares the message, try to focus on the speech content and allow the Lord to communicate to you personally. Also, pay attention to the public speaking skills employed during the delivery. It may be helpful to organize observations within the introduction, body, and conclusion parts of the speech. The speaker and listener should be consciously aware of each distinct part.

Listen carefully to the speaker's opening comments in the introduction. Did she immediately capture the attention of the audience? Did she begin with a challenging question or interesting illustration? Did she relate to the other people or elements of the program? Did she quickly gain rapport with the audience? Did she stimulate interest in the topic? Did she project energy and enthusiasm? Did she use specific words, phrases, or movements to bridge from the introduction to the body?

As the body of the speech was delivered, did the speaker transition smoothly from the introduction? Did the speaker present clear, relevant points? Did she include appropriate supportive material to strengthen her premises? Did she use nonverbal communication naturally? Did she utilize the sound system and media effectively? Did she adhere to the schedule and allot time equally to all points? Did she move smoothly into the concluding remarks?

Was the conclusion truly the conclusion? Did the speaker pause, alter tone, adjust pace, or move to denote the conclusion? Did she summarize main points or introduce new material? Did she call for response or action? Did she close in a vivid, memorable way? Did she verbalize "in conclusion" or "in closing?" Did she have a false conclusion? Did she stop before the audience finished listening?

Through the years, I (Rhonda) have developed automatic observation skills. While I am not a critical person by nature, I have learned the importance of critical thinking. These skills have been instilled through my educational studies, professional experience, and academic teaching. As I listen to other speakers, I intuitively observe the manner of presentation and methods of delivery. I have benefitted greatly through observation of others. As a speech pathologist, I am very aware of a speaker's articulation and voice. Unfortunately, I can be very distracted by unclear enunciation, rapid speech, poor projection, or vocal abuse. My greatest distraction is throat clearing. It literally sends chills up my spine. On occasion, I have resorted to tallying in my notes the number of times the speaker cleared her throat. Join me in trying not to be overly zealous when observing other speakers. Learn what you can from others when you can.

After the Speech

Recall the positives and negatives of the speech as well as the strengths and weaknesses of the speaker. Was the speaker effective? Was she well prepared and thorough? Was the message relevant to your life? Was the audience responsive? Were the major points memorable? Were personal applications realistic? What were two or three strengths of the speaker? What are one or two weaknesses needing work? What one positive comment would you like to share with the speaker?

Learning through informal observation is a key benefit to participating in an organization like Toastmasters International, a nonprofit that began in 1924. Its purpose is communication and leadership development through practice and feedback (see www.toastmasters.org). People join the local groups to improve speaking skills and leadership abilities. Group members facilitate the meetings and present impromptu talks. Meeting guidelines and speaking resources are provided. More than 13,000 clubs are located in approximately 116 countries. Members develop skills in public speaking as well as grammar, parliamentary procedure, and timekeeping. Speech evaluation and objective feedback are integral to the long-term success of Toastmasters.

Formal Examinations

There is also a role for formal examination in speech improvement. Serious public speakers benefit from objective observations of self and others in a variety of speaking contexts. More specific criteria are utilized in formal examinations and descriptive feedback is recorded. This section will describe the process of formally examining speech skills.

An evaluator has a different role when assessing the public speaking skills of others than when evaluating self. The feedback is rarely shared with the speaker unless in a teaching setting. When shared, the tone of the evaluation should be positive and constructive; the content should be useful and thorough; and objective ratings as well as descriptive comments should be helpful. Specific objectives for development should be the end result of a formal speech evaluation.

The National Communication Association provides criteria for speech assessment in a publication entitled "The Competent Speaker Speech Evaluation Form." It is suggested that these eight competencies be rated as excellent, satisfactory, or unsatisfactory.[2] (See chart on page 209.) These criteria generate specific findings that can be utilized for speech improvement.

I (Rhonda) have taken the speaking seminar with CLASServices (Christian Leaders, Authors and Speaker Services) on several occasions. The three-day workshop offers intensive training for Christians who seek to improve their communication skills. Sessions are taught by expert public speakers, including Florence Littauer who founded the organization more than thirty years ago. Training includes examination of effective oral techniques and peer evaluation of presentations. I benefitted personally from giving three different presentations during the workshops. The formal evaluations by other members in the group plus

---

[2] Sherwyn Morreale et al., *The Competent Speaker Speech Evaluation Form*, 2nd ed. (Washington, DC: National Communication Association, 2007), 12–15.

The Competent Speaker Speech Evaluation Chart

Competency #1
Chooses and narrows a topic appropriately for the audience and occasion.

Competency #2
Communicates the thesis/specific purpose in a manner appropriate for the audience and occasion.

Competency #3
Provides supporting material (including electronic and non-electronic presentational aides) appropriate to the audience and occasion.

Competency #4
Uses an organizational pattern appropriate to the topic, audience, occasion, and purpose.

Competency #5
Uses language appropriate to the audience and occasion.

Competency #6
Uses vocal variety in rate, pitch, and intensity (volume) to heighten and maintain interest appropriate to the audience and occasion.

Competency #7
Uses pronunciation, grammar, and articulation appropriate to the audience and occasion.

Competency #8
Uses physical behaviors that support the verbal message.

feedback from the teaching team helped me tremendously. My public speaking skills were definitely improved as a result of the personalized coaching. (For more information see www.classservices.org.)

In an academic setting, performance is graded on a letter scale. Because that scale is familiar, it might be helpful to assign a letter grade to the speaker's speech. Goals of delivery and techniques in performance can be rated individually and compared collectively. The grade of A would reflect a superior speech, B above average, C average, and lower grades would reflect an unacceptable speech.

Evaluation Criteria

A written form may be helpful to making speech evaluations. Observations can be rated objectively or discussed subjectively in writing. Many different speech evaluation forms may be found online on communication Web sites as well as in public speaking books.

In *An Essential Guide to Public Speaking*, Quentin Schultze suggests that vertical and horizontal listening are necessary for Christian speakers. He offers this advice to servant speakers: "Listen to other speakers to learn how they use primary and secondary research, including personal anecdotes and published sources."[3] He provides a form for evaluating speeches that includes a description of the speaker's position as well as the occasion, purpose, and thesis of the speech. Questions assess the introduction, body, and conclusion of the speech. The speaker's use of sources and technology are examined. Content organization, personal virtue, and apparent honesty as well as verbal and nonverbal expressions are critiqued. This speaker's evaluation form concludes with two open-ended questions: "What served the audience well?" and "What requires additional attention?"[4]

A general speaker evaluation form is discussed below and is presented in Appendix C. The following areas should be rated objectively on a numerical scale and discussed subjectively with brief commentary.

Appearance
    Neatness
    Appropriateness
Vocal Parameters
    Pitch
    Loudness
    Quality

---

[3] Schultze, *An Essential Guide to Public Speaking*, 52.
[4] Ibid., 105–6.

Speech Skills
  Rate of Speech
  Articulation
  Grammar
Body Language
  Facial Expression
  Gestures
  Eye Contact
  Posture
Speech Content
  Outline/Organization
  Supportive Material
  Introduction
  Body
  Conclusion
Other
  Presentation Materials
  Timing

Space is provided at the end of the form to describe specific strengths and weaknesses as well as general comments. Find a preferred speech evaluation form and use it frequently.

Permission from a speaker is not necessary to conduct a speech evaluation when the evaluator plans to use it for personal improvement. In fact, awareness of evaluation may cause a speaker to be uncomfortable or nervous. If observations are made public, the speaker's permission should be sought in all cases. Written permission may be indicated if comments are published.

I (Rhonda) had an overly zealous student who handled her speech evaluation assignment inappropriately. She went to her small group teacher immediately prior to the Bible study and announced her plan to evaluate the teacher. As you can imagine, the teacher was uncomfortable with the intrusion. The student was shocked when the Bible teacher asked her to forego the evaluation. The less-experienced teacher in an informal setting was not an appropriate candidate for a formal speech evaluation.

Ephesians 4:15 is included on the proposed speech evaluation form: "But speaking the truth in love, let us grow in every way into Him who is the head—Christ." Mature Christians who are growing in faith are to speak the truth in love and kindness. Words should build a person up, not tear her down. Informal observations and formal examinations of public speaking skills should encourage others and strengthen one's own communication efforts. Comments on a speech evaluation form should be positive and constructive. Speaker observation and self-examination contribute productively to the development of public speaking skills.

Talking Point

Awareness and observation should become
a natural mind-set for the public speaker.

Let's Talk about It

1. Identify eight personal characteristics a speaker should emulate.
2. Distinguish between informal observations and formal examinations.
3. List at least three observations that can be made about a speaker before her speech.
4. What are five areas listed on the speaker evaluation form that should be recorded objectively and discussed subjectively?
5. What do you feel is most important in evaluating a speaker? How have evaluations helped you to become a better speaker?

Part III

NONVERBAL COMMUNICATION:

What Other Factors Influence Communication?

While words are powerful in communicating a message, nonverbal language has an even greater impact. Meaning is transmitted from speaker to listener in a variety of ways. Public speakers must develop skills in nonspoken as well as spoken communication.

Psychologist Albert Mehrabian documented the impact of nonverbal communication in 1981 in his book, *Silent Messages: Implicit Communication of Emotions and Attitudes*. He found that meaning is conveyed more in how words are spoken than by what is said. Mehrabian theorized that a message is communicated in the following ways:

- 7% of meaning comes through the words that are spoken;
- 38% of meaning comes through paralanguage (the way that words are said); and
- 55% of meaning in facial expression.

These elements of communication have been labeled the "7% - 38% - 55% rule."[1] See the representation below.

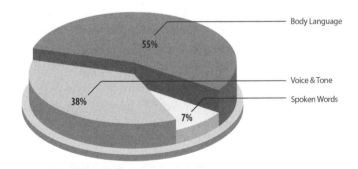

---

[1] Albert Mehrabian, *Silent Messages: Implicit Communication of Emotions and Attitudes* (Belmont, CA: Wadsworth Press, 1981), 44.

This part of the book will expand the discussion of verbal communication to include the significant arena of nonverbal communication. The first section will address the importance of nonspoken communication in public speaking. Specific attention will be given to emotions and feelings, eyes and face, gestures and posture as well as appearance and clothing. The second section will focus on the role of drama and oral interpretation in public speaking. The "what and why" as well as the "how and when" of drama will be discussed. Several advantages and disadvantages in using drama will be suggested. Public speakers should develop nonverbal as well as verbal skills in preparation for speaking opportunities.

Section I

NONSPOKEN COMMUNICATION

Several facts about nonverbal communication should be understood prior to a thorough discussion of the topic. Consider three generalizations about nonverbal communication that should guide speechmaking.[1] First, speakers reveal and reflect their emotional states through their nonverbal behaviors. Emotions and feelings are expressed more in tone of voice and manner of expression than actual words. Second, the speaker's nonverbal cues enrich or elaborate on the message communicated through words. Intensity of feeling and degree of passion are expressed best nonverbally. Third, nonverbal messages form a reciprocal interaction between speaker and listener. Even more than words, nonverbal cues connect the one speaking to the audience at a deeper level. Communication involves two distinct codes: verbal and nonverbal.

Different types of nonverbal communication include proxemics (use of space), posture (position of the body), movement (actions by the body), gestures (movements of the hands), facial expressions (emotions of the face), eye contact (connection of looks), appearance (appropriateness of looks), and paralanguage (vocal cues).

Types of Nonverbal Communication	
proxemics	use of space
posture	position of the body
movement	actions by the body
gestures	movements of the hands
facial expresssions	emotions of the face
eye contact	connection of looks
physical appearance	appropriateness of looks
paralanguage	vocal cues

---

[1] Bruce E. Gronbeck et al., *Principles of Speech Communication,* 12th brief ed. (New York: Harper Collins College Publishers, 1995), 185.

This section will explore these aspects of nonverbal communication, presenting numerous components of nonspoken communication and will discuss nonlanguage codes. Since 93 percent of a speaker's message is communicated without words, the following chapters will explore the use of vocal tone, eye contact, facial expression, gestures, and posture as well as appearance and clothing.

Chapter 21

EMOTIONS AND FEELINGS

"Warmth is the soul of the voice."[1]

I n Psalm 149:1, 6, the psalmist called for God's people to express praise to him in words and actions: "Hallelujah! Sing to the LORD a new song . . . let the exaltation of God be in their mouths." Exaltation or praise is to be reinforced by a joyful shout. The sound of the voice conveys the emotions and feelings of the heart. A Christian should offer praise to the Lord with her whole self.

Haddon Robinson explained the influence of the voice in his book, *Biblical Preaching*:

> Speech consists of more than words and sentences. The voice conveys
> ideas and feelings apart from words. We make judgments about a speaker's
> physical and emotional state—whether he is frightened, angry, fatigued,
> sick, happy, confident—based on the tenor of his voice, its loudness, rate,
> and pitch.[2]

This chapter will establish the importance of nonverbal communication to express emotions and feelings, focusing on three aspects of vocal tone that project meaning: *volume*, *variety*, and *vibrancy*. (In chap. 14, we discussed the related

---

[1] Margery Wilson, *The Woman You Want to Be: Margery Wilson's Complete Book of Charm* (Philadelphia: J. B. Lippincott, 1942), 58–59.
[2] Haddon Robinson, *Biblical Preaching* (Grand Rapids, MI: Baker, 1980), 202–3.

topic of voice quality, including the vocal mechanism, vocal hygiene, and vocal care.)

Volume

The voice can be used to shape ideas into words and convey emotions. According to Carol Kent in *Speaking Up with Confidence*, volume in sound is the loudness of the voice, and variations in loudness create interest and communicate intention.[3]

Loudness is the auditory sensation ranging from quiet to loud. Technically, it is the amplitude or intensity of sound. The human voice projects in a variety of intensities. Though the person's unique vocal mechanism determines vocal range, people can learn to control volume levels. Speech must be loud enough to be heard by listeners in every setting. Volume can also be adjusted to communicate feelings.

I (Rhonda) have a very loud voice. Sometimes I forget how strongly my voice projects during casual conversation. My dad will occasionally signal me with his hand to lower my voice. He is apparently sensitive to the loudness. I have learned to adjust my volume in different contexts, especially in personal conversations.

Increased volume also projects sound through the air so that speech may be heard. The speaker must work to improve breath support and projection in public speaking. Exercises can be practiced to increase volume (Appendix A). Amplification with a sound system helps increase volume in a larger context (as covered in chapter 13 "Microphones and Media").

My (Rhonda) husband has a pleasant speaking voice though his lower pitch and breathy quality limit his projection. Chuck has learned to project his voice louder when speaking to a larger group. In smaller settings, he turns his head and body toward the group to help his voice project. In personal conversations, he faces the listener.

Vocal stress is also influenced by volume. A speaker accents or emphasizes a sound, syllable, or word to communicate emotions. Stress can change the meaning of a message. Speech sounds monotonous without vocal stress. Unaffected speech can imply boredom or poor effort. Without changes in stress, the human voice can sound automated or computerized.

I (Rhonda) make it a point to note a speaker's vocal use when completing a speech evaluation form. I often write "pleasant voice quality," "good volume," or "voice projects well." I also make specific recommendations if the speaker needs

---

[3] Carol Kent, *Speaking Up with Confidence* (Grand Rapids, MI: Baker, 1992), 126–27.

to improve volume. It is important for speakers to evaluate volume of speech that impacts clarity, projection, and emphasis. Without these qualities, the speaker jeopardizes audience connection.

Several years ago, I (Monica) attended a women's conference at a large church. I was so excited to hear the speaker because I had recently read one of her books, and I had great expectations to hear her speak. However, I was surprised at the lack of connection she had with her audience. Although she was presenting excellent material, the speaker lacked the enthusiasm and emotion to emphasize the main points. At times, it was difficult to hear her soft, gentle voice. I left disappointed because her message would have been more effective if her vocal projection and emotional passion were better.

Keep these suggestions about vocal volume in mind when speaking publicly.

1. Monitor your voice as you are speaking.
2. Project your voice to improve audibility and express feelings.
3. Vary your volume for interest and emphasis.
4. Strengthen your voice with good breath support.
5. Convey meaning clearly through your volume.

Work on volume of sound as you speak to improve clarity, projection, and emphasis.

Variety

Variety is said to be the spice of life. Variety in the vocal parameters can communicate emotions and feelings by using fluctuations in pitch and differences in inflections to add interest and meaning to the speaking voice. Public speakers should aspire for variety in their voices. I (Monica) always try to add vocal variety while speaking to help keep the attention and interest of the audience. I once had a professor who had no variety in her speaking voice. Though I loved the subject of her class, I left disinterested and less motivated to learn. Regardless of the subject matter, vocal variety can make a profound difference to the audience.

Pitch is the frequency of sound waves that determines the highness or lowness of a tone. Each person has a natural pitch (or optimum pitch level) based on anatomical structure. Pitch range can be expanded and controlled with training and practice. In general, higher pitches communicate excitement, and lower pitches express caution or concern. Pitch is adjusted to change emotion.

Professional singers become experts in expanding pitch range. They rehearse musical scales by systematically singing different notes of increasing breadth. Vocal exercises can add to the upper and lower registers of pitch range. Public speakers should determine optimal pitch for speaking and develop pitch range to improve communication.

My (Rhonda) husband has a limited singing voice, but he sings with great enthusiasm as he "makes a joyful noise." Through the years of our marriage, I believe Chuck has increased his vocal range. Instead of one note, he can sing three or four different notes now. His frequent preaching and teaching have apparently increased his pitch range.

Inflection is related to pitch and influences the meaning of speech nonverbally. It specifically refers to changes in pitch or loudness of the voice. Changes in inflection are crucial to public speaking. Variations in inflection should enhance meaning and not distract from the message.

There are two primary types of vocal inflection: rising and falling. Most statements are spoken with falling inflection at the end of the sentence to communicate finality or authority. Questions are concluded with rising inflection to signal nonverbally the need for response. Inflection within a sentence may be varied to provide interest and reflect emotion. Exaggerated inflections are used in public speaking and theater to express suspense, fear, or uncertainty.

Remember these guidelines about vocal variety when presenting a message.

1. Listen to the pitch of your speech.
2. Notice how other speakers use variations in pitch and inflection.
3. Experiment with pitch change as you speak.
4. Expand your natural pitch range comfortably.
5. Use inflection for variety and interest as you speak.

Try to vary your pitch and inflection to communicate your thoughts and feelings more accurately.

Vibrancy

Vibrancy refers to the enthusiasm and passion communicated by the tone of a speaker's voice. An animated and energetic voice adds emotions and feelings to the spoken words. Public speakers should desire vocal vibrancy and lively delivery in their speeches. Vibrancy in the voice should make the listener want to hear the speech.

Using verbal and nonverbal communication involves energy and effort. Public speakers need to maintain physical as well as mental health to communicate more effectively. Proper nutrition, regular exercise, and adequate rest are essential ingredients of energetic speaking. Fatigue and illness hinder enthusiasm and vibrancy in speaking.

I (Rhonda) have mentioned before that in addition to my gift of talking, I have the gift of sleeping. While I am able to talk often, I do not get to sleep as much as I desire. I am grateful to have a lot of natural energy, which often compensates for my lack of sleep. My husband loves to call me the Energizer bunny, referring to the old battery commercial. I keep going and going until I can go no longer. My energy is reflected in my daily life and public speaking.

Warmth is an aspect of emotion that can be expressed verbally or nonverbally. Tender feelings can be communicated through choice of words or tone of voice. A softer, lower voice typically conveys warmth. Warmth should be a vocal quality desired by public speakers.

In an etiquette book written in 1942, Margery Wilson suggested that the voice reflects emotions as surely as a mirror reflects an image.[4] Warmth is the soul of the voice. Sweetness, generosity, and love of humanity are personal qualities of the inner person that produce warmth in a speaker's voice. Wilson recommends that people build character and virtues to speak with vocal warmth.

Excitement and eagerness should be experienced and expressed by the speaker. If the speaker does not sound excited about the topic, the audience will not want to listen. When possible, a speaker should select a topic of personal interest. If the assigned topic is less than stimulating, the speaker can express enthusiasm verbally. Vocal vibrancy depends upon energy, warmth, and excitement.

When I (Rhonda) was Director of the Division of Communicative Disorders at Ochsner Medical Center, I periodically presented in-service training to the medical staff. Because of my enthusiasm and excitement while speaking, some of my male colleagues called me the cheerleader. Other presentations were typically boring and technical. Though I did learn to adapt my communication with the male audience, I always experienced excitement during my presentations.

Consider these principles about vocal vibrancy when delivering a speech.

1. Determine the presence or absence of vibrancy in your voice.
2. Compare your vocal vibrancy to that of other speakers.
3. Prepare physically for speaking with proper sleep, nutrition, and exercise.
4. Work to soften the tone of your voice to convey warmth.
5. Expand your interests to be enthusiastic about the topics for your speeches.

The voice provides insight into the speaker's emotions and feelings. The vocal characteristics of volume, variety, and vibrancy combine with words and

---

[4] Margery Wilson, *The Woman You Want to Be*, 589.

other nonverbal cues to communicate the meaning of the speaker's message. A simple sentence such as "I have had a good day" can change meaning drastically when the voice is used differently. Soft volume may raise doubt in the listener; loud volume may cause belief in the statement. Vocal variety may keep the interest of the listener; limited variety may lose attention. Vocal vibrancy may convey passion to listeners; flat, monotonous tone sounds unconvincing. Tone of voice is the nonverbal code for expressing emotions and feelings in public speaking.

TALKING POINT

The sound of the voice
conveys the emotions and feelings of the heart.

LET'S TALK ABOUT IT

1. Discuss what the sound of the voice conveys heart.
2. List and define the three aspects of vocal tone that project meaning.
3. What are five suggestions on vocal volume that will aid a person in speaking publicly?
4. How important is variety in public speaking? Why?
5. Compare and contrast between "soft volume" and "loud volume." In what ways do you think you could improve your nonverbal cues while speaking?

Chapter 22

EYES AND FACE

"Animate—don't alienate."[1]

The eyes and face of a speaker convey mood, emotions, and character. Both interpersonal conversation and public speaking use eye contact and facial expression to amplify meaning and clarify feelings. Lack of eye contact and inconsistent facial expression can actually confuse the intended message. Poor eye contact can lead to suspicion, and limited facial expression can imply lack of interest. Effective communicators must intentionally develop skills to communicate with the eyes and face.

The word *countenance* refers to the outward expression of a person's inner being. The inward character of a person is reflected outwardly through the eyes and face. The Bible often uses the word countenance to describe the appearance of God and the people of God. God asked Moses to tell Aaron and his sons that he would "lift up His countenance upon [the children of Israel] and give [them] peace" (Num 6:26 NKJV). Samson's once-barren mother was told by an angel that she would give birth to a son. She told her husband that she had encountered a man whose "countenance *was* like an angel of God" (Judg 13:6 NKJV). David was described as a youth with a "ruddy, fair countenance" (1 Sam 17:42 KJV).

---

[1] Lillian Glass, *Say It Right: How to Talk in Any Social or Business Situation* (New York: Perigee Books, 1991), 61–66.

Psalms and Proverbs often contrast the happy or joyful countenance of one who follows God with the sad or sorrowful countenance of one who focuses on self (Ps 43:5; Prov 16:15). For example, Proverbs 15:13 (KJV) states, "A merry heart maketh a cheerful countenance: but by sorrow of the heart the spirit is broken." The prophets encountered God and spoke of his countenance also. Daniel's countenance changed when his dream was interpreted (Dan 7:28). Some in the Old Testament had sad countenances while others had happy countenances (Gen 4:5; 1 Sam 1:18; Neh 2:2–3).

The New Testament describes the countenance of Jesus and his followers. During the transfiguration, the countenance of Jesus was changed as he prayed (Luke 9:29). The countenance of the angel at his tomb was like lightening, bright and white. In his vision, John saw the risen Lord and his face (countenance) "was shining like the sun at midday" (Rev 1:16). A radiant countenance is a theme of Scripture and a trait of holiness.

The Bible describes the faces of several women, too. In 1 Samuel 1:9–18, KJV, Hannah's sad countenance became happy when the priest Eli told her she would bear a child. Abigail was described as a woman of intelligence and beautiful countenance (1 Sam 25:3 KJV). King David's son Absalom named his daughter Tamar in honor of his sister. Her countenance was described as fair and beautiful (2 Sam 14:27). Many other women of the Bible and many godly women today reflect the righteous countenance of the Lord.

His. The eyes and face should reflect the sincere emotions and godly character of those who love him. This chapter will highlight the role of eye contact and facial expression in nonverbal communication. Speakers must express thoughts and feelings in their eyes and faces as well as through words.

Eye Contact

The eyes are important organs that do more than provide vision. Eyes receive and reflect information as well as emotion and conviction. Someone has said, "The eyes are the window of the soul." They express character values and spiritual virtues. While no pair of eyes are alike, all eyes have the potential to communicate thoughts and feelings nonverbally. When two people engage each other visually in personal conversation or public speaking, a message can be transmitted more clearly.

Eye contact is the act of looking directly into another's eyes. The visual exchange influences social behavior and improves communication. When used intentionally, effective eye contact can help a good speaker become a great speaker. According to Matthew Arnold Stern's article "Maintaining Eye Contact," a speaker is able to connect with the audience, project sincerity and openness, and keep the listener's attention when she maintains eye contact.[2]

In his book, *The Psychology of Interpersonal Behavior*, Michael Argyle claims that eye contact is the most powerful type of nonverbal communication.[3] He reports that in typical conversation, people look at each other between 25 and 70 percent of the time. Less eye contact might imply disinterest, while more eye contact may prove uncomfortable. In public speaking, the speaker should engage in eye contact during at least sixty percent of the message to establish connection with each audience member or in each area of the room.

Eye contact serves several purposes in public speaking. Some believe 75 percent of nonverbal communication is through the eyes. The speaker conveys the sincerity of her heart, the intent of the message, and the intensity of her passion through her eyes. Good eye contact improves the speaker's confidence, demonstrates security, increases credibility with the audience, projects warmth, builds connection, and communicates value. Through this connection the audience may also provide visible feedback to the speaker. Smiles and nods may indicate understanding, while curious expressions or confused looks may imply poor comprehension.

A speaker can control her eye contact and connect with the audience more personally as she seeks to implement the following suggestions. *Keep the eyes open and focused.* Wide eyes are more visible in a group setting, and focus allows the speaker to see the eyes and faces of the people. *Scan the audience with the eyes and face.* Turn the head as well as the eyes to look at someone or some area of the room. *Establish eye-to-eye gaze when possible.* Connect with one person in the audience at a time. However, try not to stare or move mechanically. *Look at all areas of the room and at all people.* Try to cover all the people and the entire room with a single gaze. Try not to overlook the balcony or extreme sides. Engage in eye contact with the most important people in the room—even if they make you a little nervous. *Use steady, controlled eye contact.* Confidence and persuasion are conveyed through deliberate eye contact. *Maintain eye contact with each person or section for several seconds.* Complete a thought or sentence before gazing at another person or another area of the room. *Avoid looking at the ceiling, toward the floor, or above people's heads.* Roving eyes convey anxiety and disinterest. *Look up from any notes, and lock eyes on the audience.* Glance down to read a sentence or two; then glance up to establish eye contact with the people. *Move the eyes*

[2] Matthew Arnold Stern, "Communication Tip: Maintaining Eye Contact" in *Matthew Arnold Stern: Better Speaking, Better Writing* (Matthew Arnold Stern, 2012), http://www.matthewarnold-stern.com/tips/tipps16.html (accessed 19 March 2013).

[3] Michael Argyle, *The Psychology of Interpersonal Behavior* (New York: Penguin, 1967), 82.

about the room in a synchronized pattern. Both eyes should move together across the room and focus together on individuals. *Look at the audience while walking to the platform and before walking away.* Begin and end the speech by connecting with the audience. (See chart on page 227.)

Carol Kent's book, *Speak Up with Confidence*, supports the fact that eye contact is a powerful speaking tool. She suggests that a speaker pause for a moment before speaking the first word and look at the audience. During that time, the eyes should move around the room "connecting" with specific individuals.[4]

My (Rhonda) mother always has a pleasant expression and sincere eyes. Diane, a friend at church, once told me that she always looked for my mother in the congregation when she sang a solo because my mother looked back at her with such loving eyes. That feedback has reminded me through the years to smile as I listen to others. Nonverbal feedback from the audience can affirm and encourage a singer or speaker.

Pat and Ruth Williams, in their book, *Turning Boring Orations into Standing Ovations*, agree that good eye contact is essential when speaking. They conclude that the eyes "send invitations, reveal secrets, connect people, display love, kill dreams, capture prey, and play games." The eyes offer others a glimpse inside your world and reflect the truth in your heart.[5]

A public speaker needs to concentrate on the content of the message while at the same time thinking about the manner of delivery. Mastery of verbal and nonverbal communication improves public speaking. It boosts confidence and improves comprehension. Eye contact conveys interest and should encourage interest. If the speaker pays attention to the audience, the audience will pay attention to the speaker. Someone once said, "Once you make good eye contact with a person in the audience, they will feel like you are talking to them for the rest of the speech."

Facial Expression

Eye contact and facial expression are important aspects of nonverbal communication. It has been said, "If eyes are the windows to the soul, the face is the front of the house." In other words, the face of the speaker is the first thing a person sees. Like the eyes, the face speaks loudly. To inspire better listening facial expression should be inviting and interesting to the audience.

---

[4] Carol Kent, *Speak Up with Confidence: A Step-by-Step Guide to Successful Public Speaking* (Colorado Springs: NavPress, 2007), 129.

[5] Pat and Ruth Williams, *Turn Boring Orations into Standing Ovations: The Ultimate Guide to Dynamic Public Speaking* (Altamonte Springs, FL: Advantage Books, 2008), 151.

Suggestions for Improved Eye Contact

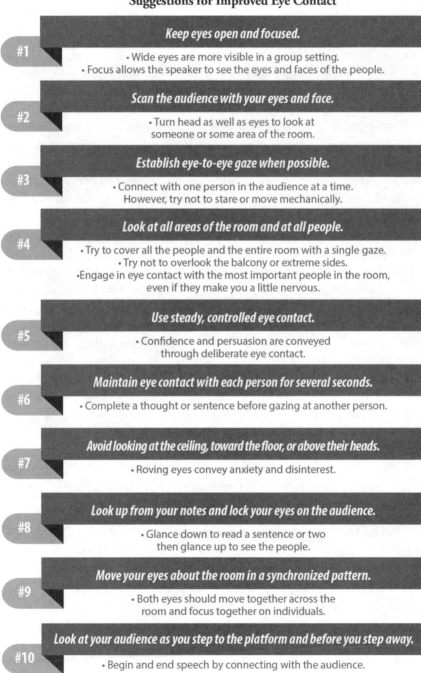

#1 Keep eyes open and focused.
• Wide eyes are more visible in a group setting.
• Focus allows the speaker to see the eyes and faces of the people.

#2 Scan the audience with your eyes and face.
• Turn head as well as eyes to look at someone or some area of the room.

#3 Establish eye-to-eye gaze when possible.
• Connect with one person in the audience at a time. However, try not to stare or move mechanically.

#4 Look at all areas of the room and at all people.
• Try to cover all the people and the entire room with a single gaze.
• Try not to overlook the balcony or extreme sides.
•Engage in eye contact with the most important people in the room, even if they make you a little nervous.

#5 Use steady, controlled eye contact.
• Confidence and persuasion are conveyed through deliberate eye contact.

#6 Maintain eye contact with each person for several seconds.
• Complete a thought or sentence before gazing at another person.

#7 Avoid looking at the ceiling, toward the floor, or above their heads.
• Roving eyes convey anxiety and disinterest.

#8 Look up from your notes and lock your eyes on the audience.
• Glance down to read a sentence or two then glance up to see the people.

#9 Move your eyes about the room in a synchronized pattern.
• Both eyes should move together across the room and focus together on individuals.

#10 Look at your audience as you step to the platform and before you step away.
• Begin and end speech by connecting with the audience.

The look on a speaker's face communicates as much meaning as her words. If verbal communication and nonverbal do not match, the listener will be confused. Facial expression involves the movement of the muscles in the face to convey the emotional state of the speaker to the listener. A wide range of emotions can be expressed through different facial movements. The muscles of the forehead, eyes, nose, cheeks, mouth, and jaws can be positioned to convey personal feelings including happiness, sadness, surprise, anger, confusion, fear, and other emotions. Speakers must develop a wide range of facial expressions in order to communicate effectively.

Facial expression is used universally to convey emotions though meaning may vary across cultures. People in different ethnic groups or countries may perceive happy, sad, or angry faces in unique ways. Cross-cultural misunderstanding may occur if a speaker and listener utilize facial expression differently. Some cultures use more facial expression while others use little expression. Facial movements can have different—even offensive—meanings in other cultures. Speakers should learn the facial expressions of other cultures and countries in order to communicate clearly with people in those lands.

My (Rhonda) husband, Chuck, and I went to Russia for a mission trip several years ago. One morning we rode the train from the suburbs into the city of Moscow with a missionary. The rush-hour crowds separated us as we boarded the train. My husband did not speak a word of English as we traveled, and he was not wearing a "Born in the USA" shirt. He just stood in the crowd smiling. A Russian man surprised him with the question, "Where do you live in America?" Chuck replied politely. However, he was curious about how the Russian man knew he was American. He asked the missionary host who commented, "You have hope on your face." No words or advertisements were needed for the passengers to know where Chuck lived. Every Christian woman speaking truth from the Bible—should have hope on her face.

Public speakers should develop nonverbal skills while understanding how the face communicates feelings. Remember these practical suggestions for effective facial expression.

1. Use a wide range of facial expressions.
2. Match your face to your words.
3. Let your emotions reflect through your face.
4. Do not allow inappropriate facial expression to misrepresent you.
5. Relax your face. Too much intensity or tension may look like anger.
6. Learn the feel of your facial muscles during different expressions.
7. Be aware of bad facial expressions.
8. Smile or frown appropriately.

9. Use more facial expression in larger venues and less in small groups.
10. Use more facial expression on radio or audio recordings and less on television or video recordings.

Rufus Jones was a Quaker scholar of the early twentieth century. After speaking to a religious group about having a radiant countenance, he was questioned by a plain-faced lady who asked what to do with a face like hers. His reply was profound: "While I have troubles of my own of that kind, I have discovered that if you light up your face from within, any old face you have is good enough." Facial expression flows from the inside out. It is not dependent upon outward beauty but inward character. Speakers who have a sincere and pure heart will have a beautiful countenance.

Facial Animation

Many different emotions can be conveyed through facial expressions. A smile can indicate happiness or approval, while a frown can signal sadness or disapproval. The look on a speaker's face can often speak louder than her words. It has been said that "words lie; the face does not." The truth is usually written all over the speaker's face.

Speakers must learn to animate their faces to express their thoughts and feelings correctly. Too little expression diminishes the message, and too much expression interferes with the message. Speakers need to use facial expression effectively to complement verbal communication with nonverbal. Animated faces intensify the meaning and amplify the message.

In her book, *Say It Right: How to Talk in Any Social or Business Situation*, Lillian Glass states that facial expression is essential to human communication. She says, "Just as inappropriate facial animation can confuse people and turn them off, too little facial expression can be a turnoff."[6] Speakers should wear emotions on their faces. Glass also encourages communicators to be aware of different expressions, to monitor facial movements in a mirror, and to practice facial animation as part of the preparation process. She suggests exercises to help speakers develop a wide range of emotional expressions including sadness, surprise, and sympathy. Speakers should balance expressions and avoid extremes. Glass says public speakers must "animate not alienate" with their faces.[7]

---

[6] Glass, *Say It Right*, 61.
[7] Lillian Glass, *Talk to Win: Six Steps to a Successful Vocal Image* (New York: Perigee Books, 1981), 63–66.

I (Rhonda) have a very expressive face. When I am worried, my forehead wrinkles. When I get excited, my eyes widen. When I am happy, my smile is huge. My expressive face speaks loudly. For years, I hosted a radio/television program for women in the New Orleans area. I needed to tone down my facial expressions for camera close-ups. My big eyes and animated face could overwhelm viewers. I need to remember: animate, do not alienate.

Psychology professor Paul Erkman has developed a technique to map or code every facial expression.[8] The Facial Action Coding System (FACS) assesses the facial muscles utilized to express different emotions and identifies the universal emotional expressions: anger, disgust, fear, happiness, sadness, and surprise. These human expressions use different combinations of muscles in the head and neck to communicate emotions and convey meanings. Though challenging to master, speakers need to be aware of facial movements that convey emotions.

Consider the complex coordination needed to express these emotions through the facial muscles.

Anger
- lower eyebrows
- fix eyes
- tighten lips

Disgust
- lower eyebrows
- wrinkle nose
- raise upper lip

Fear
- raise eyebrows
- raise eyelids
- stretch lips

Happiness
- raise eyelids
- raise cheeks
- part and raise lips

Sadness
- droop eyelids
- make eyes expression less
- lower lips

---

[8] Paul Erkman, "Description of Facial Action Coding System (FACS)," *Human Face* (Joseph C. Hager, 2003), http://face-and-emotion.com/dataface/facs/description.jsp (accessed 26 March 2013).

Surprise
- raise eyebrows
- widen eyes
- open mouth[9]

The human anatomy is an amazing creation of God. The face contains many muscles and nerves that work together in a complex manner to express emotions. Scientists have determined it takes twenty-six facial muscles to smile and sixty-two facial muscles to frown. It seems smiling takes less work and causes fewer wrinkles. Christians should smile—not frown—not only because doing so requires less effort, but also because of the positive message it communicates.

Public speakers should learn to use eye contact and facial expression to enhance communication and to project a pleasant countenance. Sincere eyes and caring faces express the love of Jesus to a hurting world. Christian speakers are challenged to let their eyes and faces, along with their words and actions, reflect the heart of God.

TALKING POINT

Speakers express thoughts and feelings
in their eyes and faces as well as through words.

LET'S TALK ABOUT IT

1. Describe what *countenance* means. What are some examples of it in Scripture?
2. How important is eye contact while speaking? What does eye contact reveal to the audience?
3. What are ten suggestions for improved eye contact?
4. How important is facial expression while speaking? What do facial expressions reveal to the audience?
5. Describe how your face can reflect the countenance of the Lord.

---

[9] Ibid.

Chapter 23

GESTURES AND POSTURE

"Hands have the power to dramatize, describe, and punctuate points to attract attention, stimulate interest, and create dynamic action."[1]

Body movements, including gestures and posture, are forms of nonverbal communication used in place of speech or in combination with words to convey meaning. In the broadest sense, gestures include movement of the hands, face, or other parts of the body. Specifically, gestures indicate expressive movements of the hands. Posture is the position of body when standing or sitting. In speaking, posture refers to the proper stance for projecting a strong voice and presenting a confident image.

A speaker can demonstrate personal poise with physical movement. Poise is the graceful and confident way a person carries herself. It is acting with dignity and composure under the pressure of public speaking. It is the opposite of being clumsy, awkward, and fidgety. For years, poise was taught to women in deportment or etiquette classes. People, especially public speakers, should exhibit grace and charm. Through poise, public speakers communicate composure, dignity, gentleness, and respect. The Bible speaks of the gentle and quiet spirit of a woman (1 Pet 3:4). Poise (including gestures, posture, and movement) suggests volumes about a person's character.

---

[1] Pat and Ruth Williams, *Turn Boring Orations into Standing Ovations: The Ultimate Guide to Dynamic Public Speaking* (Altamonte Springs, FL: Advantage Books, 2008), 156.

This chapter will summarize the impact of appropriate gestures and comfortable posture on nonverbal communication. These actions often speak louder than words in public speaking. Lack of gestures and limited movement communicates nervousness, poor self-confidence, and lack of interest. Good public speakers learn to use hand gestures and body positions to maximize communication and connect with the audience. Gestures and posture speak volumes.

Hand Movements

A gesture is any movement of the body that reinforces a verbal message or conveys a particular thought or emotion. This section will focus specifically on hand movements. The hands can encumber a speaker or enhance the message. Some speakers are unsure of how to hold their hands during a speech, while others use them naturally to illustrate the words. In their book, *Turning Boring Orations into Standing Ovations*, Pat and Ruth Williams state that hands and arms in motion have the communicative power to "dramatize, describe, and punctuate points" as well as to "attract attention, stimulate interest, and create dynamic action."[2] While some speakers are more comfortable using gestures, all public speakers need to utilize gestures to secure audience attention and emphasize meaningful points. Without varied hand movements, a speaker seems stiff and lifeless like a mannequin. A public speaker must learn why gestures are important and how to seek them effectively.

I (Rhonda) have often said that I could not talk if my hands were tied. My hands and their gestures are a part of my communication style. In one-to-one conversation and public speaking, I use my hands and my words to talk. I believe hand movements articulate my emotions and accentuate my message. So, I need to understand gestures and use them naturally.

According to Toastmasters International, all good speakers use gestures because they enhance communication in many different ways.[3] There are several specific purposes for gestures. They are used . . .

- *to clarify and support words.* Gestures strengthen the audience's understanding of the verbal message.
- *to dramatize ideas.* Together with what is said, gestures help paint vivid pictures in the listeners' minds.

---

[2] Ibid.

[3] *Toastmasters International* "Gestures: Your Body Speaks," (Toastmasters International 2011), http://www.toastmasters.org/201-Gestures (accessed 20 March 2013).

- *to lend emphasis and vitality to the spoken word.* Gestures convey feelings and attitudes more clearly than what is spoken.
- *to help dissipate nervous tension.* Purposeful gestures are a good outlet for the nervous energy inherent in a speaking situation.
- *to function as visual aids.* Gestures enhance audience attentiveness and retention.
- *to stimulate audience participation.* Gestures help indicate desired response from listeners.
- *to visualize thoughts.* Gestures provide visual support when addressing a large number of people as the entire audience may not see the speaker's eyes.

Like eye contact and facial expression, gestures may vary in usage from one culture to another. Public speakers must learn why gestures are important and how to use them across cultures as necessary.

There are several types of gestures. Emphatic gestures are used to stress or underscore a point (i.e., clenched fist, pointed finger). Descriptive gestures are used to clarify or illustrate meaning (i.e., size, shape, number). Suggestive gestures symbolize ideas and emotions (i.e., open palms, clasped hands, crossed arms). Locative gestures direct audience attention to a place, object, or person (i.e., pointing with index finger or waving with arm). Transitional gestures show movement from one part of the speech to another (i.e., finger counting, left to right arm movement). Prompting gestures stimulate a desired response from the audience (i.e., raising hand, clapping hands, taking step forward). Each type of gesture, when used appropriately, can be effective in public speaking.

I (Rhonda) saw a pastor use a prompting gesture incorrectly while extending the invitation following his Sunday morning sermon. His biblical message was powerful, but his persuasive appeal was weak. As the pastor pleaded with the congregation to "come forward and repent of their sins," he pushed his hands in an outward motion, indicating movement to the back. The audience must have been confused. When used correctly, gestures produce the desired results—clearer communication.

These guidelines for gestures should be remembered (see chart on page 236).

Guidelines for Gestures

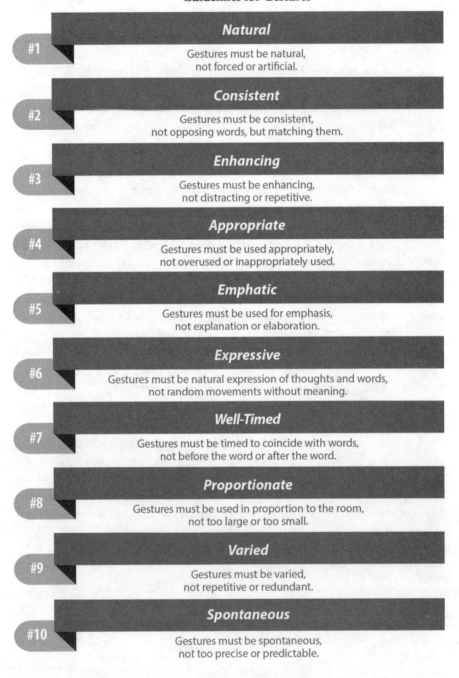

#1 Natural
Gestures must be natural,
not forced or artificial.

#2 Consistent
Gestures must be consistent,
not opposing words, but matching them.

#3 Enhancing
Gestures must be enhancing,
not distracting or repetitive.

#4 Appropriate
Gestures must be used appropriately,
not overused or inappropriately used.

#5 Emphatic
Gestures must be used for emphasis,
not explanation or elaboration.

#6 Expressive
Gestures must be natural expression of thoughts and words,
not random movements without meaning.

#7 Well-Timed
Gestures must be timed to coincide with words,
not before the word or after the word.

#8 Proportionate
Gestures must be used in proportion to the room,
not too large or too small.

#9 Varied
Gestures must be varied,
not repetitive or redundant.

#10 Spontaneous
Gestures must be spontaneous,
not too precise or predictable.

Public speakers learn to use gestures appropriately and effectively through practice, practice, practice. It is helpful to practice using natural gestures during informal conversations. Practice gestures in front of a mirror or by means of video recording. Practice gestures consciously and deliberately in every speech given to every group. In time they will flow naturally.

Body Positions

Platform movement and posture are essential elements of nonverbal communication. Like gestures, they should look and feel natural to reinforce the message and not distract. The stance and movement of the body involve the total person, mentally and physically. Thoughts and feelings can be expressed in movements and gestures. These two rules should be remembered when on the platform: move when there is reason to move and stand still when there is no reason to move.

One of my (Rhonda) doctoral professors roamed back and forth in front of the classroom during his lectures. He paced aimlessly in front of the class as he taught, apparently unwilling to make eye contact with his students. Several students attempted to alter his distracting behavior through an experiment. Students on the right side of the class paid careful attention to the professor as he paced—looking interested, nodding heads, taking notes, and asking questions. Students on the left side of the classroom ignored the professor as he taught; they took no notes and asked no questions. Within a few minutes, the professor paced back and forth only on the right side of the room. While his pacing behavior was modified, his poor eye contact remained unchanged. He served as a model of what not to do.

Posture is noticed immediately, and opinions are made about a speaker based on stance and carriage. Posture is the position of a person's body when standing or sitting. Many different organs, muscles, and nerves in the body are used to stand. While physical conditions may inhibit good posture, most people can control posture with conscious actions. A public speaker needs good posture to support vocal projection, to display confidence, and to enhance movement.

In *No Sweat Public Speaking*, Fred Miller suggests four ways that posture helps communicate a message. (1) Good, straight posture indicates leadership and confidence. (2) Leaning forward toward the audience shows concern and care. (3) Slouching the body conveys disinterest and boredom. (4) Hunched shoulders suggest low self-esteem and lack of confidence.[4] Posture is more impor-

---

[4] Fred Miller, *No Sweat Public Speaking* (St. Louis, MO: Freed, 2011), 101.

tant than many speakers realize. Evaluate your posture in a mirror or by watching video footage of a previous presentation. Remember to stand up, then speak up!

I (Rhonda) took piano lessons in my childhood. My mother sat on the bench beside me as I practiced several times a week. She often patted my back; reminding me to sit up straight. She encouraged me, "Head up, chin up." I learned in my youth that posture is important. While I may not be the most accomplished pianist, I have excellent posture at the keyboard. My mother taught me that good posture communicates confidence, energy, and poise.

There are some cardinal rules about posture and movement that a good speaker should follow. Try not to break the following posture principles.

1. Do not fidget with your hands or fingers.
2. Do not jingle change or keys in your pockets.
3. Do not cross your hands in front of your body ("fig-leaf stance") or behind your body.
4. Do not rock on your heels or toes.
5. Do not sway back and forth.
6. Do not lean on the podium.
7. Do not cross your arms across your chest.
8. Do not look down for too long.
9. Do not bob or shake your head too much.
10. Do not remain stiff or tense.

Zig Ziglar was a dynamic public speaker and powerful Christian communicator. Though small in physical stature, he had a bigger than life presence on the stage. He projected energy and enthusiasm as he moved confidently around a platform. His speech content was filled with knowledge and wisdom, and his delivery style was passionate, purposeful, and powerful. His sales experience and personal faith provided the foundational principles for his speaking and writing. A master of verbal and nonverbal communication, Ziglar said, "Your attitude, not your aptitude, will determine your altitude." Stand up and speak out like Zig Ziglar did for many years.

Correct posture is an important part of nonverbal communication in public speaking. Practice these principles and avoid these pitfalls.

1. Walk deliberately to the stage; avoid rushing onto the platform.
2. Stand upright, keeping the body core tight; avoid tension or tightness.
3. Place feet firmly on the ground and slightly apart (about shoulder width); avoid stiff legs and locked knees.
4. Face the audience directly; avoid turning the body away from listeners.

5. Position body behind podium with hands to the side or resting on lectern; avoid gripping the podium.
6. Hold head and chin up; avoid looking down.
7. Square shoulders with the audience; avoid drooping shoulders.
8. Keep chest up and stomach in; avoid tightening abdominal muscles.
9. Relax the body; avoid tension and stiffness.
10. Breathe deeply to relax; avoid short, shallow breaths.
11. Pause to look at the audience; avoid rushing into the speech.
12. Watch the posture of others speakers; avoid awkward imitation of others.

Improved posture adds strength and authority to a spoken message.

Toastmasters International teaches the importance of nonverbal communication to members developing public speaking skills. Five general methods are suggested for strengthening the body's image.[5]

1. *Eliminate distracting mannerisms.* If body movements are self-focused, repetitive, or irritating, they will hinder the speech. Replace unconscious mannerisms with conscious actions.
2. *Be natural, spontaneous, and conversational.* Try to be true to self when walking, standing, and talking. Let the body respond comfortably and spontaneously to your thoughts, feelings, and words.
3. *Let the body mirror feelings.* Believe in the speech so that your physical movements and words will naturally connect. Verify that your posture and movement reflect feelings and express thoughts.
4. *Build self-confidence through preparation.* Mental attitude and body positions as well as speech delivery are dependent upon preparation. Effective speakers prepare carefully and present confidently the message from the inside out.
5. *Develop a speaking posture.* The body position communicates its own set of visual messages to the audience. Posture reflects attitude and commands attention.

Dale Carnegie, known as the father of modern public speaking, said: "A person under the influence of his feelings projects the real self, acting naturally and spontaneously. A speaker who is interested will usually be interesting."[6]

---

[5] *Toastmasters International*, "Gestures: Your Body Speaks" (Toastmasters International 2011), 5–7, http://www.toastmasters.org/201-Gestures (accessed 20 March 2013).
[6] Dale Carnegie, "Gestures: Your Body Speaks," *Toastmasters International* (Toastmasters International 2011), 6, http://www.toastmasters.org/201-Gestures (accessed 20 March 2013).

When your name is called and you walk to the stage . . .
> rise up slowly,
> stand up erectly,
> walk out boldly,
> pause—breathe—look—then
> speak out confidently.

Good posture makes a good impression on the audience and gives good support to the speaker. Outstanding public speakers develop a platform posture to reflect their attitudes and gain the audience's attention. Body posture can reduce nervous energy and relieve physical tension. As you speak, make your body talk.

Spatial Proximity

Nonverbal communication also involves proxemics or the use of space. According to the dictionary, *proxemics* is "the study of the nature, degree, and effect of the spatial separation individuals maintain in social and interpersonal situations."[7] The space between individuals relates to environmental and cultural factors. While proxemics is controlled by the individuals in informal conversations, the setting often dictates proxemics in public speaking.

In the 1960s, the cultural anthropologist Edward T. Hall studied the impact of proxemic behavior across genders and cultures.[8] He separated territory (geographical area claimed) and personal space (immediate area around a person). He developed four types of distance to delineate the appropriate areas for personal space. (See graphic on page 241.) These findings influence interpersonal communication and public speaking. Imagine the personal space around an individual with concentric circles measuring the distance moving outward. Hall proposed four zones in varying measurements, based on relationships and preferences: intimate distance, personal distance, social distance, and public distance. This system has been used through the years to gauge the effect of the speaker's distance to the listener as well as to help speakers accomodate variation among cultural and environmental factors. In conversations, people determine the distance between speaker and listener based on personal preferences and cultural norms. In public speaking, the greater distances between people must be considered consciously and managed effectively.

---

[7] *Merriam-Webster Dictionary* (Merriam-Webster, Incorporated, 2013), s.v. "proxemics," http://www.merriam-webster.com/dictionary/proxemics (accessed 27 March 2013).

[8] M. S. Thirumalai, *Silent Talk-Nonverbal Communication* (Mysore, India: CIIL), www.ciil-ebooks.net/html/silent/ch2.htm (accessed 3 February 2013).

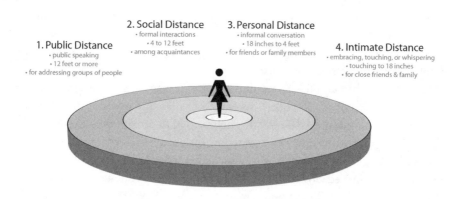

2. Social Distance
• formal interactions
• 4 to 12 feet
• among acquaintances

3. Personal Distance
• informal conversation
• 18 inches to 4 feet
• for friends or family members

1. Public Distance
• public speaking
• 12 feet or more
• for addressing groups of people

4. Intimate Distance
• embracing, touching, or whispering
• touching to 18 inches
• for close friends & family

I (Rhonda) had a friend in college who was overly sensitive about his personal space. If anyone stood within a foot or two of him, he protested, "Don't violate my space." He tried to joke about it though it was a serious matter to him. Needless to say, my friend was frequently teased. I have another friend who stands very close when speaking to anyone. It makes me feel a little uncomfortable, and I find myself stepping or leaning backward. I have learned that personal space varies among individuals in personal conversations and in public speaking venues.

Preferences in personal space can vary widely. Extroverts or outgoing personalities may enjoy less distance between speaker and listener. Introverts or withdrawn personalities may be more comfortable with greater distance. People living in cities are used to close quarters and are more comfortable with close contact, while those living in the country prefer wide open spaces in life and communication. According to Edward Hall, personal space also varies among nationalities or cultures.[9] For instance, Americans and Europeans stand sixteen to eighteen

---

[9] Ibid.

inches apart while engaging in casual conversation. The Japanese maintain a greater distance between speaker and listener (about thirty-six inches), while Middle Easterners prefer a lesser distance (eight to twelve inches). Some cultures are more tactile and expressive while others are less comfortable with contact. It is helpful to understand the role of proxemics in interpersonal communication and public speaking.

A well-loved professor at the New Orleans Baptist Theological Seminary overcomes spatial barriers to make connections with her students during class. Dr. Jeanine Bozeman does not remain behind a podium when she teaches. She walks around the classroom or sits near the students. At times, she moves directly to an individual to emphasize a point. She may reach out to touch a student's hand or pat a student's shoulder. Bozeman's passion for ministry and genuine sincerity are communicated clearly through her use of proximity as well as touch.

Public speakers must work to overcome distance barriers with the audience. Space and lighting can interfere with visual connections. When possible, the lectern should be moved closer to the people, or the speaker can move from behind a large podium. All lights should remain bright to allow the speaker to see the audience. Movement toward the crowd is effective at times. Movement around the platform promotes closeness with all in the audience. A speaker can reach out or lean over to indicate closeness. In some cases, the speaker or teacher may even ask the audience to move closer to each other or closer to the front. Proximity will help sustain attention and maintain connection.

Crowding is a concept that impacts interpersonal communication and public speaking. It is the congregating of people or things together. In *The Mind Changers: The Art of Christian Persuasion*, E. M. Griffin supports the premise that public speakers feel they are more effective when the audience is packed in tightly together. He concludes, "It isn't so much the size of the crowd that's important, but rather how tightly the people are jammed together."[10]

Crowding can have both positive and negative effects on speaking. Being too close together may be uncomfortable and sitting or standing too far apart may feel unapproachable. Typically, in public speaking, the greater the crowding, the more receptive and responsive the audience. Public speakers must learn to adjust proximity and distances when possible.

A great preacher from New Orleans handles proxemics well. As Fred Luter preaches, he moves around the platform and only references his notes occasionally. To connect with the audience and close the spatial distance, Luter frequently calls out the names of individuals in the audience, randomly mentioning a person

---

[10] E. M. Griffin, *The Mind Changers: The Art of Christian Persuasion* (Carol Stream, IL: Tyndale House, 1976), 57.

by name when he sees them in the crowd. This connects the people to each other as well as to the preacher.

Gestures, postures, and positioning are important tools for public speaking. They nonverbally communicate the speaker's message and personality. The mastery of body movement and spatial positioning are marks of an excellent public speaker.

TALKING POINT

Public speakers must work to overcome
distance barriers with the audience.

LET'S TALK ABOUT IT

1. What does your poise reveal about you? In what ways might you improve your poise as a speaker?
2. Compare and contrast gestures and posture.
3. List ten guidelines for gestures.
4. List the ten cardinal rules for posture and movement that a good speaker should follow.
5. Describe spatial proximity and the four types of distances developed by Edward T. Hall.

Chapter 24

APPEARANCE AND CLOTHING

"Regardless of your personality,
it is important to put extra effort into dressing for the platform."[1]

P ublic speakers never have a second chance to make a first impression. While a person need not be a beauty to speak to groups, appearance and clothing are an important part of the speaker's image. Neat appearance and appropriate clothing display professionalism and confidence. On the other hand, untidy appearance and inappropriate clothing can distract the listener and diminish the speaker's credibility. Christian speakers should always look their best to represent the Lord well.

Some years ago, my (Rhonda) husband came home between seminary classes to eat lunch. Before he left to teach his evangelism class, Chuck went to the mirror to mess up his hair, loosen his tie, turn up his collar, and pull out his shirt tail. I must have stared speechlessly as he said goodbye. I was relieved when he explained, "Today, my class lecture is on the appearance of the evangelist." Chuck's disheveled looks were a great visual image to make the important point that speakers should consider the impression their appearance will make.

Florence and Marita Littauer have written and spoken about personality types for many years. They discuss how personality affects style of communication.

---

[1] Florence and Marita Littauer, *Communication Plus: How to Speak So People Will Listen* (Ventura, CA: Regal, 2006), 176.

Personality is definitely expressed in the clothing, hairstyle, and makeup of a speaker.[2] While no two people are exactly alike, those of each personality tend to wear clothes of a particular style.

Popular Sanguines wear bright colors, sparkles and bling, flamboyant clothing, unique styles.

Powerful Cholerics wear bright colors, simple prints, tailored style, and business professional attire.

Perfect Melancholy personality types prefer muted tones, classic cuts, traditional styles, and simple elegance.

Peaceful Phlegmatics prefer earthy tones, flowing fabrics, relaxed fit, and unstructured styles.

Personality preferences should be considered when you are shopping for clothing, accessories, and makeup.

Public speakers need to understand how personality impacts style of speaking and type of clothing. While appearance should reflect personality, clothing styles should not be extreme. The audience and occasion should be considered as well as the fit and comfort of the clothes. Clothing should not be distracting to the speaker or listeners. According to the Littauers:

> Regardless of your personality, it is important to put extra effort into dressing for the platform. The things that work on the stage may well be things that you would never wear to the store or office. But on the stage, in front of an audience, you want to have a look that sets you apart and lends dignity to your work.[3]

Some people have a natural sense of style and dress attractively without effort. Others must work harder to look their best. General ideas can be seen in fashion magazines. Clothing consultants or sales clerks can provide professional input. Speakers must wear clothing, hairstyles, and makeup appropriate for age, setting, and ministry. Timeless classics are recommended over faddish trends. Invest money in fashions that last and are made well.

In this chapter, we will discuss appearance and clothing for female speakers. Special attention will be given to hair, makeup, and wardrobe. Most public speakers identify specific clothing items and hairstyles for a speaking wardrobe or professional look. Personal style and event setting may vary. However, a speaker's appearance should always be neat, modest, and appropriate.

---

[2] Ibid., 174–76.
[3] Ibid., 176.

Hair

Whether it seems right or wrong, people make judgments about other people based on outward appearances. Hair is the first feature noticed, especially for women. It is the only accessory worn at all times. Hair can be attractive or distracting. The Bible mentions hair, often in warnings. Women are admonished to dress with modesty, decency, and propriety, not wearing elaborate hairstyles or expensive jewelry (1 Tim 2:9). While in this passage Paul identified the inappropriate attire for women in the early church, these biblical principles apply to Christian women today. Hairstyles should not imply sensual lifestyle or wealthy status. Extreme hairstyles may hinder a speaker's ministry to all types of people.

Speakers should take hair care seriously. Style, color, and ease of preparation are important considerations for daily life as well as for speaking ministry. Stylists are professionally trained to select appropriate hairstyles for different hair textures, body types, and personal lifestyles. They color and condition as well as cut and style hair. They can also address problems like hair loss and frizz.

Public speakers should find a hairstyle that flatters the face and figure. Hair should be kept behind the ears and out of the eyes—away from the face. Be careful that bangs do not obstruct vision. Consider hairspray to keep the style in place when speaking. For facial expressions to be effective, the face and eyes must be seen.

Do not underestimate low-maintenance hairstyle. Hair that is easy to style and stays in place is the goal. Try to find a style you can achieve in thirty to forty-five minutes. Once hair is fixed, it should stay in place with the help of hairspray or gel. Try not to twist the hair or touch it while speaking. Speaker and listener alike should be able to focus on the message not be distracted by the hair.

Makeup

A woman's face needs regular care. The face should be washed morning and night with a good cleanser. Makeup should always be removed before sleeping. The face should be exfoliated weekly to remove dead skin and to open clogged pores. Scrubs for any skin type are available at little cost. The face should be moisturized regularly. Moisturizers can be applied under makeup and on a clean face before bed. Eye creams may help the delicate areas under and around the eyes. Sunscreen should be used in the daytime to minimize skin damage from ultraviolet rays: Sun damage is the number one cause of wrinkles and aging. Though some ladies prefer little or no makeup, moisturizer and sunscreen should be worn by all.

Application of makeup should begin with a foundation covering the face. Select a color to complement the natural skin tone. Foundation smoothes out uneven skin color and provides a neutral background. Concealor may be worn to cover blemishes or dark circles under the eyes. Blush may be applied to give color to the cheeks. Powder seals the makeup and reduces shine.

Eye makeup preferences vary depending upon age, personality, and fashion trends. To open the eyes yet give a natural look eyebrows should be shaped and lined. Eyeshadow may be worn on the upper eyelids to add color. Some ladies prefer neutral tones while others choose brightly colored eye shadow. Eyeliner on the upper and lower lids accentuates the eyes but should not be too dark or too harsh. Eyelashes may be curled and mascara applied to lengthen and thicken natural lashes.

More makeup should be worn when speaking before a large audience or on television. At first, heavy makeup may seem excessive. However, makeup fades quickly under bright lights. It has been suggested that a female speaker should stand about twelve feet from a mirror to examine makeup for public speaking. That distance approximates the space between speaker and audience. It helps to assess makeup from the audience's perspective.

Clothing

Clothing makes a statement. Clean, neat clothes project a sense of pride and care. Dirty, disheveled clothes indicate lack of interest or even emotional distress. Stylish, coordinated clothes display attention to detail. They can help speakers project a positive image. Therefore, speakers should wear their best to speak their best.

The speaking wardrobe should take into consideration appropriate attire, personal style, body type, and skin tones. Type of attire is determined by the occasion, setting, and audience. A speaker is wise to ask about dress for the event before arriving. It is a general rule of thumb for a speaker to wear clothing one level above that of the audience. If the audience wears jeans, the speaker should wear nice slacks. If the audience wears slacks, the speaker should wear a dressy pantsuit, skirt, or dress.

Years ago, etiquette expert Emily Post developed a dress code for every occasion from white tie affairs to casual get-togethers. A few special events may call for formal or semiformal attire. However, most speaking occasions will require festive, business formal, business casual, dressy casual, or casual attire. Christian events may specify "Sunday morning attire" to imply dressy casual, business casual, or business formal, depending on a church's preferences. Ask for clarification as needed.

The following guide for women makes wardrobe suggestions.[4]

There are four basic fashion styles among women: romantic, sporty, trendy, and classic. (Refer to the previous discussion in chap. 12.) I (Rhonda) consider

Festive Attire (usually for the holidays)	• after-five dress • long dressy skirt or pants with jacket • little black dress • holiday colors and accessories
Business Formal	• suit or business-style dress • dress with jacket • stockings (optional in summer) • heels, low or high
Business Casual	• skirt or pants • open-collar shirt, knit shirt or sweater • no spaghetti straps or décolleté • casual-style dress
Dressy Casual	• dress • skirt and dressy top • dressy pants outfit • nice jeans and dressy top
Casual	• sundress • long or short skirt • pants or nice jeans • nice shorts • plain t-shirt, polo shirt, or turtleneck • casual button-down blouse

myself to have an eclectic clothing style. I like variety based on my mood and agenda for the day. Some days, I am very sporty, wearing jeans and a simple top. On other days, I am trendy, wearing an animal print accessory or fun shoes. I also enjoy romantic styles, occasionally pairing a floral blouse or flowing skirt. I have learned to invest my money in classic wardrobe pieces. My speaking attire is typically traditional and conservative. I can enjoy a variety of clothing styles on

---

[4] Emily Post, "Dressing for the Occasion," *Emily Post* (The Emily Post Institute, 2012), http://www.emilypost.com/social-life/formal-dinners-and-parties/860-dressing-for-the-occasion (accessed 20 March 2013).

my days off, but I dress more carefully and appropriately when I teach or speak. I never want my clothes to speak louder than my words.

Four different body types determine what type of clothes look best on a person. They are called by different names, though they generally describe the same basic shapes. Several fashion sources suggest these four categories: circle (thick around the middle), triangle (larger at the bottom), hourglass (curvy but evenly proportioned), and rectangle (straight up and down). Circle figures should wear loose fitting clothes around the middle and fitted pants, avoiding high-rise pants, belts, and fitted tops. Triangle figures should wear tailored tops and fuller bottoms, avoiding oversized sweaters, skinny jeans, and clingy skirts. Hourglass figures should wear fitted waistbands and belts, avoiding shapeless tunics, baby-doll dresses, and oversized cardigans. Rectangle figures should wear fitted waists and flared bottoms to create curves avoiding clingy dresses, Empire-waist tops, and flowing skirts.[5] Women who know their body type and wear the appropriate clothing always have a more attractive and confident appearance.

Colors also matter. Solid, bright (not neon) colors are usually flattering on all women. However, certain colors look better with specific skin tones. In 1980, Carole Jackson developed a color system called "Color Me Beautiful." Based on the four seasons of the year, the system suggests that a woman's natural skin tones determine the most complementary color palate for her. See the chart listing coloration and colors for each season.[6] It is helpful to know your best colors and wear them.

Season	Skin Tone	Colors
Autumn	Fiery, earthy, golden natural	Muted, warm colors: moss, rust, terra cotta
Winter	Crisp and distinctive	Bold shades: black, white, red, jewel tones
Spring	Bright and sunny	Bright colors: turquoise, watermelon, salmon
Summer	Delicate and pale	Pastel shades: rose, periwinkle, sage

---

[5] Kristin Larson, "The Right Clothes for Your Body Type," *Real Simple* (Time Inc. 2013), www.realsimple.com/beauty-fashion/clothing/shopping-guide/right-clothes-your-body-type-00000000007925/index.html (accessed March 20, 2013).

[6] Carole Jackson, *Color Me Beautiful* (New York: Ballantine Books, 1980).

Accessories should be carefully selected for a speaking wardrobe. Accessories, including jewelry, scarves, hats, handbags, gloves, stockings, and shoes, are designed to enhance appearance, not distract from the message. They can be the finishing touches of an outfit when they complement the overall look. Accessories need not be overdone in size or number. A female speaker should limit her accessories to four or five. Accessories might include: (1) earrings, (2) necklace, (3) watch, (4) bracelet, and/or (5) ring.

It is time to talk woman to woman. Undergarments should fit properly and not be displayed. Female speakers standing before groups should wear bras, slips, and panties that fit well and cover completely. Since bra sizes change over time, women should be fitted regularly to ensure proper coverage and support. Avoid see-through and off-the-shoulder blouses when speaking. If wearing a skirt or dress, also wear a slip of the correct length and style. On stage, light can shine through and reveal the legs. Consider a body shaper to smooth out rolls and eliminate panty lines. Hose or tights are recommended with skirts and dresses worn on a platform. Hosiery pulls an outfit together and covers the legs. Pale, bare legs on a stage can be distracting and even embarrassing. Give careful consideration when choosing foundational undergarments.

In her book, *Speak Up with Confidence*, Carol Kent gives ten tips for dressing for a speaking engagement.

1. *Avoid the "sleeveless" look.* Too much exposed skin can be shiny and distracting. Wear long-sleeves, sweaters, or jackets when speaking.
2. *For a stylish "together" look, bring the color worn below the waist to the top of your body.* Bright solid colors near the neck highlight the face and focus eyes on it.
3. *Stay away from tight-fitting clothes, see-through materials, and daring skirt slits.* Inappropriate clothes draw attention to the body instead of the message. Modesty is always the key.
4. *Be conservative with jewelry.* Avoid bangle bracelets, huge earrings, or shiny necklaces.
5. *Makeup should bring your face to light, but not look "heavy."* Wear an appropriate type and amount of makeup. Department stores often provide free facial and makeup consultations, which could be very helpful.
6. *Wear nail polish only if you have attractive nails.* Do not call attention to ragged or bitten nails. No nail polish is better than chipped polish. Neat and clean nails are essential.
7. *Take a look at your hair.* Wear a flattering haircut and hairstyle. Use a little hairspray to keep it in place.

8. *Learn to use accessories.* A basic suit can be fashion-forward with a stylish accessory. Let accessories attract, not distract.

9. *Wear stylish but comfortable shoes.* If your feet hurt, it will show in your voice. Shoes should not make noise when walking on stage.

10. *Use common sense when dressing to speak.* Honestly evaluate your appearance and receive constructive feedback from others.[7]

---

10 Appearance Tips for Women Speakers

1. *Avoid the "sleeveless" look.*
2. *For a stylish "together" look, bring the color worn below the waist to the top of your body.*
3. *Stay away from tight-fitting clothes, see-through materials, and daring skirt slits.*
4. *Be conservative with jewelry.*
5. *Makeup should bring your face to light, but not look "heavy."*
6. *Wear nail polish only if you have attractive nails.*
7. *Take a look at your hair.*
8. *Learn to use accessories.*
9. *Wear stylish but comfortable shoes.*
10. *Use common sense when dressing to speak.*

Modesty is a virtue that is always in style. Christian women who speak publicly have a high calling and the privilege of walking worthy of the gospel. According to Scripture, teachers will fall under a stricter judgment (Jas 3:1). Modesty is something every Christian woman, especially speakers, should exhibit. Unfortunately, today's fashion industry promotes immodesty. In 1 Timothy 2:9–10, the apostle Paul writes: "Women are to dress themselves in modest clothing . . . with good works, as is proper for women who affirm that they worship God."

The life of a public figure, including the dress of the speaker, will be watched and examined by others. Modest appearance includes higher necklines; covered shoulders, backs, and midriffs; knee-length or longer skirts or dresses; loose-fitting garments; fitted undergarments; and classic shoes. A Christian speaker should reflect Christ not only by verbal communication but by nonverbal communication.

Recently, an older woman who happened to be a new believer, approached me (Monica) and shared the following: "I know I do not come up to you and

---

[7] Carol Kent, *Speak Up with Confidence: A Step-by-Step Guide to Successful Public Speaking* (Colorado Springs: NavPress, 2007), 146-47.

speak a lot, but I want you to know that you have been an example to me of how God has created me. You have taught me biblical femininity by the way you dress." I had no idea this believer was looking to me as an example of biblical womanhood or that my appearance was teaching her how to dress modestly, but she was learning from my nonverbal communication.

The appearance of a Christian speaker can have an enormous impact on the audience. Inappropriate or immodest clothing can be a distraction to the listeners or a contradiction of the message presented. I (Monica) recently shared at a women's conference and one of the speakers was dressed in extremely tight clothing. Her choice of wardrobe grieved my heart because so many people were looking to her as an example of godly womanhood. Although cultural styles come and go, Christian women and female speakers should make the decision to be different in their dress, wearing clothing that brings glory to God instead of attention to self.

In addition to Kent's suggestions, consider these general grooming tips.

1. *Maintain personal hygiene.* Daily showers or baths plus deodorant control body odor.
2. *Brush teeth regularly and before speaking when possible.* Brushing and flossing improve dental appearance and promote fresh breath.
3. *Wear perfume and cologne sparingly.* Since some people are allergic to fragrances, wear only a small amount of a subtle scent.
4. *Select glasses to match face shape and skin tone.* If at all possible, wear contacts. Try to use glasses only when reading aloud. Glasses obstruct eye contact and build a barrier between speaker and listener. If glasses are necessary, select smaller, neutral frames.
5. *Cover any tattoos or body piercings when speaking.* Attempt to minimize distractions.
6. *Choose lighter weight clothing when speaking.* Anxiety and stage lights may raise the body temperature, increasing perspiration and hot flashes.
7. *Wear clothes that are comfortable that will not need require adjustments.* Fidgeting with clothing or accessories is distracting.

My (Rhonda) dad often reminded my sister and me that our bodies are like packages, gifts from God. We are to take care of our packages. I think about his advice every day when I get dressed because I want my appearance to be pleasing to others and to the Lord. Care is taken as I style my hair, apply my makeup, and select my clothes. In life and ministry, I want my appearance to reflect my best and to bring honor to God. I have a responsibility to maintain my appearance so that people can hear God's message as I speak.

TALKING POINT

Speakers should look their best
to speak their best.

LET'S TALK ABOUT IT

1. Explain appropriate hair and makeup for a public speaker.
2. List Carol Kent's ten tips for dressing for a speaking engagement.
3. To what four or five accessories should a speaker limit herself while speaking?
4. How important is modesty for a Christian woman speaker? Why?
5. In what ways do you think your appearance and clothing need to change before you speak to an audience of women?

Section 2

DRAMA AND ORAL INTERPRETATION

Throughout history, the creative arts have communicated messages through music, painting, film, dance, puppetry, and magic as well as drama and oral interpretation. Pastors and worship leaders have employed dramatic presentations in the church to enhance a biblical message for members and to appeal to the unchurched in the community. Public speakers should consider using drama or oral interpretation when appropriate to capture attention and convey a thought. When considering the use of drama, a speaker should understand her own abilities, know her audience, identify a theme, and utilize available resources. The use of drama in the church and in public speaking has increased as visual communication has developed. These performing arts can glorify God and entertain.

This section will provide a brief introduction for public speakers to incorporate drama and/or oral interpretation into their presentations when appropriate. Questions will be answered about the what and why of drama plus the how and when of drama. Some practical advantages and disadvantages will also be suggested.

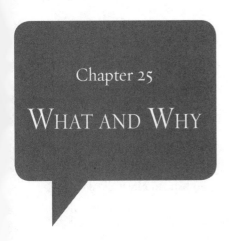

Chapter 25

WHAT AND WHY

*"Drama captures the minds, the imaginations,
and the emotions of the audience."*[1]

G od is theatrical. "All of creation is a theater for God's glory."[2] Numerous
biblical accounts demonstrate that God is powerful and mighty in his
actions and purposes. From nothing he created everything: the heavens and the
earth, the sky and land, the birds and fish, man and woman. He continues to
perform supernatural miracles, signs, and wonders to gain attention from his
children. His dramatic demonstrations of power are seen today during hurri-
canes, earthquakes, and blizzards. God is all-powerful; He is omnipotent in his
being and his behavior.

The Old Testament records numerous wonders of God. Moses experienced
the dramatic work of God when the angel of the Lord spoke to him from the
burning bush that was not consumed. When the Israelites fled Pharaoh's army,
God manifested his power in dramatic fashion by parting the Red Sea, allowing his children to cross safely to the other side. Balaam's donkey talked. The
walls of Jericho fell. The widow's son was raised from the dead. Elijah was carried into heaven. The widow's oil was multiplied. Elisha's bones were revived
from the dead. Shadrach, Meshach, and Abednego were delivered from the fiery

---

[1] Matt Tullos, *Show Me: Drama in Evangelism* (Nashville: Convention Press, 1996), 5.
[2] John Calvin, *Institutes of the Christian Religion*, ed. John T. McNeill, trans. and indexed by
Ford Lewis Battles (Philadelphia, PA: The Westminster Press, 1967), 1:6:2 (72).

furnace. Daniel was protected in the lion's den. Jonah was saved from the belly of a whale. God demonstrated his mighty power through dramatic miracles in the Old Testament.[3]

The New Testament also contains many accounts of God's dramatic intervention through the ministry of Jesus. Though Jesus refused to give a miraculous sign on command to prove his authority, he performed miraculous signs during his ministry. Jesus changed water into wine at the wedding feast in Cana. He healed Peter's mother-in-law. He calmed the storm on the Sea of Galilee. He healed the woman with a hemorrhage and raised Jairus' daughter from the dead. He fed 5,000 people with five loaves of bread and two fish, and he walked on the water. He healed a stooped woman, and he raised Lazarus from the grave. Jesus demonstrated his mighty power in dramatic ways.[4]

God has exhibited his power through wonders and signs, and Jesus performed many miracles in his ministry. These dramatic demonstrations accomplished divine purposes, met human needs, and evidenced the truth of the gospel. As God's instruments, Christian communicators may use dramatic presentations to convey a biblical message or illustrate a spiritual principle. This chapter will define drama and explain why it should be considered for public speaking.

What Is Drama?

Drama is the "compression of human experience into a story we can view on the stage."[5] The word *drama* actually comes from a Greek word meaning "to do."[6] It implies action, involving a performer and an audience. Drama is a form of literature and can be prose, verse, or dialogue. It illustrates a message and can be presented from a script, by improvisation, through mime, or spontaneously during a speech. According to *The Complete Guide to Church Play Production*, "Drama shoots darts into the hearts of the audience and pulls them out with emotions attached."[7]

The dictionary defines *drama* as "a prose or verse composition, especially one telling a serious story, that is intended for representation by actors impersonating

---

[3] Exodus 3:1–22; 14:15–31; Num 22:22–41; Josh 6:1–21; 1 Kgs 17:17–24; 2 Kgs 2:1–12; 4:1–7; 13:14–21; Dan 3:8–30; 6:10–18; Jonah 1:1–2:10.

[4] Mark 8:11–12; John 2:1–12; Matt 8:14–15; Mark 4:35–44; 5:21–43; Matt 14:13–21, 22–33; Luke 13:11–16; John 11:32–44.

[5] Alison Siewart et al., *Drama Team Handbook* (Downers Grove, IL: InterVarsity Press, 2003), 15.

[6] John Lewis, Laura Andrews, and Flip Kobler, *The Complete Guide to Church Play Production* (Nashville: Convention Press, 1997), 277.

[7] Ibid.

the characters and performing the dialogue and action."[8] When drama is used by Christian speakers, it should be God glorifying and Christ centered. The message, not the medium, is the focus of a biblical truth presented dramatically.

Drama is a powerful method of expression. It speaks to the total person— physically, intellectually, emotionally, and spiritually.[9] The body performs the actions of drama. The mind conceives and interprets drama. The emotions express feelings and portray passions. The spirit convicts through the verbal and nonverbal message. Christians can use drama to stimulate and persuade the audience to consider their personal relationship with Christ. Therefore, Christian speakers should consider adding drama to certain public presentations.

I (Monica) will never forget the many powerful dramas directed by my junior high school leader. Before becoming a youth pastor, he traveled with a drama team to different churches. He made it a priority in his ministry to implement dramas into our youth meetings and into the special events in which the youth had the opportunity to participate. It benefitted me to participate in them and the audience to experience them. The dramas always enhanced the message and many came to Christ as a result.

In his book *The Dramatic Arts in Ministry* Everett Robertson suggests that "drama is a God-given instinct in every person."[10] Since all people think and feel, they can express themselves dramatically through body language and tone of voice. Some people are more expressive naturally. All speakers should recognize their God-given potential, understanding what drama is and why it is used to improve public presentations.

I (Rhonda) am a fairly expressive person. While I rarely use skits or pantomime when speaking, I do occasionally utilize monologue and dramatic reading to accentuate a message. Like most public speakers, I need to stretch myself and step outside of my box, employing drama more often. It could be used at women's events when I read a Scripture passage or present a biblical character. It would add interest when I make an announcement in church or tell a story to illustrate a point. Holiday themes also lend themselves to dramatic presentations.

A major increase of dramatic presentations has been seen in American churches since the late 1980s. It is known as religious drama. Herbert Sennett, author of *Religion and Dramatics: The Relationship between Christianity and the Theater Arts*, pointed out: "In a sense, all drama is religious because it deals with humanity in relationships. Drama that is uniquely religious also deals with man

---

[8] *American Heritage Dictionary of the English Language*, 4th ed. (Houghton Mifflin, 2009), s.v. "drama," http://www.thefreedictionary.com/drama (accessed 20 March 2013).

[9] Everett Robertson, *The Dramatic Arts in Ministry* (Nashville: Convention Press, 1989), 7.

[10] Ibid.

and his relationship with God."[11] Everett Robertson continued this thought: "Church drama is the enlightened portrayal of the basic human situation as interpreted through the Bible."[12]

Some churches have drama teams that perform during worship services or special events. Lay leaders or staff members identify individuals with interest and talent in creative arts and develop the performance ministry. Training and practice as well as script selection are keys to building a dynamic drama team. Christians with artistic skills, who may not be involved in other church ministries, can promote discipleship growth and evangelistic outreach while participating in creative expression.

In college, I (Monica) had the privilege of traveling with a ministry team whose main purpose was to conduct teen and college retreats and conferences, presenting the gospel message. Several members of the team focused solely on dramatic performance as part of the worship services. Drama definitely promoted discipleship growth and evangelistic outreach in those youth contexts.

Oral interpretation, also called interpretive reading or dramatic reading, is a dramatic art.[13] It is the emotive presentation of a literary work for the purpose of enlightenment. Oral interpretation and dramatic performance are similar in public speaking though slightly different in academic contexts. Oral interpretation is taught typically in speech communication programs, while drama is taught in the department of theater arts. Both are appropriate for public speaking.

Oral interpretation began 3,000 years ago with the classical Greek philosophers who used formal oratory to teach and persuade. Eugene and Margaret Bahn wrote a *History of Oral Interpretation* to document its development from the classical Greek through the ancient Roman, Medieval, and Renaissance periods as well as through the seventeenth, eighteenth, nineteenth, and twentieth centuries. The oral interpretation of literature has continued into the twenty-first century, though its nature, practice, and trends have varied.[14] Oral interpretation and dramatic presentation can be essential tools for a public speaker.

Alison Siewert, in *Drama Team Handbook*, describes drama as a means of expressing deep longings and great needs. She states:

[11] Herbert Sennett, *Religion and Dramatics: The Relationship between Christianity and the Theater Arts* (Lexington, KY: University Press of America, 1995), 2.

[12] Everett Robertson, *Introduction to Church Drama* (Nashville: Convention Press, 1978), 2.

[13] *American Heritage Dictionary of the English Language*, 4th ed. (Houghton Mifflin, 2009), s.v. "oral interpretation," http://encyclopedia.thefreedictionary.com/oral+interpretation (accessed 20 March 2013).

[14] Eugene and Margaret L. Bahn, *A History of Oral Interpretation* (Minneapolis: Burgess, 1970), 174.

Dramatizing our experience is an important way we understand the world. We do it subconsciously every day. Have you ever told a story? Then in some sense you've done drama, or at least you've dramatized. You've chosen particulars—details, feelings of an event—and told the story in their terms. It wasn't just a long book about clown ministry; it was an unbelievably looooong book on clown ministry. And in the last three-and-a-half seconds of the game, you didn't just make a basket: you looked left, pivoted right, reached past the guard, caught Kevin's pass . . . and got the ball off for three, a split second before the buzzer sounded. Drama describes life.[15]

Why Drama?

Now that drama has been defined, it is time to understand why drama is used in public speaking. There are times when drama or oral interpretation could enhance a message if used effectively. Dramatic performances will not strengthen every presentation, though they will add variety and vibrancy to many. Prayerfully consider the nature of drama to determine its usefulness when you speak.

There are four primary reasons to use drama:[16]

1. Drama reveals. It helps us see ourselves and suggests that life is bigger than us. It gives us a chance to see our lives differently and to say what is needed by pointing rather than explaining.

2. Drama astonishes. It helps us see God and helps us know who we are. It provides surprising insights into how we think and feel. It can create a wow-factor.

3. Drama enlarges. It exaggerates the small story into a big story for emphasis. It calls attention to daily details, easily overlooked, and teaches a related principle.

4. Drama speaks prophetically. It interprets the present in God's terms and helps us know the future in his terms. It asks hard questions and responds indirectly. It speaks generally to all, not pointing a finger at any. God speaks through drama and listeners hear his message.

I (Rhonda) have a friend who ministers through drama. Kathy Frady inspires and entertains through the character monologues she has created. She portrays women of the Bible such as King Manasseh's wife, Job's wife, Mrs. Nicodemus, and the woman at the well. She also acts out the stories of missionary women of history such as Ann Judson, Lottie Moon, and Annie Armstrong. Among her funnier, fictional characters are Bennie the hippie, Beth the blonde bombshell,

---

[15] Siewert, *Drama Team Handbook*, 15.
[16] Ibid.

and Dr. C. C. the shrink. Her creative presentations cause laughter, stir emotions, and teach truth. Drama can be used effectively in ministry.

A primary use for drama is to give the Bible life by portraying principles and introducing characters. According to Raymond Bailey and James L. Blevins, "Bible drama is revelation of His relationship with the world and His interaction with people."[17] Drama works in sermons for several reasons. First, the inductive character of drama and story bypasses obstacles that deflect persuasive discourse. An example is the biblical account of the prophet Nathan telling David a story that paralleled his own sexual immortality (2 Sam 12:1–15). A second reason for the use of drama in public speaking is the power of symbolic action. Demonstration of a Passover meal would communicate far more than a formal discourse about it. Third, drama in a message is more likely to make a lasting impression than the mere transfer of information. Portrayal of the New Testament figure Lydia dressed in purple, sitting by a river, helps an audience remember her story (Acts 16:11–15). Fourth, drama is an appropriate vehicle for Christian truth because it subordinates the messenger to the message. The actor or speaker fades into the background as the words are heard. Finally, drama is a powerful means of presenting the gospel. Demonstration can convey God's gift of grace and a believer's response by faith in a visual display that might be clearer than words.

One form of drama that can be used by any speaker is a first-person presentation. My (Rhonda) husband, Chuck, has a powerful monologue as Joseph. He gradually builds the story of Joseph's background without giving his name. The message culminates memorably with Genesis 50:20, "You planned evil against me; God planned it for good to bring about the present result—the survival of many people." A professor in our seminary presented a dramatic monologue in chapel. His opening words were heard over the sound system as he walked in from the back of the room dressed in a beard and robe. He spoke as an aging Isaiah reflecting on his life as a prophet. The dramatization captured attention, developed interest, and improved retention.

In *Show Me: Drama in Evangelism*, Matt Tullos offers five reasons why drama should be used in worship and evangelism.

1. The Escalation of Interactivity. Advances in electronic media have brought forth a multisensory experience of sound and vision. Audiences not only visualize and hear a message, they interact with the message in multidimensional formats. Drama adds dimension and interaction to public speaking.

2. The Incredible Shrinking Attention Span. As media technology has increased, the attention span of modern man has decreased. Most images are very brief, five

---

[17] Raymond Bailey and James L. Blevins, *Dramatic Monologues: Making the Bible Live* (Nashville: Baptist Sunday School Board, 1990), 8–10.

to ten seconds. Drama chunks information into small bites requiring shorter attention, while also providing multisensory stimuli to increase attention.

3. A World of Emotions. People are emotional beings, and the Bible contains vivid drama. The world, breathed into reality by a creative God, is filled with strong, provocative emotion. Drama captivates the minds, the imaginations, and the emotions of the audience.

4. The Resurgence of Spiritual Hunger. America's "lost generation" has been born and raised outside the church. They are hungry—even desperate—for a message of hope and will search anywhere for it. Drama will communicate the gospel to spiritually hungry people.

5. The Great Time Machine of Grace. Society tends to have a misconception of church people. They caricature Christians as legalistic and judgmental, hypocritical and dogmatic. Through its parabolic nature, drama can express the true nature of the body of Christ. Drama takes God's grace onto center stage.[18]

One of the most effective dramatic presentations I (Rhonda) have experienced was a theme interpretation at a women's retreat. As the hymn "Sweet Hour of Prayer" played through the speakers, a creative young woman enacted her struggle to balance her busy life with time to pray. During the verses, she rushed around to clean the house, wash the clothes, prepare a meal, and care for the baby. As the chorus sounded, she returned to a rocking chair, Bible in hand, to spend time with God in prayer. Her dramatization communicated the theme of prayer clearly and memorably.

This chapter began with the statement, "God is theatrical." The Bible is also theatrical because it reveals the drama of human life realistically. Brothers fight. Sisters argue. Mothers sacrifice. Fathers die. There is love and loyalty, gossip and jealousy, corruption and honor. The people in the Bible live as we live, suffer as we suffer, dream as we dream. Their stories bring God's truth to life in powerful, unforgettable ways. Drama is a natural vehicle for communicating biblical messages.

---

[18] Tullos, *Show Me*, 4–6.

TALKING POINT

Drama is a natural vehicle
to convey a biblical message
or illustrate a spiritual truth.

LET'S TALK ABOUT IT

1. Define *drama* and its relevance to public speaking.
2. Define and explain the history of religious drama.
3. List and explain four primary reasons to use drama.
4. What five reasons does Matt Tullos suggest for using drama in worship and evangelism?
5. How can drama be a "natural vehicle for communicating biblical messages?"

Chapter 26

HOW AND WHEN

*"To perform Scripture drama
is to present the stories of the Bible
the way they were first presented: as well-told stories."*[1]

Women were created by God as emotional and expressive beings who convey feelings verbally and nonverbally. As public speakers, women should consider using drama, oral interpretation, and other forms of creative arts to help fulfill the purpose of the message.

Dramatist Buddy Lamb suggests four categories of skits. They apply to the general use of drama. Skits may be . . .

- *inspirational*—to encourage all Christians,
- *evangelistic*—to reach the lost,
- *teaching*—to illustrate a biblical truth, or
- *just for fun*—so that listeners may relax and enjoy.[2]

Christian women are encouraged to use drama when speaking in order to inspire, witness, teach, or entertain.

Several years ago, I (Monica) used drama to present the story of Mary Magdalene. I sang a song about her, wearing a long black dress and head covering.

---

[1] Alison Siewart, *Drama Team Handbook* (Downers Grove, IL: InterVarsity, 2003), 73.
[2] Buddy Lamb, *Clown Scripts for Churches* (Nashville, TN: Convention, 1991), 5.

The dramatic expression was a powerful tool and visually conveyed the forgiveness and freedom offered by Jesus Christ. Many people approached me after the presentation, expressing appreciation for my depiction.

Speakers throughout history have struggled to communicate without getting stuck in the rut of delivery styles. Drama or oral interpretation can be incorporated to add dimension and depth to a timeless message. Creative arts can introduce God to a new audience and communicate truth in a powerful way. This chapter will explore how different dramatic forms convey meaning while also discussing when drama might be appropriately applied to public speaking.

How Is Drama Conveyed?

Many churches today use dramatic presentations in worship services or special events. Historical and biblical information can be presented dynamically through music and drama. Large productions utilizing resources of people, time, and energy are effective for evangelistic outreach and historic celebrations.

For years, preachers have included drama in sermons to create a visual image to parallel words in the message. Some churches have used drama revivals as an evangelistic strategy to involve a large group of lay people in conveying the gospel and the Christian life to people who are unchurched.[3] Drama revivals require extensive advance preparation and skilled performers, often producing positive results in attendance and public professions of faith. Church plays involving members of the congregation and/or guest artists vividly portray stories, actions, characters, dialogues, and human situations to bring new insights to biblical truths.[4] Their effectiveness depends on the audience, the event theme, and the quality of available resources.[5]

I (Monica) had the privilege of participating in an Easter drama in church for many years during high school and college. This "drama revival" was presented with the purpose of evangelizing the lost and encouraging Christians to share their faith. Hundreds of people came to the numerous performances, and many people placed their faith in Christ after watching the drama.

While many dramatic forms involve an ensemble or cast of characters, some creative expression can be conveyed by one person. A public speaker can also be a dramatist. In public settings, speakers should consider drama for creative

[3] Matt Tullos, *Show Me: Drama in Evangelism* (Nashville, TN: Convention, 1996), 37.
[4] Everett Robertson, *The Dramatic Arts in Ministry* (Nashville, TN: Convention, 1989), 22.
[5] John Lewis, Laura Andrews, and Flip Kobler, *The Complete Guide to Church Play Production* (Nashville, TN: Convention, 1997), 15.

expression. The following forms of drama can be utilized by one individual as she delivers her message.

Monologue

In the realm of communication, the word *monologue* may carry a negative connotation of a long, boring speech or a speaker who monopolizes a conversation. However, a monologue is a dramatic expression used by a public speaker. The dictionary defines a monologue as "a dramatic soliloquy (oral discourse); a continuous series of jokes or comic stories delivered by one comedian."[6] Talk show hosts on television comedies often begin the program with a monologue.

Everett Robertson writes, "The dramatic monologue involves one actor portraying one character in a crisis situation."[7] Monologues may present biblical characters, such as Ruth or Mary the mother of Jesus, or portray an inanimate object, like the manger that held baby Jesus or the alabaster jar that held the perfume used to anoint his feet. Monologues may be short or long, presented during a portion of the message or as the entire speech. Speakers may wear costumes and makeup for dramatic effect. The script may be original or taken directly from the Scripture or another text. Monologues are most effective when they reveal a truth to the audience in dramatic details.

Dramatic Reading

Dramatic reading is defined as "a public reading or recitation of a work of literature with an interpretive use of the voice and often of gestures."[8] A speaker reads aloud a poem, essay, story, or Scripture passage with animated voice, facial expression, hand gestures, and body movements. The reader portrays the dramatic, physical, and emotional aspects of a situation. If several characters or perspectives are included, the speaker may identify them with changes of voice, posture, or gesture.

Material for dramatic reading must be selected carefully. The content must have a clear focus and appropriate emotional appeal. The audience needs to identify with, understand, and enjoy the work. Delivery requires practice and timing. Careful pronunciation and phrasing as well as a rhythmical pace enhance the presentation. Facial expression, eye contact, and gestures add to the oral expression.

---

[6] *American Heritage Dictionary of the English Language*, 4th ed. (Houghton Mifflin, 2009), s.v. "monologue," www.thefreedictionary.com/monologue (accessed 13 March 2013).

[7] Robertson, *The Dramatic Arts in Ministry*, 12.

[8] *Merriam-Webster Dictionary* (Merriam-Webster, Incorporated, 2013), s.v. "dramatic reading," www.merriam-webster.com/dictionary/dramatic reading (accessed on 13 March 2013).

Storytelling

Storytelling one of the oldest forms of drama, is "reciting tales or relating anecdotes in a captivating manner."[9] While a monologue involves a character directly, storytelling includes the character indirectly. Storytelling is typically spoken in second person, and monologue is first person. Vivid description and animated expression is a part. A real account is often exaggerated and amplified for effect. Robertson encourages the storyteller to "use every possible technique to communicate the story creatively."[10]

I (Rhonda) have two friends who have ministries of storytelling. Gwen Williams ("Miz Chocolate") writes and presents stories about real life to inspire and encourage children, youth, and adults in their faith. Becky Brown describes herself as a "song tailor and word weaver." Through her ministry, Little Brown Light, she writes and shares stories as well as songs and Bible studies to challenge Christians to live the abundant life.

Object Lesson

For years, teachers and speakers have displayed inanimate objects to explain a lesson with dramatic effect. Visual aids are helpful to most listeners. They enhance a narrative, facilitating comprehension and identity. In delivery, the speaker should carefully connect the object and the idea. Creative interaction with the audience and object may foster application.

Sermons for children often include objects. I (Rhonda) have also seen women demonstrate object lessons in teaching and speaking. One friend shares her personal testimony with four different shoes. She lines them up on the podium, holding each shoe as she describes her faith journey during each stage of life. A baby shoe represents the Christian home of her infancy. A saddle-oxford reflects her personal conversion during childhood. A tennis shoe symbolizes her commitment to ministry in her adolescence. A high-heel indicates her spiritual growth in adulthood. The objects visually embellish her verbal testimony.

Role Play

Role play is a form of drama used successfully in many areas of ministry as well as in public speaking. It is "representing in action the thoughts and feelings of another person"[11] During a message, a speaker may pause in her own discourse to

---

[9] *Merriam-Webster Dictionary* (Merriam-Webster, Incorporated, 2013), s.v. "storytelling," www.merriam-webster.com/dictionary/storytelling (accessed on 13 March 2013).

[10] Robertson, *The Dramatic Arts in Ministry*, 21.

[11] *Merriam-Webster Dictionary* (Merriam-Webster, Incorporated, 2013), s.v. "public speaking," http://www.merriam-webster.com/dictionary/public+speaking (accessed 13 March 2013).

assume the position of another person in order to emphasize or clarify a point. In teaching or training, role play may be used to demonstrate different responses or simulate varied emotions. Role playing is a creative and revealing way to present a range of emotions, values, and beliefs without threatening the audience.

Two classes that I (Rhonda) teach in our Women's Ministry Program use role play to instruct. In "Support Groups for Women," I take on the role of a group leader or participant to demonstrate group dynamics. In "Lay Counseling for Women," I assume the viewpoint of a counselor or counselee to teach the importance of peer ministry. At times, members of the class may be invited to participate in the role play. This helps me to teach key principles.

I (Monica) often use role play in the "Evangelism and Christian Life" course I teach to university students. I assume the role of a lost person as well as a Christian who is witnessing to the lost person. My goal is demonstrating witness strategies to the class. I have the students role play witness encounters to apply the principles personally. Role play has proved to be a very powerful method in teaching others how to share their faith.

Pantomime

One of the most creative forms of drama is pantomime, the process of silent expression. It is "conveying a story by bodily action or facial movements only."[12] The term *mime* may refer to the performer, though it usually refers to the more formal, classical discipline. Marcel Marceau was the famous French mime who introduced the art form to the world stage. Dick Van Dyke premiered pantomime on one of his earliest television shows as humorous, physical comedy. Pantomime communicates visually what cannot be communicated as creatively with words.

Pantomime may be used by speakers as a means of visually expressing specific actions and traits. According to Robertson, "It involves a universal language of gestures which is understood by all cultures and ages."[13] It can be serious or humorous and is often performed to music. Costumes and makeup may be worn. The audience often relates personally to the movements and emotions of the mime.

For years Christian performer Tommy Toombs has used pantomime as well as magic, juggling, and comedy in ministry. He shares his personal testimony, Bible passages, and song lyrics without saying any words. I (Rhonda) remember

---

[12] *Merriam-Webster Dictionary* (Merriam-Webster, Incorporated, 2013), s.v. "pantomime," http://www.merriam-webster.com/dictionary/pantomime (accessed 13 March 2013).

[13] Robertson, *The Dramatic Arts in Ministry*, 12.

his powerful pantomime to the song, "People Need the Lord." Through movements and expressions, he interprets the meaning of the song creatively.

Clowning

Clowns are known for entertaining in circuses and rodeos, but they can also be found ministering in churches and communities. By definition, clowning is "entertainment by jokes, antics, or tricks in a public presentation."[14] Christian clowning communicates biblical truths in a creative, nonthreatening form, often in evangelistic outreach. "A Christian dressed as a clown breaks through many of the barriers placed by the secular world against religion. The joyful nature of the clown also makes it easy to tell others about the joy and colorfulness of Christ."[15]

My (Monica) family has a dear friend with a clown ministry. She takes her ministry very seriously, using it as an opportunity to bring joy to others and present the gospel. She is very skilled and effective in her humorous presentations. Children especially love clowns and may be more apt to listen to what a clown says. Clowning is an excellent evangelistic tool to reach children and others for Christ.

One speaker can communicate a message through clowning. Some churches or Christian groups have developed clown ministries to convey the gospel and biblical truths or to promote activities and entertain. Clowning appeals to all ages. A primary purpose of clowning is to present truth in an exciting, exaggerated fashion. Robertson concludes, "Audiences laugh at the actions of the clown and see truth in themselves. A Christ-centered clown ministry can be a powerful tool in the ministry of a church."[16]

I (Rhonda) grew up watching the ventriloquist Shari Lewis and her puppet Lamb Chop on television. She sang and talked as herself and as Lamb Chop. A ventriloquist is one who is skilled at "producing voice in such a way that it seems to come from another source; an apparent conversation with a hand-manipulated dummy."[17] There are some Christian ventriloquists today, including Jacki Manna of Orlando, Florida. She projects her voice through Cowboy Eddie and Jo Jo Bean to entertain, educate, and engage the audience. Though few speakers can develop the skill of ventriloquism, it is an entertaining form of drama appropriate for some individuals.

---

[14] *American Heritage Dictionary of the English Language*, 4th ed. (Houghton Mifflin, 2009), s.v. "clowning," www.thefreedictionary.com/clowning (accessed 13 March 2013).

[15] Robertson, *The Dramatic Arts in Ministry*, 15.

[16] Ibid., 15.

[17] *Merriam-Webster Dictionary* (Merriam-Webster, Incorporated, 2013), s.v. "ventriloquist," http://www.merriam-webster.com/dictionary/ventriloquist (accessed on 13 March 2013).

Small groups of people may perform other types of drama such as dialogue, plays, skits, puppetry, dramatic improvisation, and drama games. Many different arts are helpful for communicating a message creatively. Every public speaker should develop creativity and prayerfully consider using drama to convey biblical messages and teach spiritual principles.

When Is Drama Appropriate?

Drama is not always appropriate, but when it is, it can effectively communicate the message in a dynamic method. Some biblical stories and themes lend themselves to dramatic interpretation. Some audiences seem more open to the Word of God communicated dramatically. Some occasions call for something extra like drama. Some speakers are more comfortable and experienced with drama than others. The preparation of every inspirational message, Bible study, or personal testimony should include development of nonverbal communication including the possibility of drama.

Live performances, including public speeches, provide an ideal arena for dramatic expression. Throughout history, people have related stories and presented information creatively. In fact, the Bible was recited passionately to communicate its lasting message to people in the days before the printing press. Oral proclamation of Scripture was interactive and diachronic, involving the speaker/performer and the audience. Drama and church are communal, connecting a group of people. Dramatic expression in a church setting is "an opportunity to see, experience, and feel the story with other people."[18] While video, recorded music, and electronic media can be effective means of communication, drama focuses on a live performer interacting with the audience in real time. Though rehearsed and staged, drama creates a spontaneous connection that is dynamic and memorable.

Live performances can be combined with media presentations to build up the theme of the message. Years ago, I (Rhonda) attended a statewide youth conference with my husband. As Chuck and I entered the large convention center before the service, hundreds of teenagers were jumping into the air for "rapture practice." It was a memorable sight. Later in the program, there was a dramatic reading of Matthew 24:36–41.

> Now concerning that day and hour no one knows—neither the angels in heaven, nor the Son—except the Father only . . . Two men will be in the field: one will be taken and the other left. Two women will be grinding at

---

[18] Siewert, *Drama Team Handbook*, 16.

the mill: one will be taken and one left. Therefore be alert, since you don't know what day your Lord is coming.

After the reading, a video was projected on a large screen. In the film a teenage boy was working on his car when he disappeared suddenly, leaving only his clothes on the ground. A young girl was washing dishes when she disappeared suddenly, leaving behind only her clothes. Several other teens were engaged in typical, daily activities when they were taken away suddenly in the rapture. As the video ended, the speaker challenged the young audience: "Be alert, be ready, you do not know when the Lord will return." Then he led the large gathering in rapture practice, jumping in the air to meet Jesus. The combination of dramatic forms involving the speaker and the audience added power and relevance to the message.

Drama may be appropriately employed in various settings: worship services, corporate gatherings, Bible studies, outreach events, banquets, retreats, or fellowships. In a worship service, a pantomime could be enacted to introduce a new sermon series. In a corporate gathering such as a women's conference, a skit could be presented to introduce a theme. A Bible study could begin with the dramatic reading of a focal Scripture. An outreach event could employ an object lesson to share the gospel. A banquet could begin with a monologue to portray a biblical character dramatically. A retreat could introduce a humorous character who would later present a brief vignette in each session through clowning. A fellowship could involve a storyteller to dramatize a parable from Scripture. These and many other dramatic forms are recommended in a variety of public speaking contexts.

Creative expression is also effective in publicity and promotion. Some announcements need the unique appeal and creative energy of drama to capture attention and motivate participation. Drama breaks the routine, helps people to visualize information, and conveys passion for a ministry or event. Any form of dramatic expression could be used for publicity purposes, though monologue, storytelling, object lessons, and pantomime might work most naturally. Individuals who have interest in drama could be personally involved in promotion when not involved in other areas of ministry.

My (Rhonda) friend, Christi, created a fictional character named "Fleur de Church Lady" to make women's ministry announcements for our church. Dressed in bright colors and a bouffant wig, she walked from the back of the church to the platform talking enthusiastically with the ladies about the upcoming special event. She captured attention and created interest in a unique manner. Occasionally, Fleur returns to church to make announcements in a fun, fresh way to an audience filled with anticipation.

Drama may be presented across cultures, whether in this country or abroad. Often actions and expressions have no language barriers though cultures may have different performance traditions. Some dramatic forms, such as pantomime or storytelling, may translate a message cross-culturally more clearly than spoken words alone. For many people rooted in a dominant culture, drama and other arts may be the only way they can see or hear the message. Dramatic expression nurtures a variety of cultural expressions from the stage.

Dramatization can also help an audience relate to other cultures. A foreign missionary presented a monologue to a women's conference. She spoke as a Muslim woman dressed in a traditional robe and head covering. Her first-person testimony and authentic appearance connected one culture with an audience from another culture. As a result, the participants better understood how to pray for Muslim women.

Dramatic expression helps the audience experience the message "in ways that impact, startle, renew, energize, anger, help, pester, move, and surprise. The task of drama is not only to say what is said, but to wake it up, make it fresh, let it grow."[19] Through drama, church members who have heard sermons and Bible lessons for years can hear truth in an innovative way. Visitors who are new to worship services will be intrigued and will experience the Bible coming to life. God's Word and his work can be portrayed effectively in a variety of dramatic forms. Siewert wrote, "To perform Scripture drama is to present the stories of the Bible the way they were first presented: as well-told stories."[20]

Public speakers, teachers, and preachers should consider using drama to communicate a biblical message. Though additional time is necessary for preparation, the creative delivery will offer deeper and more meaningful expression to the audience. Dramatic delivery requires a thorough understanding of the Scripture context and biblical character. The central point must be communicated verbally and visually. The voice must project the writer's or the character's perspective. Tension between the expected and the unexpected needs to be balanced, and the ending should focus on personal application of the intended biblical truth. Dramatic interpretation of Scripture can give "a fresh view and a sense of what's going on that cannot be communicated by someone reading the passage straight out."[21]

All forms of drama have a place in public speaking. When prepared thoroughly and delivered creatively, drama communicates the message and conveys the emotion of the speaker more descriptively than words alone. The audience typically gives attention, sustains interest, recalls information, and continues motivation when verbal presentation is augmented with dramatic expression.

---

[19] Ibid., 16.
[20] Ibid., 73.
[21] Ibid., 80.

TALKING POINT

God's Word and his work can be portrayed effectively
in a variety of dramatic forms.

LET'S TALK ABOUT IT

1. Describe the four types of dramas and their purposes as suggested by Buddy Lamb.
2. List six forms of drama that can be utilized by one individual in the delivery of a message.
3. When is drama appropriate?
4. Which of the six forms of drama have you personally utilized? Did you feel the inclusion of drama improved your message? Explain.
5. What does dramatic delivery require?

Chapter 27

ADVANTAGES AND DISADVANTAGES

*"A listener experiences the message through drama
like a traveler experiences the Bible on a trip to Israel—
the Bible comes to life."
(Chuck Kelley)*

This section has addressed drama as nonverbal communication in public speaking. The purpose of the discussion has been to challenge Christian speakers to utilize different forms of drama to improve communication. While professional performers have skills in the creative arts, all speakers can develop dramatic elements. The key to drama is that it must be done well. This chapter will contrast some advantages and disadvantages of drama and oral interpretation in public presentations.

My (Rhonda) husband spoke for a youth event in a statewide gathering. Before he spoke, a parade of individuals and groups performed songs, speeches, and skits. The last act, which took the stage about an hour-and-a-half later, was a drama depicting the crucifixion of Jesus. As the actors portrayed Jesus being nailed to the cross, one cast member roamed aimlessly around the stage like a lost sheep weakly bleating "baa." The teens in the audience began to laugh, even though the scene was somber. It was poorly used humor, poorly performed, and poorly timed. It did not help that the audience had been seated for so long in hard metal chairs. That was a challenging act for my husband to follow, though he transitioned into a powerful message. It is not always wise to use drama. Both

275

its advantages and disadvantages should be considered before a speaker chooses to use it.

Advantages of Drama

There are definite advantages for the use of drama in public speaking. The audience benefits from dramatic presentations in several specific ways.

- Drama adds variety, increasing attention.
- It reaches different people: children, youth, the hearing impaired, and the unchurched.
- It draws people into the message. Emotions, language, memory, and imaginations are stimulated.
- It brings Scripture to life, allowing people to "see" the Word in a different light and make application in a personal way.

Jeannette Clift George is a Christian actress in Houston, Texas. She performs with her dramatic troupe, the A. D. Players, and is a frequent speaker and dramatist. In the 1980s, I (Rhonda) had the privilege of seeing her perform a monologue of Corrie ten Boom, an inspiring character she first portrayed in the movie "The Hiding Place." She skillfully presented the story of the courageous young woman who, along with her family, hid Jewish people in their home during the Nazi invasion of Holland during World War II. After capture, Corrie and her sister suffered torture in a concentration camp. She survived, devoting her life to writing and speaking about God's love that overcomes all circumstances. George's dramatic monologue of Corrie ten Boom has preserved the influence of a great woman of God.

As a little girl, I (Monica) attended a retreat with my mother where an older lady depicted the life of Lottie Moon. Although I was very young, the monologue left a lasting impression on me, giving me a deeper, more personal knowledge of the missionary's life. I thought to myself, *This is how she really lived.*

The speaker also benefits from creative expression.

- It adds variety—presenters are inspired and challenged by different modes of delivery.
- It expands a person's speaking repertoire—dramatic expression offers creative growth and professional development.
- It provides another method for presenting Scripture—oral interpretation strengthens the proclamation of God's Word.

As the Bible states, Christians are to be diligent in correctly teaching the word of truth (2 Tim 2:15).

My (Rhonda) husband has experienced the advantages of drama through creating a monologue of King David. As he studied the extensive text of Scripture in 1 Samuel and 2 Samuel, he found the narrative flowed conversationally. His preparation focused on the details of David's life, and his delivery was dramatic. Chuck identified several advantages of his monologue. He was able to summarize a large portion of Scripture in a short period of time. He could develop a recurring theme: "I am who I never dreamed I would be." He enjoyed the diversion from standard sermon delivery, though the performance was exhausting physically and emotionally. The audience was able to experience the emotional impact plus intellectual understanding and hear a familiar story presented through a fresh method. Chuck summarized the benefits of dramatic expression: "A listener experiences the message through drama like a traveler experiences the Bible on a trip to Israel—the Bible comes to life."

Disadvantages of Drama

There are some disadvantages of using drama in public speaking. Both the audience and the speaker may struggle with creativity in communication. When taken to the extreme, any of the following factors can negate the effectiveness of the dramatic arts in public speaking.

Overuse—Drama should only be used occasionally as a special feature.

Mediocrity—If used, drama should be well done. The only thing worse than no drama is bad drama. "Bathrobe drama" is the term for bad drama performed by untrained people using ideas and materials at hand.

Overspending—Expenses for dramatic productions mount rapidly. Avoid exceeding the budget and causing financial pressure.

Shock Factor—Dramatization should be used in good taste to avoid making the audience uncomfortable. Shock usually detracts from the message.

Special Effects—Bells and whistles as well as props and noisemakers should be used to enhance drama, not distract from the message.

Embellishment—Drama should not alter the Scripture text or overstate the message. The truth should be creatively but accurately presented.

Manipulation—Emotions are a part of well-done drama. Healthy expression of feelings rather than extreme emotional control is recommended.

Camouflage—The point of the message must be clear through the drama, not lost in the creative expression.

Mismatch—The type of drama should be appropriate for the audience. Know the crowd and select drama for it.

Beware of these risks of dramatic expression. Adhere to the cautions and benefit from the advantages of drama.

Resources for Drama

One of the advantages of dramatic expression is the availability of resources. There are many reference books, Internet Web sites, and professional organizations for the dramatic arts. The most important resources for Christian drama are the Bible and life experience. The following resources for drama are helpful also. They offer general information as well as scripts, training, and networking.

Books (see the bibliography for complete details)

- *Actors Not Included: The Complete Works of Matt Tullos* by Matt Tullos
- *Art for God's Sake* by Philip Graham Ryken
- *Christian Playwriting and Self-Publishing* by Cleveland O. McLeish
- *The Complete Guide to Church Play Production* by John Lewis and others
- *Create a Drama Ministry* by Paul Miller
- *Developing the Church Drama Ministry* by Paul Miller
- *Devoted Through Drama: Monologues, Plays, and Skits for Christian Youth Groups* by Kimberly Smiley
- *Drama: Church Drama for Church Folks* by Barbara Dudley
- *Drama Ministry* by Steve Pederson
- *Drama Team Handbook* by Alison Siewert and others
- *The Dramatic Arts in Ministry* by Everett Robertson
- *Incorporating Drama in Worship* by Mike Gray
- *Producing and Directing Drama for the Church* by Robert Rucker
- *Show Me: Drama in Evangelism* by Matt Tullos
- *The Worship Drama Library*, volumes 1–14 by various authors

Many children's books and classic works of literature provide excellent scripts for drama.

Web sites

- *Christian Drama Resources* (www.christiandramaresources.com)
- *Christian Plays* (www.christplay.com)
- *Creative Pastors with Ed Young* (www.creativepastors.com)
- *Drama Share: Your Christian Drama Resource Center* (www.dramashare.org)

- *Online Journal of Christian Communication and Culture* (www.ojccc.org)
- *Wordspring Creative Resources* (www.wordspring.com)

These drama Web sites were active at the time of publication. Other Web sites may be developed to provide resources for different forms of drama.

Organizations

- *Christian Artists Network* (www.christianartists-network.org)
- *Christian Creative Arts Association* (www.christian-creative-arts -association.com)
- *Christian Performing Artists' Fellowship*—CPAF (www.christian performingart.org)
- *Christians in the Theatre Arts*—CITA (www.cita.org)
- *Christians in the Visual Arts*—CIVA (www.civa.org)
- *Church and Art Network* (www.churchandart.com)
- *Fellowship for the Performing Arts*—FPA (www. screwtapeonstage.com)
- *The Worship Arts Involvement* (www.theworshiparts.com)

In 1997 the Christian Dramatists of Southern Baptists was organized to represent all disciplines of the dramatic arts. The association involved Christian artists in drama, puppetry, clowning, mime, and interpretive movement. Its purpose was "to promote the dramatic arts in ministry and to provide information on new products, training events, and other resources for dramatic artists."[1] The association's initial newsletter was received by about 10,000 people whose names were on state Baptist convention drama lists.

The group has continued to network and meet through the years, occasionally hosting National Creative Arts Festivals. LifeWay Christian Resources of the Southern Baptist Convention and several state Baptist conventions have employed drama consultants through the years. Matt Tullos served with LifeWay for many years in several capacities including creative arts. Currently, he provides resources and support for pastors, worship leaders, teachers, and speakers through his itinerant ministry. He challenges Christian platform personalities to "augment the message you communicate so the audience will not just *know* the message but *feel* the message. Create a memory as you proclaim the gospel to this multisensory generation."[2]

---

[1] *Baptist Press* (2013) "Christian dramatists form new association," http://bpnews.net/ bpnews.asp?id=4819 (accessed on 20 March 2013).

[2] *Wordspring Creative Resources*, http://www.wordspring.com/?page_id=1416 (accessed 20 March 2013).

Drama and the creative arts have been a part of the church for centuries. In New Testament times, the church led the culture in developing the arts, specifically drama.[3] Though banned from the church at times, the dramatic arts have been powerful tools in worship when used appropriately. Dramatic arts in ministry today can reach the lost world with the gospel and the saved followers of Christ through discipleship. According to David Taylor, "Our emotions, bodies, and imaginations have a vital role, and the arts serve to bring them into an intentional and intensive participation."[4]

In the article, "Discipling the Eyes Through Art in Worship," Taylor concludes that the arts can play a powerful role in worship. He cites five ways that the arts influence a worshiper:

1. *Theologically*—beliefs about God and the Bible
2. *Morally*—convictions about right and wrong, standards of acceptable behavior
3. *Missionally*—efforts to share Christ and minister to the needs of the peoples of the world
4. *Didactically*—instructions and lessons of the Christian faith
5. *Symbolically*—visual images of abstract biblical teachings to enhance understanding[5]

Because drama is a powerful medium of communication, public speakers should consider including it in presentations when appropriate.

While there are few Christian dramatic arts associations today and few evangelical seminaries offer a Master of Communication Arts degree, the pursuit of the creative arts is encouraged. Christian speakers and dramatists need training and resources to use drama effectively in the ministry. The future of dramatic arts in the Christian arena is promising.

The Bible teaches that all people were created by God. He is the potter; we are the clay (Rom 9:20–24). He has a specific purpose for each of his creations. A child of God has no right to ask the Creator, "Why did you make me like this?"

---

[3] Julie W, "A Biblical Perspective of Drama in Ministry," *Online Journal of Christian Communication and Culture*, entry posted December 11, 2011, http://www.ojccc.org/2011/12/a-biblical-perspective-of-drama-in-ministry (accessed March 20, 2013).

[4] David Taylor, "Discipling the Eyes Through Art in Worship," *Christianity Today* (2013), http://www.christianitytoday.com/ct/2012/april/art-in-worship.html (accessed 20 March 2013).

[5] Ibid.

(v. 20). God intends the objects of his creation to bring glory to him. God is constantly at work, shaping his human creations in his image, to fulfill his purpose. God works in the lives of speakers and teachers, reshaping the human vessels into a particular design. Drama and oral interpretation may be artistic tools used by the Master Potter to refine his vessels. Let God do a divinely creative work in your life and speaking ministry through drama and oral interpretation.

TALKING POINT

Drama and oral interpretation may be artistic tools
of the Master Potter to refine his vessels.

LET'S TALK ABOUT IT

1. What is the key to an effective dramatic presentation?
2. List some of the advantages of drama in public speaking.
3. List and describe eight factors that might negate the effectiveness of drama in public speaking.
4. In what ways might you implement drama and oral interpretation in your personal speaking ministry?
5. What are some resources pertaining to drama that can help your speaking ministry?

CONCLUSION

The first words of this book, talking was identified as a spiritual gift. God created every man and woman to communicate thoughts and feelings verbally and nonverbally. Each Christian is responsible for developing the skill of communication and using the gift of talking for ministry to others. Talking connects hearts and minds.

This book has provided general principles about communication and specific information about public speaking to enhance the teaching and speaking ministries of the readers. We have discussed interpersonal, verbal, and nonverbal communication. Topics have included gender communication and listening, speech preparation and delivery, observation and follow-up, gestures and facial expression, appearance and clothing, and drama and interpretation as they apply to public speaking. A strong foundation has been presented to improve speaking abilities.

Remember what you have read and apply these principles whenever you have an opportunity to speak.

1. *Do* your best in every speaking situation.
2. *Do* continue to work on your speaking and listening skills.
3. *Do* stick with what you do well.
4. *Do* listen to other speakers.
5. *Do* keep in mind that the speaker is always on stage.
6. *Do* ask individuals what they learned, and listen to them.
7. *Do* make a check-list of what you need to have with you.
8. *Do* know it is not what you say but what they hear that counts.
9. *Do* be flexible and adapt to the speaking context.
10. *Do* affirm other speakers on the program publicly.

Try not to make these mistakes in public speaking.

1. *Don't* start with apologies or excuses.
2. *Don't* be too adamant in your opinions.

3. *Don't* say "you know" or ask "OK?"
4. *Don't* forget to pronounce all your speech sounds clearly.
5. *Don't* strain to be too funny.
6. *Don't* give opportunities for negative attitudes to develop.
7. *Don't* sigh or laugh at your own humor.
8. *Don't* jump to conclusions or make assumptions.
9. *Don't* assume listeners know denominational jargon or labels.
10. *Don't* put personal needs before those of others.

Though you will never be a perfect speaker, you can always improve your public speaking skills. God desires and deserves your best in personal communication as well as public speaking. He can minister through you in a more powerful way when you are trained and equipped. If practice makes perfect, then keep practicing your speech. Let your talking be a gift of God's love to others!

Glossary of Terms

accent—the characteristic pronunciation of a particular geographical region; distinctive pronunciation of a specific nation, locality, or social class.

articulate— to utter clearly.

articulation—shaping or forming sounds when speaking vowels and consonants.

conductive hearing loss—temporary hearing loss that occurs when sound is not conducted efficiently through the outer ear canal to the eardrum and the tiny bones of the middle ear most often due to fluid.

criticism—an act of passing judgment as to the merits of anything (usually involves finding fault).

critique—a serious examination and judgment of something (constructive criticism is always appreciated).

dialect—the local characteristics of speech that deviate from standard speech; language use—including vocabulary, grammar, and pronunciation—unique to a particular group or region.

diction—enunciation or delivery of words and phrases in speaking or singing; the speech sound quality of a speaker.

elocution—the art of public speaking; the study of formal communication dating back for centuries.

enunciate—to pronounce with clarity.

enunciation—the crispness and precision with which you form words.

ethos—from the Greek word "character"; refers to the trustworthiness or credibility of the speaker.

exegesis—the procedure one follows in Bible study to discover the Holy Spirit's intent in a Bible passage.

exposition—the process of laying open a biblical text in such a way that its original meaning is clearly understood by others.

extemporaneous speech—a speech prepared in advance and presented from abbreviated notes.

genderflex—an active process to temporarily use communication behavior typical of the other gender in order to increase potential for clear understanding.

genderlect—a variety of speech or conversational style used by a particular gender; the language of the sexes.

hermeneutics—the science of interpreting what a passage of Scripture means; hearing and correctly understanding what God says in his Word.

homiletics—the art and science of saying the same thing that the text of Scripture says.

impromptu speech—a speech delivered on the spur of the moment without preparation; speaking off the cuff or from the top of the head.

interpersonal communication—communication with other persons, including person to person (talking to individuals, one to one), small groups (talking to a few people at a time), and person to persons (public speaking to a larger group).

intrapersonal communication—communication that occurs throughout the day when an individual talks with herself during daily tasks.

logos—from the Greek term for "word"; refers to the reasoning or clarity of the speaker.

manuscript speech—a speech written out word-for-word beforehand and read word-for-word from a script or teleprompter.

memorized speech—a speech written out beforehand and memorized word-for-word then quoted for memory by the speaker without notes.

mixed hearing loss—hearing loss caused by damage in the outer or middle ear as well as in the inner ear or auditory nerve.

nonverbal communication—communication with actions—body movements, posture, positioning, gestures, facial expression, eye contact, and tone that accompany words to explain or emphasize the meaning of the message.

objective—something toward which effort is directed; an aim, goal, or end of action; a position to be attained or a purpose to be achieved.

oral communication—verbal communication including intrapersonal, interpersonal, and nonverbal communication.

pathos—from the Greek word for "suffering" or "experience;" refers to the emotional appeal or passion of the speaker.

pronounce—to produce a speech sound or word.

pronunciation—the ability to utter speech that is intelligible.

proxemics—the study of the nature, degree, and effect of the spatial separation individuals maintain in social and interpersonal situations.

sensorineural hearing loss—permanent hearing loss that occurs when there is damage to the inner ear (cochlea) or to the nerve pathways from the inner ear to the brain.

supportive material—information provided from a variety of sources that will strengthen the points of the speech.

testimony—expression of personal convictions or citation of the opinions of others that add weight or impressiveness to an idea.

theme—a topic of discourse or discussion, a subject of artistic representation, an implicit or recurrent idea.

voice—sounds produced from vibrations of the vocal cords.

Appendix A
Speech and Voice Exercises

Diction/Articulation

Goal: Minimum tension and maximum articulation; use correct articulatory posture to promote intelligibility.

1. <u>Rapid syllable drill</u>
   pu, tu, ku—putuku; buttercup

2. <u>Consonant drills (by placement—consonant followed by long vowel sounds)</u>
   a. Bilabials (two lips)

May	Me	My	Mo	Mu
Pay	Pe	Py	Po	Pu
Bay	Be	By	Bo	Bu
Way	We	Wy	Wo	Wu

   b. Labiodentals (lip-teeth)

Fay	Fe	Fy	Fo	Fu
Vay	Ve	Vy	Vo	Vu

   c. Linguadentals (tongue-teeth)
   Th- (voiceless as in "think")

Thay	The	Thy	Tho	Thu

   Th+ (voiced as in "them")

<u>Thay</u>	<u>The</u>	<u>Thy</u>	<u>Tho</u>	<u>Thu</u>

   d. Lingua–alveolars (tongue-against upper teeth)

Tay	Te	Ty	To	Tu
Day	De	Dy	Do	Du
Nay	Ne	Ny	No	Nu
Lay	Le	Ly	Lo	Lu

e.   Lingua–palatals (tongue-roof of mouth)

Chay	Che	Chy	Cho	Chu
Jay	Je	Jy	Jo	Ju
Shay	She	Shy	Sho	Shu
Zhay	Zhe	Zhy	Zho	Zhu
Ray	Re	Ry	Ro	Ru

f.   Lingua–velars (tongue-soft palate)

Kay	Ke	Ky	Ko	Ku
Gay	Ge	Gy	Go	Gu
NGay	NGe	NGy	NGo	NGu

g.   Glottal (larynx)

Hay	He	Hy	Ho	Hu

3.   <u>Vocal Drills</u>

    a.   Say the following sounds and words, going down the columns.

EE	PEEL	BEET	MEET
IH	PILL	BIT	MIT
EH	PELL	BET	MET
AH	PAL	BAT	MAT
AW	PAUL	BOUGHT	MOTT
UH	PULL	BUT	MUTT
O	POLE	BOAT	MOAT
OO	POOL	BOOT	MOOT

    b.   "eh" and "ih" —go down the columns.

LED–LID	PEN–PIN
MET–MITT	HEAD–HID
BET–BIT	HEM–HIM
PET–PIT	BEN–BIN

    c.   Dipthongs—go down the columns.

<u>O</u>	<u>AY</u>	<u>OW</u>	<u>Y</u>	<u>OI</u>	<u>EW</u>
COKE	CAKE	COW	KITE	COIN	CUE
NO	NAIL	NOW	NIGHT	NOISE	NEW
DON'T	DAY	DOWN	DIE	DOILY	DEW
BROKE	BRAID	BROWN	BRIGHT	BROIL	BREW

4. <u>Sentence Drill (includes most consonant and vowel sounds)</u>
   We brought my father two new sunlamps.
   You should choose a red coat hanger.

Breathing/Relaxation

Goal: Adequate air supply to produce speech, controlled flow of air, coordination of breathing and speaking.

1. Hand on abdomen. Breathe deeply—in through nose, out through mouth.

2. Deep breath, hold these sounds as long as you can: ah, ee, sss.

3. Deep breath, blow slowly through a straw until all air is gone. Use a small straw to limit, slow air flow.

4. Yawn–sigh. Yawn while breathing in, sigh while breathing out.

5. Sip–hiss. Take in four short sipping breaths and let out four short hissing breaths.

Pitch/Inflection

Goal: Establish vocal flexibility, use of optimum pitch, varied pitch range.

1. Find your optimum pitch range. Take a small breath in, exhale saying "ah ha" naturally to indicate natural range. Midpoint is optimum pitch level.

2. Speak the alphabet beginning with your lowest pitch and continuing until your highest pitch.

3. Read these phrases using high pitch then low pitch. Reverse the order.

<u>High</u>	<u>Low</u>	<u>Low</u>	<u>High</u>
Not	now.	Not	now.
Since	when.	Since	when.
No	good.	No	good.
Right	now.	Right	now.
Why	not?	Why	not?
At	once.	At	once.
Stay	put.	Stay	put.

4. Use varied pitch to express the emotions listed below. Say "ah" with appropriate expression.

Sadness	Disgust
Surprise	Sympathy
Anger	Love
Happiness	Doubt
Fear	Boredom

Volume/Projection

Goal: Replace volume (loudness) with projection (voice that is supported and carries).

1. Heel-Toe Bounces
    Stand on your toes and then drop to your heels as you maintain an "ah" sound. Gravity helps project tone.

2. Chair Pulls
    Sit in a chair and pull up on it as you maintain "ah" as long as you can.

3. Chair Pushes
    Push down on the chair as you maintain "ah."

4. Hand Clasps
    Clasp your finger tips together with your elbows outstretched. Try to pull your arms apart while saying "ah."

5. Tummy Flows
    Take a breath in through the mouth and breathe out as you say A-B-C-D, flowing each letter into the next as though saying one word. Do not break the air flow. Continue four letters at a time.

Appendix B
Specific Suggestions for Voice Care

1. Avoid excessively loud volume, especially screaming or shouting. Speak only when at arm's reach of the other person.
2. Avoid abrupt bursts in speaking. Use a relaxed effort.
3. Limit throat clearing and coughing, which irritate the vocal cords.
4. Drink several (6-8) glasses of water a day, especially when taking decongestants.
5. Decrease caffeinated beverages, which dry out the vocal cords.
6. Rest the voice if the throat is infected or if hoarseness persists.
7. Avoid eating milk products (ice cream, yogurt, cheese) before speaking. Dairy products coat the vocal cords and increase phlegm or mucus.
8. To decrease the possibility of reflux of stomach acid avoid eating just before going to bed.
9. Vary the pitch of the voice; however, avoid extreme high pitch and extreme low pitch.
10. See a doctor if hoarseness or throat pain persists.

APPENDIX C
SPEECH EVALUATION FORM

Speaker's Name _____

Speech Topic _____

Rate the speaker on each point: *Needs Improvement*   *Excellent*

1. **<u>Appearance</u>**   1   2   3   4   5
   Neatness
   Appropriateness

2. **<u>Vocal Parameters</u>**   1   2   3   4   5
   Pitch
   Loudness
   Quality

3. **<u>Speech Skills</u>**   1   2   3   4   5
   Rate of Speech
   Articulation
   Grammar

4. **<u>Body Language</u>**   1   2   3   4   5
   Facial Expression
   Gestures
   Eye Contact
   Posture

5. **Speech Content**   1   2   3   4   5
    Outline/Organization
    Supportive Material
    Introduction
    Body
    Conclusion

6. **Other**   1   2   3   4   5
    Presentation Materials
    Timing (__min.,___sec.)

What did the speaker do most effectively? _____

_____

_____

What should the speaker work on to improve speaking? _____

_____

_____

General Comments: _____

_____

_____

_____

_____

_____

_____

_____

_____

"Speak the truth in a spirit of love" (Eph 4:15).

_____

Evaluator's Name

Appendix D
Resources and Organizations

Organizations

- *American Speech-Language-Hearing Association* (http://www.asha.org)
  Connects professionals in the field of speech-language pathology and audiology for credentialing and training.
- *National Speakers Association* (http://www.nsaspeaker.org)
  Seeks to advance speakers eloquence, expertise, enterprise, and ethics in the professional speaking field.
- *National Communication Association* (http://www.natcom.org)
  Aids people with an interest in the field of communication through research and teaching resources.
- *POWERtalk International* (http://powertalkinternational.com)
  Trains members through public speaking clubs in countries worldwide.
- *World Speakers Association* (http://speakersassociation.org/WorldSpeakers Association.html) Assists in building successful professional speaking businesses through an international association.

Speaker Services

- *American Program Bureau* (http://www.apbspeakers.com)
  Provides professional speakers and training consultants for events held worldwide.
- *Christian Speakers Services* (http://www.christianspeakersservices.com)
  Helps Christian speakers find platforms to share their messages around the world.
- *CLASServices* (http://www.classervices.com)
  Equips Christian communicators in the arenas of speaking and writing through training workshops and speaker services.
- *Next Step Speaker Services* (http://www.nextstepspeakerservices.org)
  Helps develop the speaking and communication skills of women for Christian ministry.

- *Speak Up Speaker Services* (http://www.speakupspeakerservices.com)
  Supplies speakers for events as well as speech coaching and life coaching through a Christian network.
- *Speaker Services* (www.speakerservices.com)
  Provides a roster of public speakers as well as professional coaching and training seminars.
- *Strategic Speaker Services* (www.speakerservices.net)
  Secures speaking engagements for high profile executives who are experts in their industries.
- *Toastmasters International* (http://www.toastmasters.org)
  Assists communicators, through local clubs, in developing speaking and leadership skills necessary for succeeding in a professional career.

Other Resources

- *Dale Carnegie Training* (http://www.dalecarnegie.com)
  Improves vital skills in communication and business through performance-based training.
- *Speak Up Conference* (http://speakupconference.com)
  Sponsors training conferences for Christian communicators.
- *Speaking Without Fear* (http://www.speakingwithoutfear.com)
  Offers training to eliminate fear in public speaking.
- *Simply Speaking Inc.* (http://www.simplyspeakinginc.com)
  Provides workshops in speech coaching and presentation skills to equip speakers with skills for effective communication.

SELECT BIBLIOGRAPHY

Adams, Chris. *Transformed Lives: Taking Your Women's Ministry to the Next Level.* Nashville: LifeWay, 2011.

——. *Women Reaching Women: Beginning and Building a Growing Women's Ministry.* Nashville: LifeWay, 2005.

Argyle, Michael. *The Psychology of Interpersonal Behavior.* New York: Penguin, 1975.

Axtell, Roger E. *Do's and Taboos of Public Speaking.* New York: John Wiley & Sons, 1992.

Bahn, Eugene, and Margaret L. Bahn. *A History of Oral Interpretation.* Minneapolis: Burgess, 1970.

Bailey, Raymond, and James L. Blevins. *Dramatic Monologues: Making the Bible Live.* Nashville: Baptist Sunday School Board, 1990.

Beatty, Christopher. *Maximum Vocal Performance.* Nashville: Star Song, 1992.

——. *Vocal Workout.* Nashville, TN: Star Song, 1992.

Bounds, E. M. *Power Through Prayer.* Grand Rapids: Baker, 1991.

Brennan, Monica. *Marvelously Made: Unveil Your True Identity and Purpose as a Woman.* Ventura: Regal, 2012.

Brown, Steve. *How to Talk So People Will Listen.* Grand Rapids: Baker, 1993.

Calvin, John. *Institutes of the Christian Religion.* Edited by John T. McNeill. Translated and indexed by Ford Lewis Battles. Philadelphia: Westminster, 1967.

Capp, Glenn R., Carol C. Capp, and G. Richard Capp Jr. *Basic Oral Communication.* 5th ed. Englewood Cliffs: Prentice Hall, 1990.

Carnegie, Dale. *How to Win Friends and Influence People.* Revised ed. New York: Simon & Schuster, 2009.

CLASSeminars: Christian Leaders, Authors and Speaker Services. Available at www.classeminars.org. Accessed 19 March 2013.

Cooper, Morton. *Winning with Your Voice.* Hollywood, FL: Fell, 1990.

Corley, Bruce, Steve W. Lemke, and Grant I. Lovejoy, eds. *Biblical Hermeneutics: A Comprehensive Introduction to Interpreting Scripture*. Nashville: Broadman & Holman, 2002.

Dean, Jennifer Kennedy. *Power Praying: Prayer That Produces Power*. Mukilteo, WA: WinePress, 1997.

Decker, Bert. *Communicating with Bold Assurance*. Nashville, TN: LifeWay, 2000.

Dowis, Richard. *The Lost Art of the Great Speech*. New York: AMACOM, 2000.

Dudley, Barbara. *Drama: Church Drama for Church Folks*. Dallas, TX: St. Paul, 2013.

Duduit, Michael, ed. *Communicate with Power: Insights from America's Top Communicators*. Grand Rapids: Baker, 1996.

Elgin, Suzette Haden. *Genderspeak: Men, Women, and the Gentle Art of Verbal Self-Defense*. New York: John Wiley and Sons, 1993.

Engel, James F. *Contemporary Christian Communications: Its Theory and Practice*. Nashville: Thomas Nelson, 1979.

Erkman, Paul. *Emotions Revealed: Recognizing Faces and Feelings to Improve Communication and Emotional Life*. New York: Times Books, 2003.

Fee, Gordon D., and Douglas Stuart. *How to Read the Bible for All Its Worth*. Grand Rapids: Zondervan, 2003.

Furlong, Gary. *Conflict Resolution Toolbox: Models and Maps for Analyzing, Diagnosing, and Resolving Conflict*. San Francisco: Josory-Bass, 2005.

Gangel, Kenneth O., and Samuel L. Canine. *Communication and Conflict Management: In Churches and Christian Organizations*. Nashville: Broadman, 1992.

Glass, Lillian. *Say It Right: How to Talk in Any Social or Business Situation*. New York: Perigee, 1991.

———. *Talk to Win: Six Steps to a Successful Vocal Image*. New York: Perigee, 1981.

Gray, John. *Men Are from Mars, Women Are from Venus*. New York: Harper Collins, 1992.

Gray, Mike. *Incorporating Drama in Worship*. Brentwood, TN: Lillenas Drama, 1995.

Griffin, E. M. *The Mind Changers: The Art of Christian Persuasion*. Wheaton: Tyndale House, 1976.

Gronbeck, Bruce E., et al. *Principles of Speech Communication (12th Brief Edition)*. New York: Harper Collins, 1995.

Hale, John R. *The Art of Public Speaking: Lessons from the Greatest Speeches in History*. Chantilly, VA: The Great Courses, 2010 (DVD and book set).

Hall, Edward T. *The Hidden Dimension*. New York: Anchor, 1966.

Hamlin, Sonya. *How to Talk So People Will Listen*. New York: Harper & Row, 1988.

Hemphill, Kenneth. *You Are Gifted: Your Spiritual Gifts and the Kingdom of God*. Nashville: Broadman and Holman, 2009.

Hendricks, William, et al. *High-Impact Presentations and Training Skills*. Shawnee Mission, KS: National Press Publications, 1994.

Hoff, Ron. *I Can See You Naked: A Fearless Guide to Making Great Presentations*. Kansas City, KS: Andrews & McMeel, 1988.

Humes, James C. *The Sir Winston Method: The Five Secrets of Speaking the Language of Leadership*. New York: William Morrow, 1991.

Jackson, Carole. *Color Me Beautiful*. New York: Ballantine, 1980.

Jacobi, Jeffrey. *How to Say It with Your Voice*. Paramus, NJ: Prentice Hall, 1996.

Jahnke, Christine K. *The Well-Spoken Woman: Your Guide to Looking and Sounding Your Best*. Amherst, NY: Prometheus, 2011.

Johnson, Barbara. *Splashes of Joy in the Cesspools of Life*. Nashville: W Publishing Group, 1992.

Kelley, Rhonda H. "Communication between Men and Women in the Context of the Christian Community." *Faith and Mission* 15, no. 1 (Fall 1996): 49–56.

———. *Divine Discipline: How to Develop and Maintain Self-Control*. Gretna, LA: Pelican, 1992.

Kennedy, George. *Aristotle on Rhetoric: A Theory of Civic Discourse*. New York: Oxford University Press, 1991.

Kent, Carol. *Speak Up with Confidence: A Step-by-Step Guide to Successful Public Speaking*. Colorado Springs: NavPress, 2007.

Lamb, Buddy. *Clown Scripts for Churches*. Nashville: Convention Press, 1991.

Lehman, L. P. *How to Find and Develop Effective Illustrations*. Grand Rapids: Kregel, 1985.

Lewis, John, Laura Andrews, and Flip Kobler. *The Complete Guide to Church Play Production*. Nashville: Convention Press, 1997.

Linver, Sandy. *Speakeasy: How to Talk Your Way to the Top*. New York: Summit, 1978.

Litfin, Duane. *Public Speaking: A Handbook for Christians*. 2nd ed. Grand Rapids: Baker, 1992.

Littauer, Florence, and Marita Littauer. *Talking So People Will Listen*. Ann Arbor, MI: Servant, 1998.

———. *Communication Plus: How to Speak So People Will Listen*. Ventura, CA: Regal, 2006.

Littauer, Marita. *Communicating Effectively as a Woman.* Albuquerque, NM: CLASS (audio cassette).

Lucas, Stephen E. *The Art of Public Speaking.* New York: McGraw-Hill, 2004.

McCloskey, David Blair. *Your Voice at Its Best.* Plymouth, MA: The Memorial Press, 1975.

McComiskey, Thomas Edward. *Reading Scripture in Public: A Guide for Preachers and Lay Readers.* Grand Rapids: Baker, 1991.

McFarland, Kenneth. *Eloquence in Public Speaking: How to Set Your Words on Fire.* Englewood Cliffs: Prentice Hall, 1961.

McLeish, Cleveland O. *Christian Playwriting and Self-Publishing.* Scotts Valley, CA: CreateSpace Independent Publishing Platform, 2012.

Mehrabian, Albert. *Silent Messages: Implicit Communication of Emotions and Attitudes.* Belmont, CA: Wadsworth, 1981.

Miller, Calvin. *The Empowered Communicator: 7 Keys to Unlocking an Audience.* Nashville: Broadman & Holman, 1994.

Miller, Fred. *No Sweat Public Speaking.* St. Louis, MO: Freed, 2011.

Miller, Paul. *Create a Drama Ministry.* Brentwood, TN: Lillenas, 1984.

———. *Developing the Church Drama Ministry.* Brentwood, TN: Lillenas, 1994.

Monroe, Alan H. *Principles and Types of Speech.* Chicago: Scott, Foresman and Company, 1962.

Morreale, Sherwyn, et al. *The Competent Speaker Speech Evaluation Form.* 2nd ed. Washington, DC: National Communication Association, 2007.

Mortensen, C. David, ed. *Communication Theory.* New York: Harper and Row, 2007.

Musurillo, Herbert. "The Martyrdom of Perpetua and Felicitas." In *The Acts of the Christian Martyrs.* Oxford: Oxford University Press, 1972.

Myers, Jeff. *Secrets of Great Communicators: Simple, Powerful Strategies for Reaching Your Audience.* Nashville: Broadman & Holman, 2006.

Noonan, Peggy. *Simply Speaking: How to Communicate Your Ideas with Style, Substance and Clarity.* New York: Harper Collins, 1998.

Patterson, Dorothy Kelley, and Rhonda Harrington Kelley, eds. *Woman's Evangelical Commentary: Old Testament.* Nashville: Holman Reference, 2011.

———. *Woman's Evangelical Commentary: New Testament.* Nashville: Holman Reference, 2006.

Pederson, Steve. *Drama Ministry.* Grand Rapids: Zondervan, 1999.

Pinker, S., and P. Bloom. "Natural language and natural selection." *Behavioral and Brain Sciences* 13, no. 4 (1990): 707–84.

Poindexter, Neil. *Powerful Presentations Skills.* Overland Parks, KS: National Seminars Group, 1989.

Robertson, Everett. *The Dramatic Arts in Ministry*. Nashville: Convention Press, 1989.

———. *Introduction to Church Drama*. Nashville: Convention Press, 1978.

Robinson, Haddon W. *Biblical Preaching*. Grand Rapids: Baker, 1980.

Rozkis, Laurie. *The Complete Idiots Guide to Public Speaking*. New York, NY: Alpha, 1999.

Rucker, Robert. *Producing and Directing Drama for the Church*. Brentwood, TN: Lillenas Drama, 1993.

Ryken, Philip Graham. *Art for God's Sake*. Phillipsburg, NJ: P&R, 2006.

Sarnoff, Dorothy. *Never Be Nervous Again*. New York: Ivy, 1987.

Schultze, Quentin. *An Essential Guide to Public Speaking: Serving Your Audience with Faith, Skill, and Virtue*. Grand Rapids: Baker Academic, 2006.

Sennett, Herbert. *Religion and Dramatics: The Relationship between Christianity and the Theater Arts*. Lexington, KY: University Press of America, 1995.

Siewert, Alison. *Drama Team Handbook*. Downers Grove. IL: InterVarsity, 2003.

Smiley, Kimberly. *Devoted Through Drama: Monologues, Plays, and Skits for Christian Youth Groups*. Willoughby, OH: Holy Fire, 2005.

Stern, Matthew Arnold. "Communication Tip: Maintaining Eye Contact." Available at www.matthewarnoldstern.com. Accessed 19 March 2013.

Swindoll, Charles R. *Saying It Well: Touching Others with Your Words*. New York, NY: FaithWords, 2012.

Tannen, Deborah. *Talking from 9 to 5*. New York: William Morrow, 1994.

———. *That's Not What I Meant! How Conversational Style Makes or Breaks Relationships*. New York: Ballantine, 1986.

———. *You Just Don't Understand: Women and Men in Conversation*. New York: HarperCollins, 2001.

Taylor, David. "Discipling the Eyes Through Art in Worship." *Christianity Today*, (April 2013). Available at http://www.christianitytoday.com/ct/2012/april/art-in-worship.html. Accessed 20 March 2013.

Tingley, Judith C. *Genderflex: Men and Women Speaking Each Other's Language at Work*. New York: AMACOM, 1994.

Toastmasters International Materials. Available at www.toastmasters.org. Accessed 20 March 2013.

Tullos, Matt. *Actors Not Included: The Complete Works of Matt Tullos*. Nashville: LifeWay, 1999.

———. *Show Me: Drama in Evangelism*. Nashville: Convention Press, 1996.

Vines, Jerry, and Jim Shaddix. *Power in the Pulpit*. Chicago: Moody, 1999.

W, Julie. "A Biblical Perspective of Drama in Ministry." *Online Journal of Christian Communication and Culture*. Entry posted December 11, 2011.

Available at http://www.ojccc.org/2011/12/a-biblical-perspective-of-drama-in-ministry/. Accessed March 20, 2013.

Wakefield, Norman. *Listening: A Christian's Guide to Loving Relationships*. Dallas, TX: Word, 1981.

Williams, Pat, and Ruth Williams. *Turn Boring Orations into Standing Ovations: The Ultimate Guide to Dynamic Public Speaking*. Altamonte Springs, FL: Advantage, 2008.

Wilson, Margery. *The Woman You Want to Be: Margery Wilson's Complete Book of Charm*. Philadelphia: J. B. Lippincott, 1942.

The Worship Drama Library. Volumes 1–14. Brentwood, TN: Lillenas Drama, 1995.

Subject Index

accent 148
announcements 169–70
anxiety 125
appearance 245
   clothing 248–52
   grooming 253
   hair 247
   makeup 247–48
articulation 148–51
attention 34–35, 38
audience 66–67
audience intelligence 66–67

Bible study 52
body positions (posture) 237–39

clowning 270
conductive hearing loss 36–37, 285
connection 73–74
countenance 223

dedication 59–62
delivery methods
   extemporaneous speech 158
   impromptu speech 157–77
   manuscript speech 156
   memorized speech 157
delivery principles 159–62
devotion 51–52, 55–56
dialect 148
diction 148
discipline 56–59
documentation 105–6
drama defined 258–60
dramatic reading 267

elocution 148
enunciation 148
evaluation criteria 210–11

exegesis 47, 118–22, 285
exposition 47, 119–22, 285
eye contact 26, 43, 127, 156, 171–72,
   202, 215–16, 223–26, 231, 235, 237,
   253, 267, 286

facial animation 229–31
facial expression 226, 228–29, 231
fear 125
fluency 150–51
formal examinations 208

genderflex 18, 22, 286
genderlect 9–10, 17, 22, 286
gestures 234–35
glossophobia 125

hand movements 234–35
hearing 35–38
hermeneutics 118–22, 286
homiletics 118, 120, 122, 286
honesty 184–85
humor 185–88

ideal style 136–37
illustrations 104–5
informal observations 206–8
interpersonal communication 5, 25–26,
   135, 147, 240, 242, 286
interviews in media 177–78
intrapersonal communication 25, 286
introducing a speaker 166–69

joy 185–86

leading a meeting 174–75
listener attitude 69, 71
listener background 70–71
listener feedback 70–71